The Rise and Fall of Neoliberal Capitalism

T0310956

The Rise and Fall of
Neoliberal Capitalism

David M. Kotz

 Harvard University Press

Cambridge, Massachusetts & London, England

First Harvard University Press paperback edition, 2017
First printing

Library of Congress Cataloging-in-Publication Data

Kotz, David M. (David Michael), 1943–
    The rise and fall of neoliberal capitalism / David M. Kotz.
        pages cm
    Includes bibliographical references and index.
    ISBN 978-0-674-72565-2 (cloth : alk. paper)
    ISBN 978-0-674-98001-3 (pbk.)
    1. Neoliberalism. 2. Capitalism. 3. United States—Economic
policy—1945– I. Title.
    HB95.K67 2014
        330.12'2—dc23   2014017153

Contents

List of Figures and Tables

Figures

Tables

Preface

This book analyzes the remarkable and unforeseen transformation of capitalism that occurred around 1980 and its consequences through today. For several decades following World War II, capitalist economies around the world were actively regulated by governments. In the United States a historic compromise between labor unions and big corporations in the late 1940s granted labor a significant role in determining wages and working conditions. Then around 1980 a rapid transformation took hold in the United States and Britain, giving rise to a free-market form of capitalism that is often called "neoliberal" capitalism. Welfare states were cut back, business and banking were deregulated, public enterprises and public services were privatized, labor unions were marginalized, labor markets became "flexible," and the tax burden shifted from corporations and the rich to those in the middle. These changes soon spread to much of the world.

Advocates of this transformation promised rising investment and faster economic growth. Instead, it led to less investment and slower growth, as well as rapidly rising inequality and stagnating or declining real income for middle- and lower-income groups. The modest economic growth brought by neoliberalism has been driven by accelerating household and financial-sector debt along with a series of speculative bubbles in the stock market and real estate. This process led to a big crash in 2008, when the global financial system almost collapsed and a severe "Great Recession" set in.

This book examines the nature of the neoliberal form of capitalism—why it arose around 1980, how it has worked, why it gave rise to such a big economic crisis followed by stagnation—and possible future directions of economic and political change. Capitalism has undergone significant restructuring of its economic, political, and cultural

dimensions several times before in history. Each previous restructuring emerged from an economic crisis of the preceding form of capitalism, which occurred in the late nineteenth century, the 1930s, and the
1970s. History shows that such periods reflect a structural crisis of the
prevailing system, which means that normal economic expansion cannot resume without major institutional change. Until that occurs, stagnation and economic instability persist. That is the condition of global
capitalism at this time, a condition that cannot be resolved easily.

The analysis in this book can shed light on a number of surprising
developments since it was published in hardback in 2015. A process of
political polarization has emerged in the United States and many other
countries. In the United States, Donald Trump, a billionaire real estate
developer and reality television program producer, in quick succession
won the Republican Party presidential primaries and then the White
House. He did so without the backing of any section of the traditional
economic and political elite, in a campaign that openly abandoned
the usual norms of U.S. politics, to champion a right-wing nationalist,
program. In the Democratic Party primary campaign, self-described
socialist senator Bernie Sanders gained twelve million votes while
mounting a serious challenge to the establishment-backed campaign
of Hillary Clinton, pulling her toward the left. The venerable two-party
system, which had long served as a bedrock of political stability by
compelling both parties to compete for votes in the political center,
suddenly was overwhelmed by powerful tides toward the right and the
left.

A similar polarization has taken hold in many other countries. Non-
mainstream right-wing political figures and political parties have advanced rapidly through an appeal to nationalism, directing the blame
for economic suffering on ethnic or religious minorities or immigrants.
Right-wing nationalist regimes with authoritarian tendencies recently
have emerged in the Philippines, India, Turkey, Poland, and Hungary.
In much of Western Europe, right-wing nationalist parties have been
rapidly gaining adherents. In Latin America a tide of right-wing upsurge has suddenly replaced moderately leftist governments. At the
same time, leftist parties or individuals have recently won elections or
shown unexpected electoral strength in Greece and Spain.

The analysis presented in this book suggests that such developments
are not surprising in a period of structural crisis of capitalism. The

initial recovery from the Great Recession in 2009 was followed by a lingering stagnation in the global economy. Economic growth in the United States has faltered, stuck at around 2 percent per year, giving rise to a literature on long-term stagnation involving some of the leading U.S. macroeconomists. Western Europe's economies have oscillated between stagnation and recession. China's rapid growth, previously the main driver of the global economy, has decelerated to under 7 percent per year. A sharp decline in commodity prices has failed to stimulate the developed economies while depressing many natural-resource export economies, such as those of Brazil and Russia.

The significant decline in the U.S. official unemployment rate since 2010 does not indicate a normal economic recovery. After hitting a peak of 10.6 percent in January 2010 (a recently revised figure), the unemployment rate fell to under 5 percent in late 2016. However, this results from a remarkable decline in the active labor force relative to the population, not from vigorous job creation. The percentage of the population in the active labor force fell from 66.0 percent in 2007 to 64.7 percent in 2010, as the Great Recession eliminated millions of jobs. However, instead of recovering after 2010, the labor-force participation rate has continued to decline, to 62.6 percent in November 2016, despite the economic recovery. This results mainly from working-age people dropping out of the labor force, not from demographic changes, such as aging of the population.

Since the 2008 crisis began, the problematic trends that started in the early 1980s, such as rising inequality and stagnating household income, have only intensified. The impact has been uneven across regions and population groups, and some previously prosperous parts of the United States have seen long-term economic decline. The disappearance of millions of well-paying jobs has led to overwork, as people struggle to make ends meet on low hourly pay rates, while a tiny group of super-rich ostentatiously display their new wealth. These developments formed the soil from which the current political polarization grew. The popular legitimacy of the existing order has been undermined in stages, first by twenty-five years of increasing inequality in the name of the free market, then in 2008/9 by a government bailout of the biggest banks at taxpayer expense, and finally by a recovery that failed to create good jobs. Suddenly, millions of people became ready to abandon their past political allegiance.

The current situation has striking similarities to an earlier crisis of capitalism, the Great Depression of the 1930s. Both the Great Depression and the Great Recession followed a period of unbridled free-market capitalism, sharply rising inequality, and huge speculative bubbles. Both economic crises took the form of a steep recession and a financial crisis, followed by a stubbornly persistent stagnation. The period of the Great Depression, like that of today, gave rise to sharp political polarization. Over the course of that period, three different directions of political-economic change took hold in various countries. Fascist regimes arose in Germany, Italy, and Japan. A social-democratic (or "regulated") form of capitalism emerged in Scandinavia, France (briefly), and the United States under the New Deal. The crisis of the 1930s was not resolved until shortly after World War II, when social-democratic capitalism become the dominant mode, while a significant part of the world abandoned capitalism for state socialism.

The same economic and political forces that destabilized existing systems and led to new regimes to the right and the left some eighty years ago have reappeared with the current structural crisis of neoliberal capitalism. The neoliberal form of capitalism might survive for some time, a possibility reinforced by the nomination of hard-core neoliberal ideologues to a number of high positions in the incoming Trump administration. This book argues, though, that in such a period there is a high likelihood that some kind of more statist system will emerge as the only means to resolve the stagnation. The new system, however, can take quite different forms. Right-wing nationalist repressive regimes are one possible future, but also possible are left-wing reform regimes or even movements beyond capitalism. All three possibilities are considered in the final chapter of this book. The future is not determined by any economic law but will depend on the actions of various contending classes, groups, and organizations in the coming period, within the context of the economic and political pressures emerging from the stubbornly persistent economic stagnation.

David M. Kotz
Northampton, Massachusetts
January, 2017

Preface to the Original Edition

While I was growing up in the suburbs of New York City in the 1950s, the descriptions I read in books about the harsh conditions faced by working people in the nineteenth century seemed to be from another world. One read of dangerous working conditions, long workdays, pay too low to support a family, tenement apartments, and homeless beggars. One day some friends and I went to "the city," as we called New York, where we visited the Bowery, a neighborhood where one could see homeless alcoholic men living on the sidewalk. It seemed a museum from an earlier epoch.

In that period my local public high school added more specialty teachers and honors classes each year. We even got a new science teacher with a doctorate. In my economically diverse community, everyone was confident of getting a good job after completing either high school or college, a confidence that was borne out by the experience of older cohorts.

As I began to study the American economy in college and then graduate school in the 1960s, I learned that capitalism had changed greatly since roughly the end of World War II. The family of an average blue-collar worker could now live in moderate comfort on one income, with strong labor unions bringing job security and reasonable working conditions. Most workers lived in private homes with yards instead of tenements, possessing a car and some even a recreational boat. Those who did not find success in the labor market could turn to government social welfare programs. Of course, not everyone shared in this progress. Poverty declined but was not eliminated, the incomes of minorities remained below that of white Americans, and women were paid less than men. However, it appeared that real progress was being made toward a more just economic order.

No one knew that the prosperity and relative security of that era were not to last forever. After an economically troubled decade in the 1970s, the U.S. economy changed radically. After around 1980 many former trends went into reverse. The first sign of the change was that suddenly one did not have to visit New York City's Bowery to see homeless people—they appeared in growing numbers on the streets of every major U.S. city. Although of course conditions did not fall to nineteenth-century levels, wages now declined over time instead of rising every year. Families had difficulty making ends meet with two wage earners rather than just one. Pressure at work grew while job security plummeted. Most of the good industrial jobs fled the country. The social safety net was cut back. Public services, including public education, were squeezed year after year. Art and music shrank or disappeared in the schools, with physical education not far behind. The gap between the rich and the rest of society grew rapidly.

As a junior faculty member in economics, along with like-minded colleagues I sought to understand these unexpected new developments. At first we thought this was a temporary deviation from the previous trend of progress for the majority. How could it be otherwise? The earlier shared economic progress had seemed to stabilize capitalism and ensure its long-run survival, confounding critics who had doubted it could ever serve more than a small economic elite.

The change turned out not to be temporary. Instead the new trends grew more pronounced over time, and they appeared in many countries around the world. Starting in the late 1990s, I began to do research on the causes and consequences of these developments, which stemmed from what today is often called "free-market" or "neoliberal" capitalism. My research was guided by a key lesson taught to me as a graduate student by Professor Robert Aaron Gordon of the University of California at Berkeley: that one must listen to what the empirical evidence is saying, rather than trying to hammer it into a form that validates preconceived assumptions. Despite my personal dislike of the disequalizing trends of neoliberal capitalism, the evidence showed that it was working effectively in some respects. It did bring long-lasting, if not rapid, economic expansions, and it kept inflation to low levels. A valid analysis had to explain its successes as well as the problems it produced.

The outbreak of the financial and broader economic crisis in 2008—the most severe since the Great Depression of the 1930s—brought another return of an economic problem we had been told now belonged only to long-past history. This gave added urgency to the project of understanding neoliberal capitalism. This book is the end product of that long project. It offers an explanation of the key developments since 1980—the sharp turn in the economy around 1980, the decades of rising economic inequality and reduced public services that followed, the outbreak of a severe economic crisis in 2008, and the sluggish recovery from it. Of course, economics is a controversial subject, and there are various contending explanations of the economic problems of today. The reader will have to judge the adequacy of the analysis presented here.

This book offers a historical and analytical account of neoliberal capitalism, focused on the United States. In the book I have sought to present a serious analysis in a way that is accessible to anyone with an interest in the topic. Academic economists are encouraged to direct their work at a small audience of specialists, a practice that is in my view unfortunate. The way in which the economy develops has profound effects on the public welfare, for good or ill. Those whose profession is to seek to understand the economy, and who are given by our institutions the time and resources to do so, have an obligation to make their findings available to the general public. I hope that in this book I have succeeded in making the underlying causes of our current economic problems clear to the reader, as well as providing a basis for evaluating possible solutions to the economic problems we now face.

David M. Kotz
Amherst, Massachusetts
November, 2013

Acknowledgments

I received assistance, advice, and/or comments from a number of individuals and institutions for the project that led to this book. My editor at Harvard University Press, Michael Aronson, offered helpful comments on the manuscript, as did Dan Clawson, Barbara Epstein, Terrence McDonough, Karen Pfeifer, and two anonymous reviewers for Harvard University Press. Dan Clawson, Mary Ann Clawson, Alejandro Reuss, and Jeff Faux provided primary and secondary source documents or direct information about relevant events. Lawrence Mishel helped to locate economic data not available from the usual government websites. Discussions with Mimi Abramovitz, James Crotty, Terrence McDonough, and Martin Wolfson over a period of years made significant contributions to the development of the analysis in this book. Jennifer Fronc, Laura Lovett, and Rob Weir offered their expertise on the recent historical literature on topics relevant for this book. Olivia Geiger provided invaluable research assistance. Michelle Rosenfield provided technical advice and assisted with literature searches. Doruk Cengiz prepared the index for this book. My colleagues in the Economics Department of the University of Massachusetts Amherst offered helpful comments when I gave presentations on the topics that are the subject of this book. The Department of Economics and the Political Economy Research Institute of the University of Massachusetts Amherst provided financial support for the project. Kathleen Drummy of Harvard University Press patiently responded to my many questions about the technical side of the publication process. Of course, none of the foregoing individuals or institutions is responsible for the analysis or the conclusions in this book.

1

Introduction

In 2008 a severe financial and broader economic crisis broke out in the United States. It rapidly spread to much of the global financial and economic system. As will be shown in detail in Chapter 5, this has been the most severe crisis since the Great Depression of the 1930s. While the acute stage of financial collapse and economic free-fall at the start of the crisis has passed, it has been followed by a period of stagnation and economic instability continuing up to the time of this writing five years later. The term "crisis" aptly captures the ongoing condition of the U.S. economy and that of much of the rest of the world economy.

The crisis came as a surprise to most of the leading economists and policy-makers in the United States, who believed that depressions were no longer possible in contemporary capitalism. Robert Lucas, a leading representative of the free-market Chicago School of academic economics, claimed in his 2003 presidential address to the American Economic Association that the "central problem of depression-prevention has been solved, for all practical purposes, and has in fact been solved for many decades."[1] Ben Bernanke, a noted Princeton University economist who was appointed chairman of the Federal Reserve in 2006, told a meeting of Federal Reserve officials in March of that year that "I think we are unlikely to see growth being derailed by the housing market." At the same 2006 meeting Janet Yellen, a Berkeley economist and Federal Reserve official who later succeeded Bernanke as head of the Federal Reserve, added "Of course, housing is a relatively small sector of the economy, and its decline should be self-correcting."[2] Thus, leading representatives of the mainstream of the American economics profession could not see the impending economic crisis, and many were convinced that a serious crisis could not happen again.

This crisis issued from the particular form of capitalism in the United States in recent decades, often called free-market, or neoliberal, capitalism.[3] Neoliberal capitalism arose around 1980, first in the United States and the United Kingdom, replacing the quite different "regulated capitalism" that had preceded it. It soon spread to many, although not all, other countries and came to dominate the global-level economic institutions of this era.

The full meanings of neoliberal and regulated capitalism will be explored in Chapter 2. In brief, in neoliberal capitalism market relations and market forces operate relatively freely and play the predominant role in the economy. By regulated capitalism we mean a form of capitalism in which such non-market institutions as states, corporate bureaucracies, and trade unions play a major role in regulating economic activity, restricting market relations and market forces to a lesser role in the economy.[4] The aim of this book is to uncover the roots of this crisis in neoliberal capitalism, as well as to provide an understanding of the neoliberal form of capitalism that gave rise to the crisis. This requires an examination of several related questions. What is neoliberal capitalism? Why did it arise after several decades of regulated capitalism, a development that, like the current crisis, surprised most analysts at the time? How has this form of capitalism worked since its inception around 1980, a period that has seen a series of historically long economic expansions, low rates of inflation, and high and rising levels of inequality and debt?

Finding answers to the foregoing questions prepares the way to understand the roots and character of the crisis that began in 2008, as well as the state responses to the crisis. The analysis offered in this book suggests that significant economic and political change is likely in the coming years. While it is not possible to foresee with any certainty the future course of developments, this analysis sheds some light on the kinds of future economic and political change that could potentially resolve the current crisis.

The approach followed in this book views capitalism as a system that evolves and changes over time. However, such change is not simply partial or gradual. While capitalism has retained certain fundamental defining features since its origin centuries ago, it has assumed a series of distinct institutional forms over time. Each form of capitalism has displayed internal coherence, with a set of economic and political institutions, as well as dominant ideas, that reinforce one another. Each form of capitalism has also persisted for a significant period of time, from a decade to several decades in duration. Transitions from one institutional form of capitalism to the next have been punctuated by crisis and restructuring.

The defining features of capitalism are the ownership/control of enterprises by a part of the population, the capitalists, who employ wage earners to produce products for sale in the market, with the aim of gaining a profit. However, that is a sparse account of a socioeconomic system, and a much richer set of economic and political institutions has developed in every historical period of the capitalist era. The view that such sets of institutions tend both to be coherent and to last for significant periods of time was put forward by two theories that arose in the late 1970s and early 1980s, the social structure of accumulation theory and the regulation theory. The former arose in the United States (Gordon et al., 1982; Kotz et al., 1994) and the latter in France (Aglietta, 1979).

The analysis in this book is based on a modified version of the social structure of accumulation theory, which holds that each coherent institutional structure in capitalist history, referred to as a social structure of accumulation, centers around promoting profit-making and a stable capital accumulation process (Wolfson and Kotz, 2010). After one or several decades, each social structure of accumulation turns from a structure that promotes profit-making and accumulation into an obstacle to it, ushering in a period of economic crisis. The crisis period lasts until a new social structure of accumulation is constructed. This theoretical approach does not in itself explain why a particular form of capitalism gives rise to a severe crisis at a given time and place, but rather it provides a framework for investigating the roots of a crisis.

Like every preceding form of capitalism, neoliberal capitalism has a particular configuration of economic and political institutions, as well as dominant economic theories and ideas. As argued in Wolfson and Kotz (2010), each social structure of accumulation provides a way to stabilize the main conflicts and resolve the main problems that capitalism tends to produce. This includes stabilizing the relation between capital and labor as well as relations among capitalists. To promote profit-making and stable accumulation, a social structure of accumulation also must assure growing markets for the output of an expanding capitalist economy. Central to each social structure of accumulation is the role of the state in relation to the economy.[5]

This approach to analyzing capitalist growth and crisis combines theoretical considerations with historical analysis of particular conjunctures. In this book the most important actors are not individuals but classes and groups, which engage in struggles and enter into alliances and coalitions as each seeks to advance its interests in the face of economic developments. The broadest category of actors is classes, such as capitalists and workers. The capitalist class is not an undifferentiated group, and our analysis will pay attention to the sometimes conflicting interests of different segments of the capitalist class.

The neoliberal era has seen two related developments that have stirred much debate, globalization and financialization. While capitalism has shown a powerful tendency to expand globally since its inception, in the neoliberal era it became significantly more globally integrated than in the past by some measures. Another feature of capitalism in the neoliberal era has been the "increasing role of financial motives, financial markets, financial actors and financial institutions in the operation of domestic and international economies" (Epstein, 2005, 3), a development that has been given the awkward name "financialization." Some analysts view the character of the economic system during this period mainly through the lens of globalization or financialization rather than neoliberalism. In Chapter 2 we will argue that neoliberalism is the most useful concept for understanding the current form of capitalism, with globalization and financialization best understood as important features of neoliberal capitalism.

A number of books have appeared that offer analysis of neoliberal capitalism and/or the crisis to which it has given rise. Examples are Harvey (2005, 2010), Dumenil and Levy (2004, 2011), Stiglitz (2010), Foster and Magdoff (2009), Sweezy (1994), Palley (2012), Howard and King (2008), and Rogers (2011). There are some points of agreement and some differences between the conclusions found in those works and this book. A distinguishing feature of this book is the approach taken, which utilizes the concept of successive institutional forms of capitalism underlying periods of growth and crisis, offers a combination of theoretical and historical analysis, and presents a focus on classes and class segments. This approach can yield insights into the past, present, and future of capitalist society that cannot be found by other methodological approaches.

A central argument of this book is that the crisis that began in 2008 is not just a financial crisis, or a particularly severe recession—or a combination of the two. It is a structural crisis of the neoliberal form of capitalism. By a structural crisis is meant not only that the crisis emerges from the current structural form of the economy but that the crisis, unlike an ordinary business cycle recession, cannot be resolved within the current structural form. A structural crisis cannot be resolved by well-chosen economic policies. Even a bold Keynesian policy of fiscal expansion through big increases in public spending, while capable of stimulating faster economic growth and creating more jobs for a time, would not in itself resolve the underlying structural problem that is blocking a resumption of a normal trajectory of profit-making and economic expansion over the long run. Rather, major structural change in the economy and other related aspects of society represents the only route to resolving the current crisis, a view that finds support from the history of the resolution of past structural crises in the United States such as that of the 1930s.

Chapters 2, 3, and 4 present an analysis of neoliberal capitalism— what it is, how it arose, and how it has worked. Chapter 5 analyzes the roots and character of the current economic crisis, as well as the evolving state response to the crisis. Chapter 6 delves into the U.S. past, seeking lessons from earlier institutional forms of capitalism, and the transitions from one to another, that can inform a consideration of what will come next at this time. Chapter 7 concludes with a discussion of possible future directions of economic and political change.

This book focuses on the United States. The United States is of course the dominant economic, political, and military power in the world, as well as having a culture that exercises a substantial influence over the rest of the world. Neoliberal capitalism originated in the United States, along with the United Kingdom, and it was U.S. power that spread neoliberal institutions and policies throughout the global system. The current crisis emerged from the United States. However, both neoliberal capitalism and the crisis it has produced have important international dimensions, and the analysis in this book will take account of the major relevant developments in the global political economy.

In order to analyze the neoliberal form of capitalism, various economic data series will be introduced. (See the appendix to this book for information about data sources.) We will make comparisons to the previous dominant form of capitalism, which we call regulated capitalism. When using data for this kind of analysis, assessment, and comparison, the question of how to date the beginning and end of each period inevitably arises. The choice of beginning and ending years is more important than one might expect, because the business cycle—the periodic short-run ups and downs in the economy—can distort long-run comparisons of economic performance if the end-point years are not carefully chosen. A good way to remove such distorting effects is to choose a business cycle peak year for both the initial and final year of the period.

We regard the period of regulated capitalism as starting roughly in the late 1940s and continuing until the late 1970s, while neoliberal capitalism runs from the early 1980s to the present. According to the approach followed here, each form of capitalism has a period in which the social structure of accumulation works effectively to promote profit-making and economic expansion, followed by a period of structural crisis when the social structure of accumulation no longer works effectively. We will show in later chapters that regulated capitalism stopped working effectively as seen in most data series around 1973, although the average rate of profit in the U.S. began to fall earlier, after 1966. Hence, for most data series, we will treat the period 1948 to 1973—both business cycle peak years—as representing the regulated capitalist era in the sense of the interval when that system was in its effective phase. The interval 1973 to 1979—again both peak years—will represent the period of structural crisis of regulated capitalism, although for profit data we will examine 1948–66 and 1966–79 as the periods of effective working and crisis, respectively.[6]

Although neoliberal capitalism was not well established until the early 1980s in our view, we will regard the period 1979 to 2007, both business cycle peak years in the U.S., as the period when it was working effectively. While the year 1979 is a bit on the early side, the next normal business cycle peak was not until 1990, long after neoliberal institutions had become well established.[7] The year 1979 marked a turning point in many economic data series, and it is common to regard that year as a break point between these two quite different periods. Following the business cycle peak year of 2007, the U.S. economy entered a period of structural crisis, which has not reached its end as of this writing. Additional details about the dating of these periods will be supplied in later chapters.

2

What Is Neoliberalism?

Because the current economic crisis emerged from the particular form of capitalism that has prevailed since about 1980, the first step toward understanding the roots of the crisis is to determine just what this form of capitalism is. There is disagreement about how to characterize the contemporary form of capitalism. In this book post-1980 capitalism is regarded as "free-market" or "neoliberal" capitalism. Some analysts have a different understanding of contemporary capitalism, arguing that the best defining concept is either "globalization" or "financialization." This chapter examines the radically changed form of capitalism that emerged after around 1980 and presents a case that "neoliberalism" captures its main features—and hence is the best starting point for analyzing the roots of the current economic crisis.

The term "neoliberalism" is confusing to those schooled in U.S. politics, since in the United States a "liberal" political stance favors active state intervention in the economy aimed at benefiting the average person. However, the term "liberal" has long had more or less the opposite meaning in every other country, where a liberal political party is one that calls for a free-market economic policy. When a free-market form of capitalism began to emerge in the United States in the late 1970s and early 1980s, at first various names were applied, such as conservative economics, Reaganomics, or simply free-market economics. As this form of capitalism spread around the world, the term "neoliberalism" gradually came into common use to indicate a new form of "liberal" (free-market) ideas, policies, and institutions. In the 2000s the term "neoliberalism" became the most common name for the current form of capitalism and/or the ideas and policies associated with it. While some analysts use the term to refer only to a set of ideas, or to certain policies, we use the concept of neoliberalism, or neoliberal capitalism, more broadly to refer to a particular institutional form of capitalism along with the dominant ideas associated with that form of capitalism.[1]

The concept of neoliberal, or free-market, capitalism does not mean that the state plays no role in the economy. Market relations and market exchange require a state, or state-like institution, to define and protect private property and to enforce the contracts that are an essential feature of market exchange. Every large-scale society requires a state, or a state-like institution, to preserve order. The maintenance of a strong military is fully consistent with the neoliberal view of the proper role of the state. The meaning of "free-market" in this context is that the state role in regulating economic activity is limited, apart from the preceding essential state functions, leaving market relations and market forces as the main regulators of economic activity—but of course operating within a framework provided by the state.[2]

Neoliberalism should not be associated solely with conservative governments. As we will see in Chapter 3, neoliberal restructuring in the United States began under a Democratic Party administration, that of President Jimmy Carter, in the late 1970s. While it intensified under the successive Republican administrations of Ronald Reagan and George H. Bush, there was no reversal after Bill Clinton took office. Similarly, in Western Europe during this period social democratic parties would run for office against liberal parties, promising a reversal of neoliberalism, but once in office they have maintained the direction of neoliberal restructuring.[3] The continuity of neoliberalism despite changes in ruling political parties will be considered in some detail in Chapter 4.

To understand the current historical moment, the best starting point is a close examination of what neoliberal capitalism has been. It emerged from the crisis of the very different regulated capitalism of the post-World War II decades, and to some extent neoliberalism was a reaction to problems that were seen as stemming from regulated capitalism. Hence, the distinctive features of neoliberalism are best understood against the background of the preceding system.

Both regulated capitalism and neoliberalism are complex entities with many features. To understand them both, it is best to start with the dominant economic ideas of each period and then proceed to the main institutions of each. The reasons why the big change in the dominant economic ideas took place and why such radical institutional change occurred will be examined in Chapter 3. Here the aim is to establish what it is that needs explanation.

A Sudden Shift in the Dominant Economic Ideas

The dominant economic ideas in the neoliberal era diverged sharply from those that had reigned in the regulated capitalist era. The dominant economic orthodoxy in the post-World War II decades in the U.S. and U.K. is often identified with the British economist John Maynard Keynes.[4] His book *The General Theory of Employment, Interest, and Money* was published in 1936, in the midst of the Great Depression. Keynesian economics holds that capitalist economies have a fundamental flaw at the level of the economy as a whole. The Keynesians argue that there is no automatic mechanism in the economy to assure full employment of labor or to avoid occasional severe and prolonged depressions.

According to the Keynesians, this flaw stems from the impact on the economy of the highly variable level of business investment in capital goods. Business investment decisions must be made based on guesses about the inherently unknowable future economic conditions that a firm will encounter, which makes the level of total investment unstable and subject to waves of optimism or pessimism. If business investment declines, total demand in the economy will decline as a result, and unsold goods will pile up on the shelves. This prompts firms to cut production and lay off workers, causing household income and spending to fall, driving the economy downward further into a mild recession or even a severe depression.

This theory of the macroeconomy underpinned a new view of the proper role of the state in a capitalist economy. Keynes's followers were reformists, not revolutionaries, and argued that the flaw he had identified in capitalist economies had a remedy ready at hand—active state intervention in the economy. When private investment declines, state spending should rise by a similar amount, keeping total demand at the level required to maintain full employment. Just as private business borrows to finance investment, the state should borrow to finance such increased spending; that is, it should run a deficit if necessary. Once private investment recovers, state spending can relinquish its expanded share of total demand.

The dominant economic orthodoxy of the period of regulated capitalism went beyond calls for an active fiscal policy.[5] The state came to be seen as an important actor in the economy, providing an expanding supply of such public goods as education and infrastructure (transportation, power, communication, sanitary facilities), which contribute not just to economic progress but also to the profitability of private business. The state was also seen as responsible for pursuing other goals such as correcting market failures (environmental destruction, for example), reducing income inequality, and bringing greater individual economic security.[6] In the postwar decades, the term "capitalism" practically disappeared from public discourse, replaced by the"mixed economy," in which private and state institutions both had major contributions to make. We will refer to this dominant economic orthodoxy as Keynesian, although it included a belief in the need for interventions in the market that went beyond the aim of stabilizing the business cycle, for which Keynesian economics is best known.

The new Keynesian economic theory was embodied in MIT economist Paul Samuelson's textbook *Economics,* introduced in 1948. That book provided the model for all major college introductory economics textbooks over the following several decades. The reign of Keynesian economics reached its peak in the 1960s, during the administrations of Presidents John F. Kennedy and Lyndon B. Johnson. Advocates of this economic theory occupied key economic policy posts and dominated the policy debates. Even President Richard Nixon announced in 1971, "I am now a Keynesian in economics."[7]

However, during the course of the 1970s the Keynesian economic orthodoxy was replaced, quite rapidly, by a new one—free-market, or neoliberal, economic thought. Neoliberal thought rests upon a highly individualistic conception of human society.[8] Individual freedom of choice is seen as the fundamental basis of human welfare, with market relations understood as the institution that allows individual choice to drive the economy. The state, by contrast, is seen as an enemy of individual liberty, a threat to private property, and a parasite living off the hard work of individuals.[9] In the mid/late 1970s Milton Friedman of the University of Chicago, having survived a long period in the intellectual wilderness, emerged, along with Frederick Hayek, as the guru of the newly dominant neoliberal economic thought.

The new neoliberal economic theories came in several variants, bearing such names as monetarism, rational expectations theory, supply side economics, crowding-out theory, and real business cycle theory. However, they are all based on the elevation of individual choice in unregulated markets to the position of the central economic act, while state economic activities are portrayed as either ineffectual and thereby wasteful, or actively harmful.[10] Exceptions are made for the military and public order functions of the state. Neoliberal theory asserts that a "free" (meaning unregulated) market system assures optimal economic outcomes in every respect—efficiency, income distribution, economic growth, and technological progress—as well as securing individual liberty.[11] This theory claims that a capitalist economy naturally maintains full employment and an optimal rate of economic growth, and any state interventions aimed at promoting those goals are not just unnecessary but will worsen economic performance.

While the emergence of a newly dominant neoliberal theory cannot by itself explain the big changes in economic and political institutions in the neoliberal era, it provided a powerful justification for them. Neoliberal theory asserted that the institutional changes that took place beginning around 1980 were necessary for economic prosperity and would benefit everyone.

Neoliberalism is often described by reference to a trilogy of policies known as liberalization, privatization, and stabilization. However, the policies associated with those terms are best understood as means to transform the institutions of regulated capitalism into the institutions of neoliberal capitalism. The main institutions that radically changed with the rise of neoliberal capitalism fall into four categories: 1) the global economy; 2) the role of government in the economy; 3) the capital-labor relation; and 4) the corporate sector. Each institution of neoliberal capitalism will be examined against the background of the contrasting institution of the regulated capitalist era from which it evolved.

The Global Economy

The Bretton Woods system governed the international economy in the period of regulated capitalism. That system originated in a 1944 conference in Bretton Woods, New Hampshire, at which the United States and its allies laid down the design of the postwar international economic system. It gave birth to the International Monetary Fund (IMF) and the World Bank, which were to oversee the new global system. While the Bretton Woods system encouraged trade in goods, calling for the gradual reduction of barriers, significant tariffs were allowed under certain conditions and states had the right to regulate capital movements in various ways. This produced a global system that was somewhat open to international trade but with significant barriers, particularly for capital movements. The U.S. dollar, backed by gold at a fixed rate, assumed the role of global trading and reserve currency. The other major powers' currencies were tied to the dollar, creating a system of fixed exchange rates for the major world currencies. IMF approval was required for any change in a major nation's relative currency value.

During 1967–73 the Bretton Woods system broke down in stages, fully collapsing in 1973 when the U.S. government announced that the dollar would be allowed to "float"—that is, to rise and fall based on market forces in international currency markets. This ended the system of fixed exchange rates that had been at the center of the Bretton Woods system. After a period of chaos in the international monetary system in the 1970s, a new system emerged in the early 1980s that had two main features. First, a "managed float" developed, with governments allowing international currency markets to play a major role in setting currency values but with significant interventions by central banks aimed at influencing the result.[12]

Second, and more importantly, the new system emphasized free movement of goods, services, capital, and money across national boundaries.[13] The IMF and World Bank remained in business but their roles changed, as they became the enforcers of a new, more open global system of trade, investment, and money, as well as major promoters of other features of neoliberalism around the world. Some new international organizations arose over time, the most important of which is the World Trade Organization, born in 1995, whose aim is to enforce free trade. In the neoliberal era, the global economy became much more open than it had been in the regulated capitalist era. Figure 2.1 shows that world exports relative to world GDP, which had begun to increase significantly after the mid 1960s, grew much more rapidly after the early 1980s.

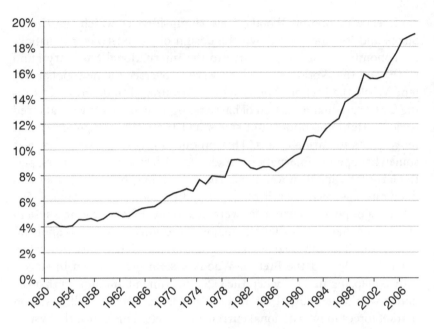

Figure 2.1. World exports as a percentage of world gross domestic product, 1950–2009.

Source: International Monetary Fund, 2013b; Maddison, 2010.

Note: World exports and world gross domestic product are in 2005 U.S. dollars.

The Role of Government in the Economy

While not all of the important institutional changes in the neoliberal era directly involved the role of the government in the economy, the latter represented a major part of the neoliberal restructuring that began in the late 1970s. In the United States a series of changes in the role of the state together transformed the relation between state and economy. Among the most important were the following: 1) renunciation of Keynesian-inspired government demand management policy; 2) deregulation of basic industries; 3) deregulation of the financial sector; 4) weakening of environmental, consumer product safety, and job safety regulation; 5) reduced enforcement of anti-trust laws; 6) privatization or contracting out of public functions; 7) elimination of or cutbacks in social welfare programs; and 8) enactment of tax cuts for business and wealthy households.

First, in the neoliberal era the former Keynesian-inspired "demand management" policies were renounced. In the previous period the federal government had been committed to using spending, taxing, and monetary policy to counterbalance swings in private sector demand to stabilize the business cycle, to keep unemployment low as well as prevent high inflation, and to promote economic growth over the long run. Neoliberal economists believe such state interventions are unnecessary and even harmful. In the neoliberal era these active government policies were given up, as the official aim of fiscal policy became a balanced budget while monetary policy shifted to a sole focus on stable prices rather than a combination of low unemployment and low inflation. The appointment of Paul Volcker to the position of chairman of the Federal Reserve (Fed) by President Jimmy Carter in 1979 marked the beginning of this policy shift. Volcker drove interest rates up to 20%, stopping the rapid inflation of that period by driving the economy into a deep recession and pushing the unemployment rate into the double-digit range. Thereafter a low unemployment rate was no longer a goal of the Fed.[14]

Some observers mistakenly thought that the Reagan administration actually continued Keynesian fiscal policies, since among its first acts in 1981 was a big tax cut intended to stimulate economic growth. However, the rationale for the Reagan tax cut was not the Keynesian idea of increasing demand by leaving more income in consumers' pockets. President Reagan, in his message to Congress on February 10, 1982, stated, "As a result of passage of the historic Economic Recovery Tax Act of 1981, we have set in place a fundamental reorientation of our tax laws . . . we have significantly restructured it [the tax system] to encourage people to work, save, and invest more" (Peters and Wooley, 2013). The Reagan tax cuts were intended to encourage investment and greater work effort through the incentive effect of allowing households and businesses to keep more of what they earned. Neoliberal theory advocated simultaneous reductions in government spending to keep the budget balanced.[15] The underlying idea was that smaller government, on both the revenue and spending sides, would lead to faster growth in the private sector.[16]

The second shift in the state role in the economy involved government regulation of key industries. The railroads and the telephone industry had come under effective government regulation by the early twentieth century. A regulatory structure was later extended to electric power, airlines, long-distance trucking, and radio and television broad-casting.[17] Such infrastructure sectors were viewed as basic industries that had important elements of natural monopoly, requiring govern-ment oversight to assure that prices would be stable and not excessively high.[18] While the details of the regulatory structure varied among these sectors, the regulatory agencies generally set prices, regulated business practices, restricted entry into the industry, and had some control over investment in additional productive capacity. In some cases, such as telephone regulation, the company was guaranteed a fixed rate of profit on its investment.

Neoliberal economists argued that such regulation was unnecessary and harmful, stifling efficiency and technological innovation. Starting in the mid 1970s, the aforementioned types of government regulation of business were dismantled, leaving only a few elements of regulation at the local level for electric power and cable systems where natural monopoly was undeniable. Deregulation actually got its start in air-lines and trucking during the administration of a Democrat, President Jimmy Carter, in the late 1970s. Cornell economist Alfred Kahn was named by Carter to oversee airline deregulation, while Congress pro-moted trucking deregulation. As deregulation took hold in the basic industries, market forces came to operate in those parts of the economy, replacing state regulation.

The third change in the state economic role was a shift from strict regulation of the financial sector to a largely deregulated financial sec-tor. In the 1930s, following the collapse of the U.S. banking system in 1933 and spurred by congressional hearings that exposed questionable activities by the leading bankers of the day, the federal government en-acted a comprehensive system of regulation of the financial sector. The aim of this regulatory system was to assure the stability of the banks, to prevent bank failures and panics, and to promote what was seen as the proper productive role of the financial sector while discouraging speculative activity. In the period of regulated capitalism following World War II, the banks were closely controlled by several regulatory agencies, which set interest rate ceilings for some types of loans, deter-mined allowable interest rates for some kinds of consumer deposits, and restricted the types of financial activities permitted for each type of financial institution. This produced a segmented financial system, with commercial banks lending to businesses, savings banks making commercial and home mortgage loans, insurance companies selling conventional insurance, and the less-regulated investment banks underwriting corporate security issues but forbidden to offer depository services. Commercial and savings bank deposits were federally insured, and their books were regularly inspected. Under this system there were no big bank failures or financial panics from the end of World War II through 1973 in the U.S.

In the 1970s the financial regulatory system began to experience strains, as mutual funds intruded on the territory of banks by offering money market fund accounts paying high interest rates, while rising inflation put pressure on the interest rate ceilings set by the regulators. Neoliberal economists began a campaign against government regulation of finance, bringing out the same arguments used against regulation of infrastructure sectors, arguing that it led to inefficiency and stifled innovation.[19] They claimed that market competition among financial institutions was sufficient to assure optimum performance by the financial sector. Some even called for the repeal of federal deposit insurance, arguing that vigilant oversight by ordinary bank depositors made it unnecessary.[20]

In 1980, the last year of the Carter administration, the first bank deregulation act was signed into law, followed by another in 1982.[21] The process of bank deregulation continued through 2000. The Financial Services Modernization Act of 1999 finally largely repealed the Glass-Steagall Act of 1933 which had forced financial institutions to choose among deposit banking, investment banking, and sale of insurance. This allowed the formation of financial conglomerates for the first time since the Great Depression, which raised the possibility that funds in government-insured deposits could be invested in risky financial activities. In 2000 the Commodity Futures Modernization Act forbade government regulation of derivative securities, the collapse of which was to play a big role in the financial meltdown of 2008.[22] Thus, a largely unregulated financial system gradually emerged in the U.S. during the neoliberal era, and by 2000 financial institutions had been fully freed to pursue virtually whatever activity promised the highest rate of return.

The fourth change in the state role involved what is sometimes called "social regulation," to distinguish it from the "economic regulation" aimed at natural monopolies and key sectors of the economy described above. Social regulation includes oversight of consumer product safety, job safety, and environmental quality. While the first steps toward government social regulation in the United States were taken in the early twentieth century, or even earlier, such regulation was greatly expanded in the decades following World War II. Consumer product safety regulation first appeared in 1906 with passage of the Pure Food and Drug Act and the Meat Inspection Act. In 1972 the Consumer Product Safety Act broadened the role of the federal government in assuring that consumer products would be safe. In the 1970s the Federal Trade Commission became more active in the area of consumer protection.

Modest efforts to make jobs safer in particularly dangerous industries, such as railroads and mining, occurred at both state and federal levels starting in the nineteenth century. In 1969 coal mining regulation was tightened with the passage of the Federal Coal Mine Safety and Health Act. Then in 1970 Congress passed the comprehensive Occupational Safety and Health Act, a major step toward inserting the federal government into the regulation of job safety in the United States.[23]

Environmental protection legislation also has a long history going back to the early twentieth century. Congress enacted a series of federal laws regulating environmental quality in the 1950s and 1960s, culminating in the Clean Air Acts of 1963 and 1970 and the National Environmental Policy Act of 1969. In 1970 the Nixon administration created the Environmental Protection Agency to implement the recently passed legislation.

All three types of social regulation addressed harmful effects of business behavior on the population, as consumers, workers, and community residents. The significant expansion of social regulation during the postwar decades was driven by popular movements demanding that government should compel business to avoid harm to those groups in its pursuit of profit. The dominant economic ideas of that period justified such social regulation as necessary to address "market failures," in which the profit interests of business might lead companies to engage in practices that harm individuals who have little or no ability to avoid such harm.[24]

In 1978 President Carter took some tentative steps to ease social regulations (Ferguson and Rogers, 1986, 106). However, the tide turned after Ronald Reagan took office in 1981. The Reagan administration sought to weaken social regulation, viewing it as anti-business and an obstacle to economic growth. Reagan's 1981 statement that "trees cause more pollution than automobiles do" set the tone for his administration's environmental policies. He named long-time opponents of government regulation to key positions in his administration, such as James Watt as secretary of the interior and Anne Gorsuch as head of the Environmental Protection Agency.[25] From fiscal year 1980 to 1984, authorized permanent personnel declined by 21% in the Environmental Protection Agency, by 22% in the Occupational Safety and Health Administration, and by 38% in the Consumer Product Safety Commission.[26] From fiscal year 1980 to 1982 initial complaint inspections by the Occupational Safety and Health Administration fell by 52% and follow-up inspections by 87% (Ferguson and Rogers, 1986, 131, 134).

The newly influential neoliberal economic theories provided support for social deregulation, arguing that individual actions such as lawsuits were a more effective means than government regulation to resolve any problems that business decisions might cause. James C. Miller III, an economist named as Reagan's first chairman of the Federal Trade Commission in 1981, tried to reign in the activist lawyers in the commission's Bureau of Consumer Protection by requiring that any action they initiated against unsafe products first get approval from one of the agency's free-market economists. In 1982 a Federal Trade Commission economist temporarily blocked a proposed order requiring the repair of leaky valves in the cold-water survival suits kept on merchant vessels and off-shore oil rigs. The Coast Guard had found that some 90% of the suits, meant to keep a worker alive if plunged into cold ocean waters, had defective valves, whose repair would cost about ten cents per valve. The Federal Trade Commission economist ruled that no government regulatory action was needed, on the grounds that lawsuits by affected parties or their survivors were a superior way to handle the problem.[27]

Unlike in the case of bank regulation and regulation of natural monopolies, social regulation was not eliminated, due to the strong public support for it. However, enforcement was significantly weakened in the neoliberal era. A key means of weakening social regulation was the introduction of so-called cost-benefit analysis of proposed social regulations. Neoliberal economists made the seemingly reasonable argument that, to be justified, a regulation should yield benefits that exceed its costs. However, the Environmental Protection Act had cited as its basic principle the prevention of environmental destruction, not a balancing of costs and benefits. Supporters of social regulation pointed out that in cost-benefit studies the cost of regulations tends to be derived from affected businesses' estimates of their cost of compliance, which they have a strong incentive to overstate, while the benefits of social regulation are very difficult and in some cases impossible to quantify. Hence, cost-benefit analysis tends to be stacked against regulation.

The fifth change in the role of government was a significant pull-back from enforcement of anti-trust laws. America's major anti-monopoly laws were passed in two waves, the Sherman Anti-Trust Act in 1890, when large corporations were first arising, and the Clayton Anti-Trust Act and Federal Trade Commission Act in 1914, passed in the Progressive Era after big corporations and banks had become well established. There is historical controversy about the political origin of anti-trust, which emerged from a complex political process involving a mass movement of small farmers and small businesses, newly active middle class social reformers, a growing Socialist Party, and representatives of the new big businesses, a political battle that is examined in Chapter 6.

As we shall see in Chapter 6, the Progressive Era initially produced a period of vigorous anti-monopoly enforcement that included suits to break up the new large corporations, two of which (the Standard Oil Trust and the American Tobacco Company) were broken up. However, over the course of the Progressive Era and the years immediately following it, anti-trust enforcement evolved to accept the legitimacy of large corporations, emphasizing regulation of business behavior to prevent certain kinds of monopolistic tactics rather than seeking to restructure the economy through the breakup of large corporations. After World War I there was little anti-trust enforcement until the tide reversed again in the 1930s under the New Deal. In the post-World War II decades, anti-trust laws were enforced relatively vigorously, but contrary to the popular impression, almost all anti-trust actions responded to complaints, not from ordinary consumers, but from businesses. The majority of market exchanges in a modern economy are between two business firms as seller and buyer, and the anti-trust laws became a framework for regulation and stabilization of the competitive process aimed at preventing any one company or small group of companies from taking undue advantage of other companies in either buyer-seller or competitive rival relationships.

Toward the end of the period of regulated capitalism, proposals arose in the U.S. Senate to use anti-trust law to undertake a major downsizing

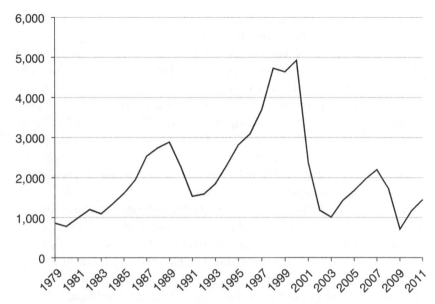

Figure 2.2. Merger transactions reported to the Federal Trade Commission, 1979–2011.
Source: Federal Trade Commission, various years.

of big business. The proposed Hart Deconcentration bill threatened to break up leading firms in every industry in which the top four firms had a large share of the business.[28] Although the proposal never became law, just its introduction by a well-respected senator was unnerving to large corporations.

After 1981 anti-trust enforcement was significantly eased. Proposed corporate mergers received less scrutiny, and a merger wave occurred in the 1980s, followed by a much larger one in the 1990s, as Figure 2.2 shows.[29] As they did for other areas of state withdrawal, neoliberal economists provided justifications. A theory of "contestable markets" arose arguing that even an industry with only one firm could be a competitive one, as long as the firm faced potential entry of new firms. Some economists claimed that domination of many industries by a few giants with very high profits did not indicate monopoly power but rather that the most efficient ones in the industry had grown and displaced their less efficient rivals. According to the new neoliberal theory of competition, where monopoly power exists in the economy it is the product of government coercion through such practices as requiring a license to enter a profession, not the actions of private firms.

The sixth change in the role of government was the privatization of public functions. The previous process of building an expanded public sector providing public goods and services directly to the population was reversed, as privatization became the order of the day. In the regulated capitalist era following World War II, in many West European countries, such as France and the U.K., state-owned enterprises came to compose a large part of industry. Unlike most other developed capitalist countries, the United States never developed a large sector of state-owned enterprises.[30] In Europe privatization meant selling off state-owned enterprises. In developing countries where publicly owned oil companies and other natural resources companies had been formed in the postwar decades, many governments sold them off, usually to investors from the United States or Europe. However, in the United States privatization took the form mainly of contracting out public services to private companies rather than the sell-off of state-owned enterprises.

Not only were auxiliary aspects of public services contracted out, such as cafeterias in public buildings, but core public functions as well. This took place in social services, housing for the poor, schools, prisons, and even military functions, as during the Iraq War when private contractors supplied a significant proportion of those under arms. A proposal even surfaced in Congress in the 2000s to contract out federal tax collection to private firms, although this proposal was buried by charges of the revival of medieval tax farming with its notorious abuses. In 2007 the government, concerned about possible fraud and abuse by federal contractors, decided to investigate by hiring a contractor. The contractor, CACI International, itself had been criticized for its practices, and it charged the government $104 per hour for each person supplied to investigate other contractors.[31]

The dominant economic theory of the regulated capitalist era had granted a place for direct government provision of public goods and services. By contrast, a core principle of neoliberal economic theory is that government is inherently inefficient while private for-profit companies are optimally efficient. Hence, it follows that whatever goods and services government must be responsible for can be provided more effectively by private for-profit companies.

The seventh area of pullback by the state was the elimination or cutback of social welfare and income maintenance programs. In the regulated capitalist era such government programs as welfare payments for low-income people, social security retirement pensions, unemployment compensation, and minimum wage laws were viewed as measures that reduced the poverty and inequality that resulted from the operation of the market economy while increasing economic security in the face of the unpredictability of market forces. By contrast, neoliberal economists argued that such programs interfered with work incentives, created a government-dependent population, absorbed resources better devoted to private saving and investment, and in the case of the minimum wage, led to unemployment of low-skilled workers. A significant theme was that such programs only harmed the very groups they were intended to help.

After 1980 America's social welfare programs were weakened and some were eliminated. In 1996 the main income support program for poor people, Aid to Families with Dependent Children (AFDC), was abolished and replaced by Temporary Assistance for Needy Families (TANF), which provided support that was temporary and less generous. As Figure 2.3 shows, the benefit level under AFDC/TANF rose to a peak

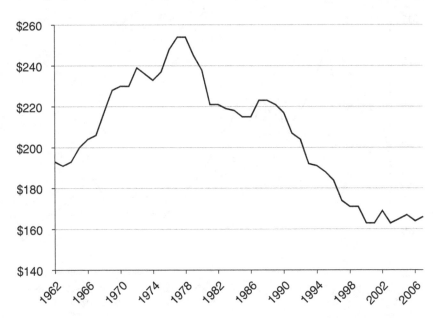

Figure 2.3. Monthly benefit per recipient under aid to families with dependent children or temporary assistance for needy families in 2009 dollars, 1962–2007.

Source: U.S. Department of Health and Human Services, 2013.

in 1977–78, after which it trended downward to a level 35% below its 1978 value by 2007. While Social Security was too popular to eliminate (or privatize), even it suffered marginal cutbacks over the neoliberal era, as the retirement age was raised.

The buying power of the federal minimum wage fell significantly in the neoliberal era. Figure 2.4 shows the federal minimum wage corrected for inflation. In the mid-1960s the real minimum wage was briefly over $10 an hour in 2011 dollars, then varied around $9 an hour in the 1970s. Starting in 1979 it declined steadily to $6.08 an hour in 1989, a drop of almost one-third, because Congress did not increase it in the face of inflation in that period. In the 1990s and 2000s it ranged between about $6 and $7 an hour in 2011 dollars. A declining real minimum wage affects a much larger share of the labor force than those who earn only that level of pay, since an increase in the minimum wage tends to cause the wages in the entire lower-wage segment of jobs to rise as well.

Eighth, and last in our list of changes in the government role, the tax system underwent major revisions in the neoliberal era. In the early

Figure 2.4. Federal hourly minimum wage in 2011 dollars, 1960–2007.
Source: U.S. Department of Labor, Wage and Hour Division, 2009; U.S. Bureau of Labor Statistics, 2013.

Ordinary Income — — — Corporate Income

····· Capital Gains

Figure 2.5. Top federal marginal tax rates, 1952–2007.
Source: Saez et al., 2012, Table A1.

part of the regulated capitalist era, the U.S. tax system was relatively progressive, despite some regressive elements, with high tax rates on the highest household incomes and a 50% tax rate on corporate profits. As Figure 2.5 shows, in the 1950s the marginal tax rate on the highest incomes was 91%, which was reduced to 70% in the 1960s. Then after 1981 it fell steeply, reaching a low of 28% in 1988, before rising somewhat in the 1990s. The corporate income tax rate remained near 50% until 1988, when it fell to 34%. The tax rate on capital gains, almost all of which falls on the rich, was lowered to 15% in 2003. Overall, in the neoliberal era tax incidence shifted significantly away from business and the rich toward those at the middle of the income distribution.[32]

While income tax rates declined for corporations and high-income households, payroll taxes for Social Security and Medicare, which are regressive taxes that take a smaller share of income from high-income earners, rose during the period. One partially offsetting program to this trend has been the Earned Income Tax Credit, which was expanded in the 1990s. This program has provided significant additional income to low-income working families with children. However, as we shall see in Chapter 3, this was not sufficient to counter the sharp trend of increasing income inequality over the whole course of the neoliberal era.

The Capital-Labor Relation

The institutions governing the relation between employers and employees changed radically in the neoliberal era. This change is as important for understanding neoliberal capitalism as the changes in the state role in the economy discussed above. A central institution of the regulated capitalist era in the U.S. was a stable form of collective bargaining between large corporations and trade unions that emerged after World War II. For the first time in U.S. history, wages, hours, and working conditions in a major part of the economy were set by negotiation between companies and labor unions. This took place in most of the manufacturing industries that had come to be dominated by large corporations as well as in mining, construction, transportation, power, communication, some sections of wholesale and retail trade, and various services. Collective bargaining was established mainly among large corporations, although it also played a role in some sectors where small companies predominate, such as in construction.

While the postwar capital-labor relation was not entirely peaceful, and strikes frequently occurred in major industries in the 1950s and 1960s, big corporations that engaged in collective bargaining normally did not try to get rid of the practice or drive out the unions, but accepted the legitimacy of trade unions.[33] That this was the case is suggested by the following statement by Republican presidential candidate Dwight D. Eisenhower during the general election campaign in 1952:

> I have no use for those—regardless of their political party—who hold some foolish dream of spinning the clock back to days when unorganized labor was a huddled, almost helpless mass. . . . Today in America unions have a secure place in our industrial life. Only a handful of unreconstructed reactionaries harbor the ugly thought of breaking

unions. Only a fool would try to deprive working men and women of the right to join the union of their choice.[34]

In the neoliberal era the collective bargaining relation between employers and labor unions rapidly eroded. Big corporations that had previously accepted collective bargaining began to aggressively seek to reduce or eliminate any union role in the setting of wages and working conditions, and the federal government's stance toward unions shifted to one of hostility. From the mid-1930s through the early 1950s, union membership as a percentage of employment had grown steadily, reaching 35.7% in 1953 (Hirsch, 2007). The impact of collective bargaining was significantly greater than the 35.7% figure might suggest, for two reasons. First, the number of employees covered by collective bargaining contracts exceeds the number of union members. Second, when a substantial percentage of companies are unionized, non-unionized companies are under pressure to offer wages and working conditions that approximate those won through collective bargaining in order to discourage their employees from unionizing.

From its peak in 1953 the unionization rate declined gradually to 29.1% in 1970. From 1970–73 it fell further, to 24.0% in 1973.[35] As Figure 2.6 shows, the rate then stabilized until 1979, as rising public sector unionization compensated for a decline in the private sector. After 1979 the unionization rate fell steadily, to 11.2% in 2012, which was below the rate in 1929 prior to the long expansion of unionization during the Great Depression and World War II. While various factors explain the decline in unionization after 1979, one factor was the marked shift in the rulings of the National Labor Relations Board, whose members are appointed by the president. Unfair labor practice complaints against employers had been sustained 84% of the time in 1979–80 but the rate declined to 51% of cases in 1983–84. While board decisions on contested issues in union representation campaigns favored the union complaint in 54% of the cases in 1979–80, the rate fell to 28% in 1983–84 (Ferguson and Rogers, 1986, 136).

In the neoliberal era the determination of wages and working conditions passed from labor-management negotiation to market forces. As unions' power waned, even formerly strong unions, that had previously won regular wage increases, were forced to accept wage freezes, large wage cuts, or two-tier wage structures providing wages for new

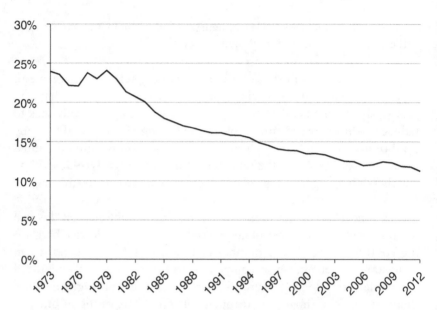

Figure 2.6. Union members as a percentage of all employees, 1973–2012.
Source: Hirsch 2007, data appendix; Hirsch and Macpherson, 2013.

hires as low as half the pay rate for current workers.[36] Starting in the 1980s and spreading rapidly in the 1990s and 2000s, such two-tier wage structures appeared in basic manufacturing industries such as autos and steel as well as in airlines, the retail sector, and state and local government.[37]

Employers, now largely free from having to bargain with unions, began to transform the nature of jobs in many industries. There followed another institutional change in the capital-labor relation: the "casualization" of jobs. Over time a growing proportion of jobs in the United States became part-time or temporary. In the regulated capitalist era what has been called the "primary sector" of employment—that is, stable, long-term jobs with relatively high pay, good fringe benefits, and regular pay increases over time—made up an estimated 63.8% of all jobs in the U.S. in 1970 (Gordon et al., 1982, 211), while most of the remainder of employment, although lacking such good conditions, at least involved a standard, full-time employment relation. In the neoliberal era the number of such jobs shrank rapidly, as business demanded "flexible labor markets." One study found that all forms of contingent jobs constituted one-third of total employment in the U.S. in 1997 (Kallberg, 2003, 162). A study of OECD countries found that temporary employment in 2006 was 21% of total employment in Spain and 20% in France, having risen from 15% and 3%, respectively, in 1983–85 (Vosko, 2010, 132).[38] The term "flexible labor markets" has different meanings for employers and workers, in that flexibility means for employers that they are free to define the terms of employment, while for workers it means they have lost any say in their conditions and must accept whatever terms employers offer them.

The Corporate Sector

Several changes took place in the corporate sector during the neoliberal era. First, competition among large corporations took a new form. Under regulated capitalism, large firms had engaged in a restrained form of competition, sometimes called "co-respective competition." While large companies sought to increase their market share at the expense of rivals through advertising and product innovation, they followed accepted ground rules of competition. The most important rule was avoidance of price wars, or even price reductions. In the post-World War II period price leadership was a widespread practice in industries dominated by a few large firms. The largest or most powerful firm would set the price and the others would follow suit. If the price leader raised the price, the others would resist the temptation to undersell the price leader, instead raising their prices in lock-step. As long as there were no meetings or communications among the rival firms, price leadership did not run afoul of the anti-trust laws. Such co-respective competition brought stability to both prices and profits of large corporations, which typically made positive profits even in recession years as they resisted the temptation to cut prices when sales were falling.[39]

In the neoliberal era co-respective competition gave way to an unrestrained competition reminiscent of the late nineteenth-century U.S. economy. Large price cuts, and price wars, returned to the world of large corporations. The relatively secure world of co-respective competition was replaced by a very different environment, in which even the largest firms were forced to confront the possibility not just of losing money for a period of time but of being driven out of business. In 1999 Jeffrey Garten, dean of the Yale School of Management, stated that CEOs of large corporations now "feel they are in a brutally competitive world, and they think they are in a race for their lives."[40] This contrasts sharply with the life of the large corporate CEO in the regulated capitalist era.[41]

A second change in the corporate sector involved the manner of selection of the top corporate official, the CEO. In the regulated capitalist era, the normal practice in large corporations was to fill that position by promotion from within. Almost all CEOs were individuals who had spent their career working for the company, rising through the ranks and finally attaining the top position. This practice produced CEOs who were "company men" (virtually all were male that era), who strongly identified with the company. The channel through which a CEO had risen varied across companies, with some often promoting managers who specialized in production (frequently the case in oil companies) while others saw managers from sales or finance rise to the top—but whatever the specialty, the norm was promotion from within.

In the neoliberal era a market in CEOs developed as it became common for CEOs of large corporations to be hired from outside the company, often from another industry.[42] Top corporate officials often moved from one company to another over time. Rather than being a lifetime "company man," many CEOs of large corporations now had a material self-interest in creating the appearance of successful management over a few years, to be positioned for getting a higher paying CEO position at another company.

A third change was the penetration of market principles within large corporations. In the nineteenth century Marx observed that large capitalist firms were internally much like planned economies. Within the firm, economic activity proceeds according to a plan laid out by the management. The relation among the employees is not that of market exchange but of jointly carrying out a plan. Market exchange takes over after the product is produced and ready for sale (and of course in the purchase of inputs by the firm). However, in the neoliberal era market relations intruded inside large corporations to some extent. Divisions came to be viewed as so many profit centers competing against one another, with those that showed success being allowed to expand while those with subpar profit would be downsized or sold off.[43]

Fourth, and last, a particularly important change in the corporate sector occurred in the relation between financial institutions and nonfinancial corporations. Under regulated capitalism, financial institutions were forced by the regulatory system of that era to basically serve the nonfinancial sector. Financial institutions could not pursue whatever activity they expected would gain the highest rate of profit but were required to offer only those financial services allowed to each type of institution. As noted above, commercial banks took deposits and made loans, largely to the business sector. Savings banks took deposits, paying slightly higher allowed interest rates, and made mortgage loans to homeowners. Insurance companies offered various types of conventional insurance. Investment banks floated bond and stock issues.[44]

In the neoliberal era, financial institutions gradually shifted their activities as the regulations were lifted in stages. As they became free to pursue whatever activity appeared most profitable, financial institutions increasingly engaged in risky and speculative activities. As will be discussed in Chapter 5, they created an array of complex new financial instruments, through a process referred to as "financial innovation," some of which had little or no relation to the nonfinancial sector, or only an indirect relation to it. The financial sector became largely independent of the nonfinancial sector, increasingly pursuing profit from the creation and buying and selling of financial assets, which was far more profitable than the traditional financial activities they had been constrained to engage in under regulated capitalism. However, such activities were far more profitable only until the financial structure they built came crashing down in 2008.

The Uneven Spread of Neoliberal Capitalism

When regulated capitalism arose after World War II, it soon became the dominant form of capitalism in practically the entire developed capitalist world, including Western Europe and Japan, as well as in the developing countries in Asia, Africa, and Latin America. There were differences in the exact form of regulated capitalism in the various parts of the world. In much of Western Europe it was often called social democracy, in which state intervention in the economy was greater than in the United States, the welfare programs were more generous, and labor had a stronger role than in the United States.[45] In Japan, a somewhat different form of regulated capitalism developed, with a high degree of state intervention but weaker social welfare programs and little influence for labor. In many developing countries, regulated capitalism took the form of a "developmental state," in which the group controlling the government sought to use state power to promote rapid economic development

The global distribution of neoliberal capitalism has differed from that of postwar regulated capitalism. Neoliberalism emerged first in the United States and United Kingdom. It was adopted even more fully in some other countries, such as the formerly Communist Party-ruled states of Eastern and Central Europe and those developing countries whose external debt caused them to fall under the control of the IMF, which imposed neoliberal restructuring on them. Limited neoliberal restructuring took place in some continental Western European countries and practically not at all in Japan.

For a time after 1980 several East Asian countries maintained a developmental state, most notably South Korea. However, following the Asian financial crisis of 1997, a number of former developmental states underwent significant neoliberal restructuring. As China shifted away from an economy based on central planning and state-owned enterprises after 1978, it adopted a form of developmental state system with a mixture of market and plan as well as private and state enterprises. While China underwent neoliberal restructuring of its social programs and eliminated the former promise of guaranteed employment, it retained an interventionist state that has guided economic development in the neoliberal era.

Perhaps the location in which neoliberalism has been most fully installed is in the institutions of the global economy, particularly the IMF, World Bank, and World Trade Organization (Kotz and McDonough, 2010). In individual nation-states the extent of neoliberal restructuring has varied significantly and changed over time. Nevertheless, this period well deserves the title of the "neoliberal era," given the significant neoliberal restructuring in the dominant capitalist state—the United States—and the need for every state to adjust to operating within a neoliberal global system dominated by the United States.

Financialization and Globalization

During the neoliberal era, the role of finance and financial institutions in the economy expanded significantly. The term "financialization" came into use, meaning, as was noted in Chapter 1, "the increasing role of financial motives, financial markets, financial actors and financial institutions in the operation of domestic and international economies" (Epstein, 2005, 3). Evidence of this development can be found in the increase in activity in financial markets, a rise in the value of financial assets, an increase in foreign exchange transactions compared to the volume of international trade, and other indicators of financial activity.[46] Some analysts view financialization as the main change in capitalism in recent decades, interpreting the form of capitalism since around 1980 through the lens of financialization rather than neoliberalism.[47]

Financialization has two limitations as an overall conception of post-1980 capitalism. First, it arrived too late. By some measures, such as the increase in foreign exchange transactions relative to the volume of international trade, financialization appeared to begin in the 1970s.[48] However, financialization did not develop until a later date by most measures. Figure 2.7 shows the gross value added by financial corporations as a percentage of value added by all corporations in the United States. From 1948 to 1981 financial gross value added rose gradually, from 4.2% to 7.8% of all corporate value added. After the first major financial deregulation laws were passed in 1980 and 1982, a steeper upward trend in financial value added as a share of the total took hold, reaching 13.8% in 2006.[49] The financial deregulation laws, an important part of neoliberal restructuring, allowed the financialization process to get underway. This suggests that financialization was to a significant extent a consequence of neoliberal restructuring.

It was the rise in financial profit that propelled the financial sector to a place of rapidly growing importance in the economy. Measured by value added, the financial sector did not loom large in the U.S. economy even by 2006, as Figure 2.7 indicates. On the other hand, financial profit rose spectacularly and its rise came later than for financial sector value added. Figure 2.8 shows the percentage of financial corporate profit in total corporate profit in the U.S. From 1948 to 1970 financial profit rose gradually, if unevenly, from about 10% to 20% of total profit. However, after 1970 financial profit showed no growth trend through 1989, when it again hit 20%. Only after 1989 did financial profit begin a long and steep climb, interrupted by a fall in the mid-1990s, rising to a remarkable 40% of total profit in 2001–03.[50] It was only in the 2000s that financialization fully blossomed, long after the neoliberal era had begun.

Figure 2.7. Gross value added of financial corporations as a percentage of gross value added of all corporations in the U.S., 1948–2012.

Source: U.S. Bureau of Economic Analysis, 2013, NIPA Table 1.14.

The second limitation of financialization as an overall concept for post-1980 capitalism is that it is not a good basis for explaining most of the institutional changes in the neoliberal era. Financialization does not provide an adequate framework for explaining the many changes in the role of the state in the economy in the neoliberal era discussed above, nor the changes in the institutions of the capital-labor relation. It is not an adequate basis for explaining the big rise in inequality during the neoliberal era.

The evidence supports the view that financialization in recent decades was driven by neoliberal restructuring. Chapter 4 will consider the ways in which the overall neoliberal institutional structure enabled financial institutions to appropriate a rapidly growing share of profit in the economy and the problems that eventually resulted. Thus, despite its undoubted importance, the financialization process does not provide an adequate overall framework for understanding the development of capitalism in this period.[51]

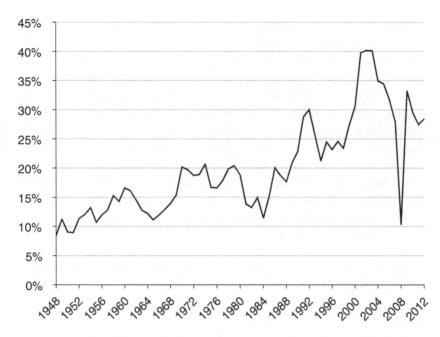

Figure 2.8. Profits of financial corporations as a percentage of the profits of all corporations in the U.S., 1948–2012.

Source: U.S. Bureau of Economic Analysis, 2013, NIPA Table 1.14.

Globalization is another much discussed feature of contemporary capitalism. By globalization is meant a significant increase in the movement of goods, services, capital, and money across national boundaries, resulting in a capitalism that is more globally integrated than before, including the creation of global production and distribution chains far more developed than those existing in earlier periods. Even more so than for financialization, globalization has been presented as a framework for understanding the contemporary form of capitalism. For example, Bowles et al. (2005, 162–164), which like this book uses the social structure of accumulation theory, specifically reject the view that the state role in the economy has been reduced in this era. They refer to contemporary capitalism, which they date from about 1991, not as neoliberal capitalism but as "transnational capitalism." They argue that "its most distinctive feature, compared to what came before, is the integration of the U.S. economy into a world system of trade in goods, migration of people, exchange of knowledge, and footloose investors" (163).

Capitalism became increasingly globalized in the decades prior to World War I. Then the interwar period saw a reduction in global economic integration. After World War II, the process of globalization resumed, gradually at first. However, by the late 1960s and early 1970s the degree of global economic integration was increasing, as Figure 2.1 showed. For the United States, Figure 2.9 shows that import penetration began to increase in the late 1960s, rising rapidly in the 1970s. Thus, in contrast to financialization, which emerged after the rise of neoliberalism, the globalization process in this era began before neoliberalism had emerged, although globalization did increase further in the neoliberal era, particularly after 1990.

In Chapter 3, it will be argued that the increasing global economic integration of capitalism in the late 1960s through the 1970s was one

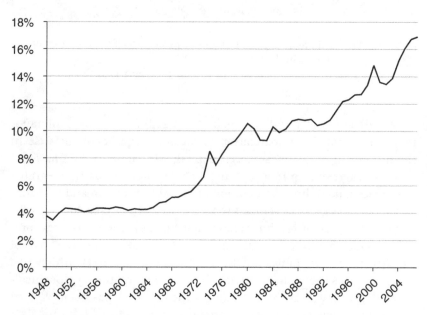

Figure 2.9. U.S. imports as a percentage of gross domestic product, 1948–2007.

Source: U.S. Bureau of Economic Analysis, 2013, International Transactions Table 1, NIPA Table 1.1.5.

Note: Imports include goods and services.

factor that led to the emergence of neoliberalism. However, many of the most important features of capitalism since 1980 cannot be understood or explained based on globalization. Globalization cannot explain the financialization process and the rise of a speculatively oriented financial sector, which have played a major role in contemporary capitalism. It cannot explain the succession of big asset bubbles that has been an important feature of neoliberal capitalism. Globalizalization has been one factor strengthening the bargaining power of capital relative to labor, but it is by no means the only factor. Globalization cannot fully explain the rapidly rising inequality in the contemporary era, which has been quite extreme in the United States compared to some other countries that are even more integrated into the global economy than is the United States, such as Germany. The belief that globalization is the central feature of capitalism in this period had led some analysts to predict, prior to 2008, that global economic and financial imbalances would bring the next big economic crisis, but that prediction turned out to be wrong. Like financialization, globalization has been an important feature of the neoliberal form of capitalism, but it is not the best defining concept for understanding the development of capitalism in this era.[52]

The best way to resolve the debates over these different lenses for viewing contemporary capitalism is to see how effectively each can focus attention on and explain the most important economic developments in this period. This book seeks to show what can be explained through the lens of neoliberal capitalism, and the reader can judge the adequacy of the resulting analysis.

Is It Liberal?

The concept "neoliberalism" might suggest a reduction in the size of the state. Has this actually happened in the neoliberal era? As the size of the economy grew, the state was bound to grow in absolute terms. A reasonable measure must be the size of the state in relation to the size of the overall economy.

There are several ways to measure the size of the state. Economists distinguish three traditional measures, with the broadest one called government expenditure. That measure includes the value of goods and services produced by public employees, the cost of items purchased from the private sector, and transfer payments such as social security retirement pensions, disability payments, and medical care payments for individual health care.[53] Furthermore, one can examine the federal government only or include state and local governments as well.

Figure 2.10 shows the broadest measure, government expenditure, as a percentage of GDP.[54] Since the business cycle greatly affects this measure, long-run trends can be seen by comparing business cycle peak years,[55] which are indicated by vertical lines in the figure.[56] Total government expenditure rose rapidly relative to GDP from 1948 to 1973 in the regulated capitalist period. During 1979 to 2007, it increased somewhat further from 1979 to 1990, from 31.1% to 34.3% of GDP, then fell somewhat in 2000 and rose again in 2007. Looking at the series as a whole over the two periods, the trend was rising in 1948–73 and relatively flat in 1979–2007. If military spending—a type of spending

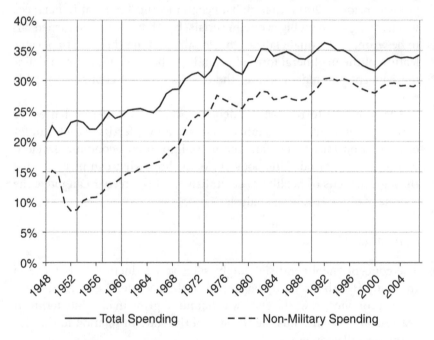

Figure 2.10.   Government expenditure as percentage of gross domestic product, 1948–2007.

Sources: U.S. Bureau of Economic Analysis, 2013, NIPA Tables 1.1.5, 3.2, 3.3, 3.9.5.

Note: Vertical lines indicate business cycle peaks.

that is supported by neoliberal ideology and that is greatly influenced by war and cold war—is excluded, there is a sharp upward trend from 1953–73, followed by a more gradual upward trend during 1979–2007. The two narrower measures of the size of government, called government value added and government consumption and investment, show rapid growth relative to GDP in 1948–73, followed by no growth or a slight decline relative to GDP during 1979–2007, both including and excluding the military category.

Thus, the data suggest that the size of government relative to GDP in the United States rose significantly in the regulated capitalist era and showed little change in the neoliberal era. While the sharply rising trend was arrested in the neoliberal era, the growth of the state was not significantly reversed by any of the measures. One could interpret this as a small success for the neoliberal agenda, yet it fell short of the goal its promoters had set.

The size of the state is one indicator, but not the best indicator, of whether this form of capitalism can be considered "neoliberal." Liberalism calls for a state that does not "interfere" in the economy, letting the "free market" operate undisturbed. Has the state actually withdrawn significantly from regulation of the economy in the neoliberal era?

Some critics of the concept of neoliberalism argue that the state has remained just as active, or has even become more active, in regulation of the economy, although with a shift in government intervention away from programs that benefit the majority and toward those that benefit big business and the rich. An example is the expansion in the enforcement of so-called intellectual property rights in the neoliberal era. This has been cited as an example of the hypocrisy of neoliberal advocates, who decry government intervention in the market while taking draconian steps to prevent free-market trading of intellectual creations whose distribution and use have almost no costs.

On the contrary, active enforcement of intellectual property rights is entirely consistent with the neoliberal view of the proper role of the state. Neoliberal ideology is not anarchist ideology. As was noted above, it views the protection of private property rights as a proper role of the state, along with maintaining public order and providing a strong national defense. The defense of intellectual property rights, it is claimed, protects the rights of everyone from individual inventors and writers to corporations, although in practice it often benefits large corporations at the expense of individual knowledge producers. Private property cannot exist without state protection, if society is to avoid incessant conflict over control of property among its members. The extension of protection of intellectual property rights by the U.S. government, within the United States and outside its borders, falls well within the neoliberal concept of the proper role of the state. Once property rights are defined and enforced by the state, then the exercise of such property rights is left to the decisions of the property owners (and their attorneys) in market transactions. Similarly, the active use of military force and the massive increase in incarceration in the neoliberal era in the United States fit within the neoliberal concept of the proper role of the state.

On the other hand, as was noted above, the state did withdraw from regulation and intervention in the economy in many respects during

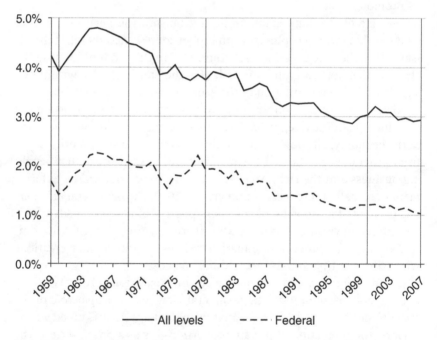

Figure 2.11. Government infrastructure spending as a percentage of gross domestic product, 1959–2007.

Source: U.S. Bureau of Economic Analysis, 2013, NIPA Tables 3.17, 1.1.5.

Notes: Vertical lines indicate business cycle peaks. Infrastructure spending includes investment and current consumption in the economic affairs category.

the neoliberal era. Even some types of government intervention in the economy that mainly benefit business were cut back, such as public infrastructure spending. Figure 2.11 provides an estimate of infrastructure spending by the federal government and by all levels of government as a percentage of GDP. After 1960 federal infrastructure spending rose and then remained stable through 1973 at about 2% of GDP. After 1979 federal infrastructure spending declined, including in the 1990s despite the Clinton administration's promise to increase it, falling to 1% of GDP by 2007. Infrastructure spending by all levels of government rose to 4.8% of GDP in the mid-1960s, then gradually declined to 3.8% in 1973. After 1979 the trend was downward, reaching 2.9% in 2007. Weakened anti-trust enforcement is another example of a regulatory withdrawal that can be interpreted as harmful for business as a whole, since it has largely functioned to protect the majority of companies against monopoly power on the part of their suppliers.

Some large government programs have survived in the neoliberal era, despite their contradiction to the neoliberal agenda, due to the political power of their beneficiaries. A good example is farm subsidy programs, whose beneficiaries reside in many congressional districts. But it is difficult to deny that the U.S. state significantly reduced its regulation of and intervention in the economy during this period, with the exception of those government roles approved by the neoliberal view as within the proper role of the state, which center around protecting private property, maintaining order, and providing a strong military. On this ground, it is reasonable to view the current form of capitalism as a liberal one, by comparison to the previous regulated form of capitalism.

Although neoliberal capitalism has been presented so far as a list of ideas and institutions, it does have a unifying principle, as was suggested in the brief definition given in Chapter 1. Table 2.1 summarizes the main ideas and institutions of neoliberal capitalism in the United States. The unifying principle is the greatly expanded role of market relations and market forces in the regulation of economic activity, with a reduced role for regulation by other types of relations and institutions such as states, corporate bureaucracies, trade unions, and professional associations. This explains why the term "regulated capitalism" is more accurate than "state-regulated capitalism"—the state is not the only institution partially taking the place of market relations and market forces.

Table 2.1 The Ideas and Institutions of Neoliberal Capitalism

1.	Dominance of neoliberal ideas and theories
2.	The Global Economy: Removal of barriers to the movement of goods, services, capital, and money across national boundaries
3.	The Role of Government in the Economy

    a)   Renunciation of aggregate demand management

    b)   Deregulation of basic industries

    c)   Deregulation of the financial sector

    d)   Weakening of regulation of consumer product safety, job safety, and the environment

    e)   Weakening of anti-trust enforcement

    f)   Privatization and contracting out of public goods and services

    g)   Cutbacks in or elimination of social welfare programs

    h)   Tax cuts for business and the rich

4.   The Capital-Labor Relation

    a)   Marginalization of collective bargaining

    b)   Casualization of jobs

5.   The Corporate Sector

    a)   Unrestrained competition

    b)   Corporate CEOs hired from outside the corporation

    c)   Market principles penetrate inside corporations

    d)   Financial institutions shift toward new types of activities and become relatively independent of the nonfinancial sector

Every one of the institutional changes in Table 2.1 involves an expansion of the market. For a few, that may not be so obvious, such as tax cuts for business and the rich, or the separation of the financial sector from its traditional relation to the real sector. However, tax cuts for business and the rich are a way to redirect funds that had been in the hands of the state back to their original private recipients, who thereby have additional funds for market transactions. The financial sector, now free of government regulation, is therefore able to follow market incentives which lead it away from traditional roles and practices. Neoliberal ideas, with their glorification of unfettered market relations and their denial of any need to intervene in the face of market failures, provide a powerful justification for the shift away from non-market forms of regulation and toward an expanded role for the market. Neoliberal ideology presents a case that such a shift will secure both economic prosperity and individual freedom.

Neoliberal Institutions and the Capital-Labor Class Relation

In Chapter 1 it was noted that every institutional form of capitalism, or social structure of accumulation, must stabilize the relation between capital and labor, which is necessary if the social structure of accumulation is to promote profit-making and stable economic expansion.[57] There are two ways this relation can be stabilized under capitalism—via a compromise between the two sides or through capitalist domination of labor sufficiently great that labor has little ability to defend its interests.[58] Postwar regulated capitalism was based on the former mode of stabilization of the capital-labor relation—capital-labor compromise—while neoliberal capitalism is based on a thorough domination of labor by capital. The thorough domination of labor by capital in the neoliberal era can be seen in various developments, including the sharp break in the trend of real wages after the 1970s—from regular annual increases to stagnation—as well as the decline in unionization, the sharp increase in income inequality, and the remarkable rise in corporate CEO salaries. The latter developments will be documented in Chapter 4.

This raises the following question: What is the connection between the unifying principle embodied in the ideas and institutions of neoliberal capitalism—the greatly expanded role for market relations and market forces—and the shift from capital-labor compromise to thorough domination of capital over labor? Neoliberal ideology says nothing explicitly about the power relation between capital and labor. While a few of the institutions listed in Table 2.1 obviously are related to this change in the capital-labor relation—particularly the marginalization of collective bargaining and the casualization of jobs—for some others the connection to the increased power of capital is not so obvious.

Whether obvious or not, most, if not all, of the institutions in Table 2.1 directly or indirectly reinforce the thorough domination of capital over labor. Globalization empowers capital to move wherever labor is cheapest. Renunciation of aggregate demand management aimed at a low unemployment rate weakens labor's bargaining power, as do the cutbacks in social welfare programs. Deregulation of basic industries, where unions had been strong and wages relatively high, was followed by sharp drops in wages in those industries. Privatization and contracting out often replaced well-paid, unionized public sector jobs by low-wage private sector jobs in non-unionized companies. Unrestrained competition among large corporations makes it difficult for them to afford union wages and puts pressure on them to get rid of the union in their company.

Some analysts interpret the current form of capitalism as centered around thorough capitalist domination of labor while others view it as characterized by the expansion of market relations and market forces. The interpretation presented here holds that these two features of neoliberal capitalism are consistent with, and related to, one another. The neoliberal transformation of capitalism, from a form of capitalism in which non-market institutions played a major role in regulating economic activity to the current form in which market relations and forces predominate, has promoted the increasing power of capital over labor.

What explains this curious connection between expanded market relations and increased power of capital over labor? The best way to explore that question is to examine how neoliberal capitalism emerged in the late 1970s and early 1980s. In doing so, we can uncover the connection between these two aspects of neoliberal capitalism, while also learning some lessons about the nature of dominant ideas and their role in economic and social change. That is the subject of the following chapter.

3

The Rise of Neoliberal Capitalism

The rise of neoliberal capitalism and its associated ideas came as a surprise to most analysts. By the 1960s, after some two decades of regulated capitalism in the United States, it was widely believed that an expanded state role, unionization of the workplace, the building of a welfare state, and the other changes that had emerged in the 1930s and 1940s represented real progress for the economy and society. If capitalism had been harsh in its early days, that was now ancient history. The economic benefits of capitalism, no longer flowing only to a few plutocrats, were now widely shared among most, if not all, of the population. As was noted above, the very term "capitalism" had largely disappeared from public discourse, replaced by "mixed economy."

Keynesian ideas seemed to be permanently ensconced in academic economics as well as in the policy realm. The old free-market economic theories were widely regarded as outmoded, relegated to the proverbial dustbin of history. At the leading U.S. university economics departments other than that of the University of Chicago, the old free-market economic theories were considered relevant only in courses in the history of economic thought.[1] "Modern" economics was assumed to be the dominant Keynesian theory.[2]

Neoliberalism first arose in the realm of ideas, starting in the late 1960s and steadily gathering strength over the course of the 1970s.[3] The sudden emergence and rapid spread of new versions of free-market economic theory were startling and inexplicable to many leading economists. By the end of the 1970s, the new free-market theories, increasingly advocated by younger academic economists, were pushing the established Keynesian orthodoxy aside.

45

As was noted in the preceding chapter, neoliberal institutional transformation, which many associate with the Reagan administration, began before Reagan took office in January 1981. During 1978–80 airline and trucking deregulation were underway, the first major bank deregulation act was passed, and the Federal Reserve drove interest rates up rapidly despite the very high unemployment rate that resulted. The average real AFDC benefit hit a peak in 1978, after which it began its long decline, as did the real value of the federal minimum wage (see Figures 2.3 and 2.4). After Ronald Reagan assumed the presidency in 1981, neoliberal restructuring accelerated. A defining event took place when President Reagan broke a national strike of air traffic controllers in August 1981, which sent a signal to business that direct action to roll back unions, long considered taboo, was now legitimate.[4]

Why did this major, unexpected transformation take place? Why did an old form of capitalism, albeit with some new features, suddenly emerge in the late 1970s to early 1980s? The underlying cause lay in a shift on the part of big business.[5] Regulated capitalism had been the product of a coalition that emerged in the 1940s between two key groups in American society, big business and organized labor.[6] The main opposition to regulated capitalism came from smaller businesses, which were too weak to prevent the consolidation of regulated capitalism.[7] Over the course of the 1970s, big business shifted from support for regulated capitalism to endorsement of neoliberal transformation. In a new alliance with small business, this created an overwhelmingly powerful force that was able to rapidly install the neoliberal form of capitalism. Organized labor, deserted by its erstwhile coalition partner, was left as the main opposition, and it was in no position to prevent the transformation on its own.

This interpretation of the rise of neoliberal capitalism will be presented in several stages in this chapter. First, we consider three alternative explanations for the rise of neoliberal capitalism, finding none of them to be persuasive. Second, we provide evidence that the introduction of key features of regulated capitalism received support from a major part of big business in the 1940s, and we offer an explanation for that position on the part of big business. An understanding of the role of big business in the formation of regulated capitalism is a necessary foundation for explaining why big business later shifted to support for neoliberal transformation in the 1970s. Third, the historical context for the rise of neoliberal capitalism is briefly examined: the economic crisis of the 1970s. Fourth, we present evidence that big business did indeed shift its support to neoliberalism in the 1970s. Fifth—and this is the heart of the case—we offer an explanation of why this shift on the part of big business occurred. Sixth, some lessons are drawn about the role of ideas and ideology in economic continuity and economic change.

Alternative Explanations of the Rise of Neoliberalism

Neoliberal theory itself suggests a simple explanation of neoliberalism's rise to dominance. That is the view that state intervention in the economy not only restricts individual freedom but also undermines economic performance. Thus, free-market ideas and institutions re-emerged once people realized the economic damage done by several decades of statism.

The problem with this explanation is that, for twenty-five years from the late 1940s to the early 1970s, the U.S. economy had the fastest, and most widely shared, economic growth of any long period in U.S. history. A study by Maddison (1995, 60, Table 3.1) found that period showed by far the fastest growth in GDP and in GDP per person of any period since 1820 for every region of the world.[8] In Chapter 4 we present evidence about economic performance during that period, which was sufficiently impressive to inspire the term "golden age of capitalism" to describe the quarter-century following World War II.[9]

Thus, it appeared that the "statism" of the postwar decades was working rather well in promoting economic progress. Indeed, that was a key reason for the continuing widespread acceptance of regulated capitalism and the inability of its opponents to derail it prior to the 1970s. However, eventually serious economic problems did emerge. One can trace their roots to the second half of the 1960s, although the problems did not fully emerge until after 1973. Following that year the U.S. economy, and the global capitalist economy, entered a period of long-term economic crisis. Although advocates of neoliberalism could point to serious economic problems after 1973, the argument that regulated capitalism could not bring economic progress is not supported by the historical evidence.

A second explanation of the rise of neoliberalism is that the financial sector of big business, after decades of subordination under regulated capitalism, was able to emerge as the dominant force in the 1970s (Arrighi, 1994; Dumenil and Levy, 2004). There are several variants of this view, but the idea common to the different variants is that regulated capitalism had been the creation of an alliance involving some subset of the following groups: corporate managers, industrial (or nonfinancial) capitalists, and labor. Left out of power were the financial capitalists, under a regime that closely regulated financial institutions and restricted their activities. Then, in the conditions of the economic crisis of the 1970s, financial capitalists were able to assert their dominance over the other groups, and the new version of capitalism they built is what we know as neoliberalism.[10] According to this interpretation, the neoliberal era can be understood as a return to a kind of finance capitalism somewhat akin to the era of J. P. Morgan before World War I.

If this explanation of the rise of neoliberalism is to have any explanatory power, then one should be able to identify a shift in dominance from one section of business to another in the 1970s. It assumes that financial capitalists displaced from power industrial capitalists, corporate managers, or both. Presumably the ousted groups would have contested their demise, but no one has found evidence of resistance to the rise of neoliberalism from either industrial capitalists or corporate managers, although labor did resist. Indeed, high-level corporate managers became far richer under neoliberal capitalism than they had previously been, as we will document in Chapter 4. We will present evidence below that, contrary to the financial dominance explanation, both financial and nonfinancial big capitalists first supported regulated capitalism, then in the 1970s both shifted to support for neoliberal transformation.

A third explanation points to technological factors. Howard and King (2008) present such an explanation based on the traditional Marxist theory of social change, although versions of the technological change explanation have been offered by mainstream analysts as well. Howard and King's understanding of what neoliberalism is has significant similarities to the interpretation presented in this book, including regarding globalization as an aspect of neoliberalism (Howard and King, 2008, 5).

The traditional version of the Marxist theory of social change asserts that, over very long periods of time, changes in technology (referred to as the development of the forces of production) lead to accommodating changes in social relations, economic and political institutions, and the dominant ideas.[11] Howard and King apply this theory to explain the rise of neoliberalism in the 1970s. They explicitly reject the view that attempts by capitalists to raise the rate of profit led to neoliberal restructuring. They argue that new technologies, particularly in information processing and communication, undermined the advantages of centralized production and decision-making while lowering the cost of decentralized production systems coordinated by market relations (Howard and King, 2008, chap. 6). Outsourcing was encouraged by such new technologies. The resulting expansion of market relations, which foster individual self-interested behavior, weakened the trade unions. Neoliberalism is seen as an institutional transformation that arose because it was a consequence of new technologies as well as fostering the effective utilization of the new technologies.

The traditional Marxist theory of social change can be used effectively to account for some major historical developments, such as the rise of capitalism in Europe many centuries ago, as well as some institutional changes during the capitalist era such as the rise of large corporations in the late nineteenth century. However, an explanation of the rise of neoliberalism as a consequence of technological developments is not persuasive. There are at least three weaknesses in this explanation.

One weakness is conceptual. The claim that the new technologies in information-processing and communication tended to move society toward decentralization in the form of expansion of market relations is not persuasive. Those technologies make centralized decision-making more effective by reducing the cost of gathering a lot of information in one place. One would think that these new technologies would make a more centralized form of economy more efficient as well as more flexible in response to unforeseen developments. Indeed, economic concentration has proceeded rapidly in some sectors of the economy in the neoliberal era, such as finance, telecommunications, restaurants, and retail trade.

Second, the timing of the key technological developments does not appear to fit this explanation. The most important of these new technologies—the personal computer, the internet, and cellular telephones—arose or became important only after the 1970s. This timing is not consistent with the theory of social change which holds that first new technologies develop, followed by resistance to their effective use from existing institutions, which eventually leads to institutional transformation.

Third, the idea that initial technological advance leads to institutional change which in turn frees the forces of production to develop rapidly does not appear to be supported by the evidence about economic performance in the neoliberal era. The next chapter will take a close look at economic performance after 1980. While important new technologies have indeed been introduced in the neoliberal era, those changes did not lead to accelerated economic advance for the economy as a whole if judged by the usual measures. It will be shown that the most commonly used measures of economic progress, such as the GDP growth rate and labor productivity growth rate, show inferior performance compared to that of the regulated capitalist era. As we will see in Chapter 4, GDP growth in the neoliberal era in United States even showed no discernible improvement over that of the crisis phase of regulated capitalism in the 1970s.

While the idea that technological change can help explain social, political, and ideological change may be applicable in some historical contexts, it does not appear to offer explanatory assistance in this case. Neoliberal capitalism has displayed some strengths in economic performance, such as price stability and a series of relatively long economic expansions punctuated, prior to 2008, by relatively brief and mild recessions. However, there is not a persuasive case that it has promoted rapid economic progress by the usual measures. Indeed, in our view neoliberalism has been a step backward with regard to economic progress as well as in other respects, and a rather big step at that. While steps backward do occur in history, such developments are not typical and, when they do occur, they present a puzzle that requires an explanation other than technological progressivity.[12]

Big Business and the Rise of Regulated Capitalism

The ideas and institutions that made up post-World War II regulated capitalism in the United States did not all arise simultaneously.[13] Table 3.1 lists the dominant ideas and the main institutions of regulated capitalism in the United States, in a manner parallel to the list for neoliberal capitalism in Table 2.1 of the previous chapter (the institutions listed in Table 3.1 were explained in Chapter 2).[14] A few of the institutions in Table 3.1 arose even before the 1930s but later came to make up part of the postwar system: regulation of basic industries, promotion of corporate CEOs from within, and governance of relations within corporations by bureaucratic principles. Several emerged, or were revived, during the

Table 3.1 The Ideas and Institutions of Regulated Capitalism

1. Dominance of Keynesian ideas and theories

2. The Global Economy: The Bretton Woods System, with fixed exchange
    rates, a gold-backed U.S. dollar as the world currency, and a moderately
    open world economy although with tariffs and some obstacles to free
    capital movement

3. The Role of Government in the Economy

    a) Keynesian fiscal and monetary policies aimed at a low
        unemployment rate and an acceptable inflation rate

    b) Government regulation of basic industries

    c) Government regulation of the financial sector

    d) Social regulation: environmental, occupational safety and health,
        and consumer product safety

    e) Strong anti-trust enforcement

    f) A high level of provision of public goods and services including
        infrastructure and education

    g) Welfare state

    h) Progressive income tax

4. The Capital-Labor Relation

    a) A major role for collective bargaining between companies and unions

    b) Large proportion of stable, long-term jobs

5. The Corporate Sector

    a) Co-respective competition

    b) Corporate CEOs promoted from within the corporation

    c) Bureaucratic principles govern relations within corporations

    d) Financial institutions mainly provide financing for nonfinancial
        businesses and households

New Deal in the 1930s and remained in place after World War II: financial regulation, strong enforcement of anti-trust legislation, a welfare
state, and a progressive income tax system.

However, the institutions of regulated capitalism that had emerged
by the 1930s fell short of constituting a new social structure of accumulation that could promote high profits and stable economic expansion.
Through the end of the 1930s, sharp conflict between labor and business continued to create instability and uncertainty, and the economy

failed to fully recover from the depression. U.S. entry into World War II at the end of 1941 introduced a special period in which the capital-labor conflict was temporarily suspended by both sides to support the war effort. It was not until shortly after World War II that a new, viable social structure of accumulation was constructed. The key new institutions that emerged in the 1940s were the Bretton Woods system, the rise to dominance of Keynesian ideas, government macroeconomic policies aimed at a low unemployment rate as well as avoiding high inflation, and, of particular importance, a stable system of collective bargaining between big corporations and unions.[15]

The key role of big business in the construction of regulated capitalism unfolded toward the end of, and shortly after, World War II. The Bretton Woods system, which was explained in Chapter 2, emerged gradually starting in 1944, and the International Monetary Fund started to operate in 1946.[16] Block (1977) provides an insightful analysis of the complex struggles among key groups in the creation of the Bretton Woods system, making a convincing case that the most powerful players were large U.S. transnational corporations and big banks. Block refers to that group as the "multilateralists," who sought a relatively open world economy and stable currency values. While the banks were skeptical of the proposed IMF and preferred a return to the gold standard, they went along as long as the IMF rules excluded the more radical restrictions on capital flows favored by some U.S. Treasury Department officials.

The Treasury Department was the power base of a group dubbed the "national planners" by Block. Led by the famous Harry Dexter White, the national planners found support among the new industrial unions in the Congress of Industrial Organizations (CIO). White proposed a plan that would have insulated nation-states that pursued pro-labor economic reforms from pressures stemming from international currency markets. White's original draft of the Bretton Woods agreement was extensively rewritten by the multilateralists. A third group, made up of smaller domestically oriented business, supported the position Block characterizes as "isolationist," which opposed the U.S. taking the lead in creating a new global monetary system, but it was soundly defeated by the big corporations and banks.[17]

The most important domestic institution that arose after World War II was collective bargaining between big business and trade unions.

Closely related to that institution was the acceptance of Keynesian macropolicy to maintain a low unemployment rate and guard against another depression. Keynesian macropolicy would enable large corporations to agree to wage increases in a three-year collective bargaining contract without fearing that a depression would leave the company unable to afford to pay rising wages. The intellectual justification for Keynesian macropolicy was provided by the rise to dominance of Keynesian economic ideas and theories.

A central claim of the analysis in this book is that a decisive part of big business in the U.S. came to support collective bargaining, Keynesian macropolicy, Keynesian economic ideas, and a welfare state during the mid to late 1940s. During the 1930s only a few big business leaders supported the New Deal, particularly its embrace of trade union rights. In 1935 the relatively conciliatory Business Council, the leading big business policy organization in that period, had joined with the National Association of Manufacturers and the U.S. Chamber of Commerce in a futile opposition to the proposed National Labor Relations Act, which guaranteed the right to collective bargaining. The Business Council continued to resist trade unions after the United States entered World War II (McQuaid, 1982, 47–48, 96). However, as the war ground toward its conclusion and big business leaders pondered the experience of the past decade of depression, intense labor strife, and wartime mobilization, a growing part of big business shifted its position.

The Committee for Economic Development (CED) was the most important channel through which big business came to express its support for collective bargaining, Keynesian macropolicy, and the welfare state, as well as seeking to influence the specific features of those institutions. The CED, which grew out of the Business Council, was formed in September 1942 "as a private, non-profit, non-political association . . . composed of some of the nation's leading businessmen."[18] The CED's two official objectives were to help with postwar reconversion and to "determine . . . those economic policies that would encourage both the attainment and maintenance of high production and employment" (CED, 1948, 57). At first a small number of big corporations were represented on the CED board of trustees, totaling thirteen in 1944, shown in Table 3.2. By 1948 the number had grown to forty-three, as shown in Table 3.3. For those two years, the list of big business officials who served on the Board of Trustees or the

Research Committee of the CED is almost a who's who of U.S. big business in that period, although with some omissions. The lists for 1944 and 1948 included the top officials of major financial and non-financial companies, such as J. P. Morgan, Bankers Trust Company (long connected with the Morgan financial group), Goldman Sachs, Lehman Brothers, General Electric, Union Pacific Railroad, Ford Motor Company, Eastman Kodak, General Foods, Goodrich Tire, Federated Department Stores, New York Life Insurance, and Shell Oil. By 1964 the list had expanded to ninety-one big corporate members, including such titans as AT&T, Bank of America, First National City Bank (predecessor of Citibank), General Motors, U.S. Steel Corporation, and Standard Oil of New Jersey (which later became Exxon).[19]

What did the CED advocate? In 1944, two years after its founding, the CED issued a report, *The Economics of a Free Society,* authored by one of its founders, William Benton.[20] This report advocated acceptance of three key institutions of what is called here regulated capitalism: collective bargaining with trade unions, Keynesian policies to regulate the business cycle, and government provision of social welfare programs.

Table 3.2. Big Business Representatives Affiliated with the Committee for Economic Development, 1944

Champion Paper
Coca-Cola
Eastman Kodak
Fidelity & Casualty Co
General Foods
Goldman, Sachs & Co
Hormel Foods
J.P. Morgan & Co.
Quaker Oats
R.H. Macy and Company
Scott Paper
Studebaker
Union Pacific Railroad Co.

Source: CED, 1944.
Note: Includes representation on the CED Board of Trustees or Research Committee.

For example, it argued, "To compensate for the weakness of their individual bargaining position, wage earners need the right to combine into organizations for collective bargaining" (Benton, 1944, 6). It advocated active government policy aimed at "maintaining the flow of buying power needed to sustain high levels of employment" and even

Table 3.3. Big Business Representatives Affiliated with the Committee for Economic Development, 1948

Allegheny Ludlum Steel	Goldman, Sachs & Co
Anderson, Clayton and Co	Hormel Foods
Arkansas Power & Light Company	International Harvester
B.F. Goodrich	J.P. Stevens
Bankers Trust Company	Lehman Brothers
Bausch and Lomb Optical	Libbey-Owens-Ford Glass
Bristol-Myers	National Broadcasting Co
Champion Paper	New York Life Insurance Co
Chicago, Indianapolis & Louisville Railway	Northern Pacific Railway Company
Cincinnati Street Railway Company	Northwest Bancorporation
Cleveland Electric Illuminating Company	Owens-Illinois Glass
Coca-Cola	Pennsylvania Railroad Company
Colgate-Palmolive	Philco
Continental Insurance Co	Procter & Gamble
Corning Glass Works	Quaker Oats
Crown Zellerbach	R.H. Macy
Eastman Kodak	Scott Paper
Federated Department Stores	Shell Union Oil Co
Ford Motor	Sinclair Coal Company
General Electric	Texas Power and Light Company
General Foods	United Air Lines
General Mills	

Source: CED, 1948.
Note: Big corporate trustees of CED. In 1948 all corporate members of the Research and Policy Committee were also on the Board of Trustees.

endorsed public jobs for the unemployed when necessary (7). It not only endorsed social security retirement pensions and unemployment compensation but argued, "Such individual protection . . . should be extended as rapidly as possible" (7).

In 1944 the number of big corporations represented on the CED board was still relatively small, at thirteen, and it may be that in 1944 such ideas had not yet gained widespread acceptance among big business. However, by 1948 the CED's trustees included forty-three big business representatives. By 1964 CED's trustees even included corporations that had been staunchly anti-union in the mid-1930s, such as General Motors.[21]

In 1947 the CED's Research and Policy Committee, consisting largely of corporate CEOs from its Board of Trustees, issued a "Statement on National Policy" titled *Collective Bargaining: How to Make It More Effective*.[22] The statement accepted collective bargaining with unions and discussed ways to make it less disruptive to business. It warned that "industrial strife" jeopardized the U.S. economy while threatening "international peace and prosperity" given the leading role of the United States in the world in 1947 (CED, 1947, 7). It insisted that the CED Research and Policy Committee "believes in true collective bargaining" and warned against returning to the past state of "civil war" between labor and business (7–8). It called for "mutual trust and understanding" between companies and unions, endorsed the use of grievance procedures, and called for amending the Wagner Act to require unions as well as employers to engage in collective bargaining (9, 12–13).

Seventeen years later, in 1964, another report by the CED's Research and Policy Committee, titled *Union Powers and Union Functions: Toward a Better Balance,* stated, "Workers should be able to form unions of sufficient power to represent them effectively in negotiations with employers that affect terms and conditions of their employment" (CED, 1964, 9), although it warned against unions accumulating too much power.[23] After briefly reviewing the history of the labor upsurge starting in the mid-1930s and the series of labor laws passed by Congress since 1932, the report concluded with the following lines:

> We believe that the national labor legislation adopted in the past generation, taken as a whole, has been constructive. To return to the situation which existed before 1932, or before 1947, or before 1959, would be highly undesirable. (12)[24]

In 1948 the CED issued a statement on government policy titled *Monetary and Fiscal Policy for Greater Stability*. The statement spelled out in detail its support for the Keynesian view of the proper role of the federal government in stabilizing the economy and promoting high employment through monetary and fiscal policy. The statement observed that "monetary and fiscal policies are essential functions of government . . . [that] encourage or discourage financial expansion" (CED, 1948, 57).[25]

Why would the leading big business policy advocacy organization of that era offer support for trade unions, collective bargaining, Keynesian macropolicies, and the welfare state? There are several reasons for this, rooted in the conditions of the 1940s in the United States and the world.[26] The first stemmed from the evolution of labor-management relations in the United States after the early 1930s. Before the 1930s, with few exceptions big business in the United States had strenuously resisted recognizing trade unions, much more so than big business in most other developed capitalist countries. In the depth of the Great Depression, a major labor upsurge began in the United States, as workers in many industries launched campaigns for union recognition, including in autos, steel, tires, electrical machinery, trucking, and longshoring. Fierce and often violent battles resulted, with labor gaining strength over time, compelling many giant corporations to recognize and bargain with unions.[27] When the United States entered World War II, the labor leadership accepted a truce, agreeing to a no-strike pledge for the duration of the war. During the war, with full employment bolstering labor's bargaining power and the success of the war effort dependent on labor's cooperation, the unions made several further gains, including dues checkoff, grievance procedures, seniority as the basis for promotion and as protection against layoff, and further expansion of union membership.

After the war's end, a nationwide strike wave broke out in 1946 in several major industries, after the lifting of wartime wage-price controls and the end of the no-strike pledge. However, as the Cold War got underway, U.S. politics swung to the right. Many of the most effective union leaders were Communists, Socialists, or independent radicals, and the union movement was portrayed as "subversive." The 1946 congressional election brought big gains for Republican opponents of the labor movement. Big business now allied with smaller business to push for new restrictive labor legislation, leading to the passage of the Taft-Hartley Act over President Truman's veto in 1947, an act which outlawed secondary boycotts and other effective union tactics. As the Cold War took root, and with it fear of radicals, in 1948 the more moderate leaders of the new industrial union federation, the CIO, turned against the left-wing union leaders in their midst who had played a central role in most of the major labor confrontations with big corporations since the 1930s. This culminated in the expulsion of several major national unions led by Communists and other leftists from the CIO in 1949–50. Many left-wing union activists were fired from their jobs by management.

It was in this context that a critical mass of corporate leaders concluded the time was right to make a deal with a labor leadership that was now more moderate and hemmed in by Taft-Hartley. Big business had tried to defeat the labor upsurge for some fifteen years, but they had failed to do so. They apparently decided that accepting unions and engaging in collective bargaining over wages and working conditions was their best option available. The newly tamed union leadership, shorn of many of its most militant officials and battered by the shift in public sentiment which had previously been favorable to unions, agreed to the deal, which involved giving up the most militant union tactics, accepting many management rights, and promising to enforce collective bargaining contracts on their often unruly members once they were signed. Had the elimination of unions been a possibility, it is likely that few, if any, of the big corporations would have signed onto this deal, but the option of continuing the effort to drive out unions was not a realistic one.

Ford Motor Company provides a good example of a company that vigorously fought unionization in the 1930s before shifting its position in the late 1940s. In a famous incident on May 26, 1937, United Auto Workers Union leader Walter Reuther was severely beaten by security guards in the employ of Ford Motor Company while he was leafletting near a Ford plant gate. In a remarkable turnaround, in 1946 Henry Ford II, recently ascended to head of the company, stated that the corporation had "no desire . . . to turn back the clock. . . . We do not want to destroy the unions" (McQuaid, 1982, 143).

A revealing passage in the 1964 CED Research and Policy Committee statement on unions indicated an advantage, from the companies' viewpoint, of accepting a stable relation with trade unions. The statement expressed some discontent with the political activism of unions, but noted the following:

However, the system [of union activism in politics] also has some advantages. It probably tends to focus attention of American labor on collective bargaining rather than on the effort to invoke the power of government to change conditions best left to private decisionmaking. . . . A major accomplishment of American labor policy is the degree to which it has kept government out of the determination of specific employment conditions. (CED, 1964, 13–14)

This expressed a preference for the politically moderate politics that emerged from union political activism in the United States. By contrast, in most European countries in that period, labor played a more radical political role, supporting Socialist and Communist parties that pressed for greater state intervention in business while proclaiming an ultimate objective of replacing capitalism with socialism.

A second reason for big business to support key institutions of regulated capitalism was fear that the Great Depression would return. Big business had good reason to endorse Keynesian macropolicy and Keynesian ideas after World War II. Everyone knew that the huge spending and mobilization of World War II had abruptly ended the Great Depression. In 1939, a decade after the start of the Great Depression, the unemployment rate, while having fallen from its high of 25% in 1933, was still at 17.2%, and business fixed investment was only 58% of its 1929 level. The economic effect of entry into the war quickly ended the depression, driving the unemployment rate down to 1.2% in 1944. There was widespread fear, including among big companies, that once the war conditions ended, the depression would return. Most of big business decided a big federal government could stabilize the economy and prevent a return of depression.

The 1948 CED statement on monetary and fiscal policy observed, "This generation, after the worst depression and one of the most severe inflations [after World War II price controls were ended] in our history, knows that our economy can have great fluctuations of production, employment, and prices" (CED, 1948, 9). To avoid a recurrence of the depression, the report endorsed counter-cyclical government policy, including monetary expansion and tax cuts if a depression threatened, even if it meant running a government budget deficit. The report noted that after the war the size of the federal government had greatly expanded relative to the economy, to 15 to 25% of the national income depending on military spending needs. It concluded, "Wise policy with respect to budgets of this size can exert a great stabilizing influence upon the economy" (14).[28]

The statement also made clear that big business regarded the stakes as very high in the effort to prevent another depression. After enumerating the obvious costs of a depression in output lost, unemployment, bankruptcies, and home foreclosures, it added the following consequences: "the resulting deep sense of injustice and frustration" and "the growing receptivity to futile or dangerous ideas that appear to promise relief from all ills" (9–10). That is, big business was fearful that, if severe depression returned and people became convinced that this was an inevitable experience in a capitalist system, the result would be growing support for a socialist alternative to capitalism. Keynesian policy seemed far preferable to losing capitalism.

The third factor pushing big business toward support for the new institutions of regulated capitalism was the significant popular support for Socialist and Communist parties in many of the major developed capitalist countries. In Britain the then radical Labor Party won a big election victory in 1945 and initiated a program of nationalizing major industries. Communist and Socialist parties were vying for power in France and Italy. Left-wing parties were also strong in Japan. Even in the United States, the Communist Party had played a significant role from the late 1930s through the mid-1940s, although it was easily crushed in the Cold War conditions that arose after World War II. It is likely that American big business feared that support for socialism might spread to the United States even in the absence of another massive depression. A policy of recognizing some labor rights and the pursuit of full employment must have appeared to be a bulwark against the spread of socialist sentiment in the United States. Similarly, the acceptance by big business of the modest social welfare programs initiated in the 1930s, expressed in the 1944 CED document (Benton, 1944), which opposed an effort to roll back Social Security or unemployment compensation, must have seemed a small price to pay for warding off socialism.

Fourth, and last, following the end of World War II the number of Communist Party-ruled states suddenly jumped, from one—the USSR—to nine. Communist parties came to power in six Eastern European countries under occupation by the Soviet army, as well as in two Eastern European states without Soviet assistance (Yugoslavia and Albania). A few years later, in 1949, the Chinese Communist Party came to power in the world's most populous country, which meant that about one-third of the world's population was living under Communist Party rule. Thus, a powerful Communist bloc emerged for the first time. The Communist-ruled states claimed to be workers' states that had eliminated the problems that capitalism posed for workers. This pressed big business to make concessions to labor, to prevent American workers from viewing the now globally influential socialist system as an appealing model.[29]

A few big business leaders had supported the New Deal in the 1930s, such as Joseph Kennedy, whom Roosevelt named to be the first head of the Securities and Exchange Commission.[30] However, such renegades were a minority in the 1930s, as most of big business opposed the New Deal's initial attempts to establish a regulated form of capitalism. It was only during and after World War II, under the changed conditions recounted above, that a decisive part of big business shifted in favor of regulated capitalism. As big business entered a coalition with organized labor in support of regulated capitalism, this powerful coalition was able to establish and consolidate the new system.

Not all of business supported regulated capitalism. Two segments remained in opposition. One was composed of particular big business leaders who held onto their long-standing hostility to trade unions and government efforts to stabilize the economy. For example, the du Pont family, one of the wealthiest in the U.S., remained in diehard opposition. Their base was the DuPont Chemical Company and, for a time after World War I, General Motors, which they controlled until the late 1930s.[31] However, the big business opponents of regulated capitalism were now in a minority.

The main opposition to regulated capitalism came from smaller business and its associations. The U.S. Chamber of Commerce, which had long been the major representative of small business, did not give up its opposition to regulated capitalism, particularly to the acceptance of trade unions, social welfare programs, and budget deficits (Collins, 1981). In congressional hearings in the 1950s on economic policy issues, the Chamber of Commerce regularly sent its experts to testify that trade unions infringed on the rights of workers, that Social Security undermined work incentives, and that America was heading down a slippery slope toward socialism. The opposition to regulated capitalism from small business was understandable. Unlike big business, small businesses struggle to survive from day to day, typically operating on razor-thin profit margins in highly competitive sectors of the economy. A significant proportion of small business goes bankrupt every year. They have difficulty paying union wages, affording taxes to support social welfare programs, and handling the expense of complying with government regulatory programs.

In the post-World War II period, big business faced a quite different environment from that of small business. Typically operating in industries with only a few major competitors and possessing large financial resources, they could afford to pay union wages and the taxes required to support social welfare programs. If necessary they could use their market power to pass on cost increases via price rises. Unlike small businesses, they did not face the fear of being driven out of business, which made it possible to take account of potential long-run benefits of the new arrangements that might outweigh their costs. A large federal government that would intervene in the economy was a fearsome prospect to the typical small business, which had little power to affect the direction of federal government policy, whereas big business was confident of its power to prevent a big federal government from turning against its core interests. While these features of the situation of big business by no means guaranteed its support for a regulated form of capitalism, in the conditions of the late 1940s they made it palatable to big business.[32]

Regulated capitalism ended up working remarkably well for big business, probably better than had been expected. As the "golden age of capitalism" proceeded in the United States, it brought many benefits for big business, including stable labor relations, predictable labor costs, an absence of severe recessions, rapid economic growth, and a high rate of labor productivity growth. Workers' wages rose but, over the long run, no faster than output per worker, and by the mid-1960s the rate of profit hit a post-World War II high, as we shall see below.

Yet regulated capitalism did have features that were not optimal for big business. They had to contend with relatively powerful trade unions. They had to help pay the cost of social welfare programs. They had to endure various kinds of state regulation. Nevertheless, workers' struggles, fear of another depression, and fear of communism/socialism had led big business to reluctantly accept reforms that they undoubtedly would have been happier to do without.

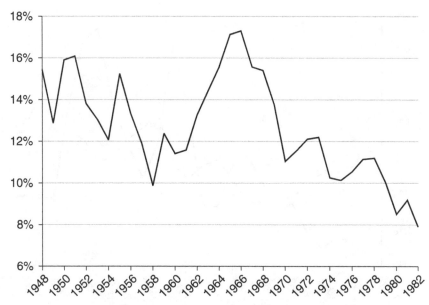

Figure 3.1. Rate of profit of the U.S. nonfinancial corporate business sector, 1948–1982.

Sources: U.S. Bureau of Economic Analysis, 2013, NIPA Table 1.14, Fixed Assets Table 4.1.

End of the Golden Age: The Crisis of the 1970s

As was noted above, regulated capitalism brought relatively rapid economic growth in the United States from the late 1940s through the early 1970s. From 1948 to 1973 there was rapid growth in GDP, in private sector output, and in labor productivity. While poverty and inequality were not eliminated, the economic growth of that period was widely shared as real hourly wages grew rapidly and consistently (with only one year of decline in 1959) and the degree of income inequality decreased over the period. Detailed data on these trends are presented in Chapter 4.

Business was not left behind in the golden age of capitalism. Figure 3.1 shows the rate of profit for the nonfinancial corporate business sector in the United States While the profit rate trended downward from the early 1950s through the early 1960s, in the mid-1960s it rose to its highest rate of the postwar period, reaching 17.3% in 1966.

However, after 1966 a problem arose from the viewpoint of business. While real wages kept growing, if somewhat more slowly than

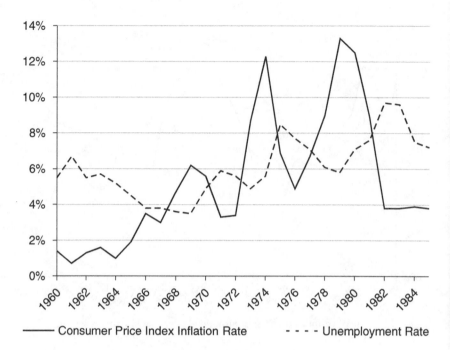

Figure 3.2. Annual inflation and unemployment rates, 1960–1985.
Source: U.S. Bureau of Labor Statistics, 2013.
Note: Consumer price inflation is measured from December to December.

previously, profits began to perform badly. From 1966–73 the real hourly wage grew at 1.7% per year, down from its growth rate of 2.5% per year from 1948–66 (*Economic Report of the President,* 1990).[33] However, as Figure 3.1 shows, the rate of profit trended sharply downward during 1966–73, losing 29.5% of its 1966 value by 1973.[34] From 1966 to 1973 the share of labor compensation in national income rose by 2.8 percentage points, while the share of corporate profits fell by almost the same amount, 3.0 percentage points (U.S. Bureau of Economic Analysis, 2013, NIPA Tables 1.1.4, 1.12, and 1.14).

After 1973 both labor and business experienced a squeeze. During 1973–79 the real wage fell by 4.4%, while the rate of profit continued its decline, falling by 17.8% over that period. Output per hour in the nonfarm business sector rose at a rate of only 1.1% per year in 1973–79 (U.S. Bureau of Labor Statistics, 2013). The years 1973–79 are rightly considered a period of economic crisis.

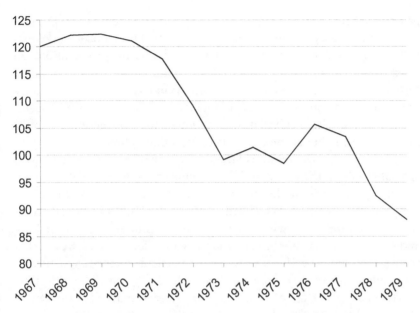

Figure 3.3. Multilateral trade weighted value of the U.S. dollar, 1967–1979 (March 1973=100).

Source: Economic Report of the President, 1990, 418, Table C-109.

After 1973 not only did wages and the rate of profit fall while productivity stagnated, but the economy entered a period of instability. An inflation that had been building since the late 1960s accelerated in 1973–74, as the newly empowered Organization of Petroleum Exporting Countries sharply boosted oil prices in late 1973 while at the same time wage-price controls in place since 1971 were lifted. As Figure 3.2 shows, the dreaded condition of stagflation gripped the American economy in 1974–75, as a relatively sharp recession drove the unemployment rate to 9.0% in May 1975, while inflation, despite subsiding somewhat, remained high. Consumer prices rose by 8.3% in 1973, 12.3% in 1974, and 6.9% in 1975. Both the unemployment rate and the inflation rate trended noticeably upward after 1973.

At the same time, international currency markets became unstable as the Bretton Woods monetary system, with its fixed exchange rates, collapsed during 1971–73. The international value of the dollar, which remained the world's trading currency, fell sharply and had sizeable wobbles after 1971, as Figure 3.3 shows. During 1973–79 there was a generalized sense in the United States that the economy was spinning out of control. Keynesian techniques, which had previously worked effectively, proved powerless to simultaneously solve the problems of high unemployment, rapid inflation, and international currency instability. Fiscal and monetary expansion would stimulate growth and reduce unemployment, but before unemployment reached what was considered an acceptable level, inflation would take off. Contractionary policy slowed inflation but at the cost of very high unemployment.

As for the Great Depression of the 1930s, there is no agreement among specialists about the cause of the economic crisis of the 1970s. The social structure of accumulation theory locates the underlying cause of a long-lasting economic crisis in the end of the ability of a social structure of accumulation, which had previously promoted profit-making and economic expansion, to any longer work effectively. However, that theory does not specify exactly why a particular social structure of accumulation will stop working effectively at a given time and place. Bowles et al. (1990, chap. 5) provide a persuasive analysis of the causes of the 1970s economic crisis within a social structure of accumulation framework. They argue that the major underlying reason why the postwar regulated capitalism that had worked so well since the late 1940s had turned into an obstacle to stability, profit-making, and growth in the 1970s was the emergence of increasing conflict between American big business and subordinate groups in the United States and internationally. This conflict destabilized regulated capitalism and led to the crisis of the 1970s.

Workers resisted bad working conditions and job speedups and fought for a larger share of the pie. The labor movement and its allies succeeded in expanding the welfare state through such measures as Medicare, the food stamp program, and improvements in the Social Security system. Citizens mounted increasingly effective campaigns to stop corporations from imposing the rising costs of their profit-making activities on society in the form of dangerous products, unsafe jobs, and environmental destruction. Oil-exporting states in the Middle East and Latin America demanded and received a better price for their oil exports. U.S. manufacturing companies, which had faced no serious competition from imports since the 1940s, suddenly faced effective competition from West European and Japanese companies starting in the late 1960s.

Bowles et al. (1990) argue that U.S. big business sought to clamp down on each of the above groups, but the multiple conflicts remained unresolved through the end of the 1970s. That is, intensifying conflict between big business in the United States on the one hand and U.S. labor, U.S. citizens, poor countries, and capitalists in other developed countries on the other rendered the social structure of accumulation no longer effective. The result was a falling profit rate, stagnant productivity growth, rising inflation, increasing unemployment, the breakdown of the Bretton Woods system, and international monetary chaos.

While we consider this explanation for the 1970s crisis to be persuasive, it is not necessary for our purposes to evaluate it or to consider alternative explanations. The following economic facts are not in dispute: 1) an economic crisis emerged in the 1970s; 2) the crisis was preceded by a steep drop in what matters most to business, the rate of profit, and the decline continued through the end of the 1970s; 3) labor productivity growth, which is a key variable that underlies the ability of business to gain rising profits over time, practically disappeared; 4) the smoothly functioning "mixed economy" promised by regulated capitalism had stopped functioning smoothly, and the remedy it endorsed for fixing economic problems—Keynesian demand management—was not able to solve the problems.

During the course of the 1970s, debates raged about the cause of the problems afflicting the economy. Various business groups argued for a variety of solutions, as did representatives of other segments of society. One prominent investment banker, Felix Rohatyn of Lazard Freres and Company, advocated a still more regulated form of capitalism based on tripartite deals among representatives of business, labor, and government. However, that direction never gained traction among big business which, in the context of the economic crisis of the 1970s, gradually coalesced around a different solution. That solution is what we know today as neoliberalism.

Evidence That Big Business Shifted to Support of Neoliberalism in the Late 1970s

In October 1972 a new big business organization, the Business Roundtable, was formed from the merger of two little-known predecessor organizations. Unlike earlier business organizations, its membership was

Table 3.4. Selected Business Roundtable Members, 1972 and 1979

AT&T[+]	Firestone Tire & Rubber Co.[*+]
Allied Chemical Corporation[*+]	Ford Motor Company[*+]
Aluminum Company of America[*]	General Dynamics Corporation[*+]
American Can Company[*+]	General Electric Company[*+]
American Electric Power Company[*]	General Foods Corp.[*+]
Atlantic Richfield Company[*+]	General Mills, Inc.[*+]
B.F. Goodrich[+]	General Motors Corporation[*+]
Bank of America[+]	Gulf Oil Corp.[*+]
Bethlehem Steel Corporation[*+]	International Harvester Company[*+]
Burlington Industries, Inc.[*+]	International Nickel Co.[*+]
Burlington Northern, Inc.[*+]	International Paper Co.[*+]
Campbell Soup Company[*+]	J.C. Penney Co., Inc.[*+]
Champion International Corp.[*+]	J.P. Stevens[+]
Chase Manhattan Bank[*+]	Kennecott Copper Corporation[*+]
Chrysler Corporation[*+]	Mobil Oil Corporation[*+]
Citibank[*+]	Morgan Guaranty Trust Co. of N.Y.[+]
Coca-Cola[+]	Morgan Stanley & Co., Inc.[+]
Consolidated Edison[*]	Procter and Gamble[+]
Corning Glass Works[*+]	R.H. Macy & Co., Inc.[*+]
Crown Zellerbach Corp.[*+]	Scott Paper Company[*+]
Dow Chemical Company[*+]	Sears, Roebuck and Co.[*+]
E.I. du Pont de Nemours & Co[*+]	Shell Oil Company[*+]
Eastern Air Lines[*+]	Texas Power & Light Co.[*]
Eastman Kodak Company[*+]	United Aircraft Corp.[*]
Exxon Corporation[*+]	United States Steel Corporation[*+]
Federated Department Stores, Inc.[*+]	

[*] Member in 1972.
[+] Member in 1979.
Source: Business Roundtable, 1972; Green and Buchsbaum, 1980, Appendix A.
Note: From the membership list of the Business Roundtable for October 16, 1972, and August 1, 1979.

restricted to corporate CEOs. At its founding it had eighty-two corporate members, including the heads of more than half of the hundred largest industrial companies in the United States, and by 1979 it had nearly seventy of the top hundred (Reuss, 2013, 69–70). Its membership was not limited to industrial companies but included large corporations from across the nonfinancial and financial sectors of U.S. big business. A sampling of its big corporate members in 1972 and 1979 is shown in Table 3.4.[35] Forty-five big corporations (or their predecessor companies) on the membership list of the Business Roundtable had previously been affiliated with the CED at some point between 1943 and 1964, including AT&T, Bank of America, Citicorp, Exxon, Ford, General Electric, General Motors, J.P. Morgan, and U.S. Steel.

Unlike the CED, the Business Roundtable was set up as a lobbying group. With broad representation of big companies from the major sectors of U.S. business, it sought to represent the interests that big business had in common. It became the most important organization pressing the interests of big business in the United States in that period (Clawson and Clawson, 1987; Ferguson and Rogers, 1986; Vogel, 1989; McQuaid, 1982). It managed to achieve a significant degree of unity of purpose among the various corporate interests it represented, which greatly enhanced its influence. For example, in a key battle over labor law reform in 1978, even CEOs who had dissented from the Business Roundtable's decision to oppose that bill nevertheless publicly lobbied against it, as described below (Vogel, 1989, 154–155).

The founding document of the Business Roundtable, issued in April 1973, was cautious and relatively bland. It described its mission as economic education, better public communication, application of law through litigation, improved government relations, and better balance in labor-management relations, although the last aim did foreshadow what would a few years later become an aggressive stance toward labor (Business Roundtable, 1973). However, over the course of the 1970s the Business Roundtable became increasingly assertive in its policy advocacy.[36]

Although the Business Roundtable was a lobbying group rather than a policy organization, it occasionally issued papers and reports that showed support for various elements of neoliberal restructuring. In 1977 its Task Force on Taxation Proposals argued that greater incentives were needed to spur business investment, including a reduction in the corporate income tax, bigger tax deductions for depreciation, and reduced taxation of capital gains (Business Roundtable, 1977). Two years later, in 1979, another report addressed Social Security retirement pensions. It emphasized that they should be regarded as just a "floor" to meet "basic needs" and that benefits "should be reviewed critically to determine if they are really necessary" (Business Roundtable, 1979, 3–4). The "floor" provided by the Social Security retirement program should be supplemented by individual workers' savings and private pension plans, which "offer greater flexibility to meet individual desires and circumstances" (4). It also called for raising the retirement age (6).

A series of reports by or for the Business Roundtable in 1979–81 called for cutbacks in social regulation. A 1979 study for the Business Roundtable by Arthur Andersen found that a sample of forty-eight large corporations incurred $2.6 billion in regulatory compliance costs in 1977, which was 15.7% of the companies' net income after taxes and 43.4% of total R&D spending (Arthur Andersen, 1979, iii). A multi-volume study of air quality for the Business Roundtable urged a change in the method of assessing health damage from poor air quality, proposing that the finding of an "adverse health effect" from bad air quality should be limited to conditions resulting in "permanent damage or incapacitating illness" (Ferris and Speizer, 1980, iv). Rejecting the current approach of adding a margin of safety in deciding on air quality standards, the report supported substituting "acceptable risk" (iv). A 1981 report on productivity growth cited the "burden of excessive government regulation" as a key cause of the lagging productivity growth of that period (Business Roundtable, 1981, 1). It called for cost-benefit analysis to decide whether regulations were justified and cited a much-criticized estimate that government regulations cost $126 billion in 1980 made by Murray Weidenbaum, the first chairman of the Council of Economic Advisors in the Reagan administration and a longtime critic of government regulation of business (8).

However, the Business Roundtable's lobbying activities in the 1970s are the best indicator of what it stood for. During 1975–78 the Business Roundtable fought a largely defensive battle against labor and public interest groups to stave off their attempts to strengthen the labor movement and tighten social regulation. The Watergate scandal of 1973 had led to a big increase in the Democratic majorities in both houses of Congress after the 1974 election, and the labor and public interest movements pushed to advance their political agendas. While President

Ford vetoed a number of the resulting bills, Democrat Jimmy Carter's election in 1976 seemed to create favorable conditions for passing laws long sought by labor and public interest groups.

Starting in 1977 the Business Roundtable was able to block a succession of such bills. In 1977 it was instrumental in defeating in Congress a measure, called "common situs," that would have strengthened the bargaining power of construction unions. In 1978 it was able to block passage of a bill that would have created a new overarching consumer protection agency long favored by the regulatory movement, handing consumer advocate Ralph Nader an unaccustomed defeat (Vogel, 1989).

The most dramatic, and unexpected, victory for the Business Roundtable was the defeat of a labor law reform bill in the first half of 1978. The proposed Labor Law Reform Act of 1978 was labor's top legislative priority, intended to reverse the decline in union representation. While existing labor law supported workers' right to organize or join a union, in practice non-union companies often used illegal tactics to defeat unionization, including firing workers for supporting a union. The resulting legal actions took many years to resolve, and penalties were very small. The Labor Law Reform Act would have shortened the time period for National Labor Relations Board decisions and modestly increased fines for such violations as firing workers for union activity. The bill had gathered large majorities of supporters in both houses of Congress, and President Carter promised to sign such a bill.

While several business organizations lobbied against the bill, including those representing small businesses, the Business Roundtable played a central role in its defeat. Working together with the Chamber of Commerce and the National Association of Manufacturers, the Business Roundtable lobbied actively against the bill. General Electric's CEO, Reginald Jones, had supported neutrality on this bill in the Business Roundtable's Policy Committee—GE workers were already unionized so the bill would have no direct effect on GE. However, when the vote in the Policy Committee went heavily in favor of working against the bill, GE nevertheless then publicly opposed the bill and lobbied against it. Big corporations used their corporate jets to fly small businessmen from around the country to the Capitol to see their representatives. The effort succeeded when enough Senate supporters were peeled away to narrowly sustain a Senate filibuster of the bill in June 1978, and the bill died (Vogel, 1989, 154–156). Labor leaders concluded, correctly, that the big corporations that had for decades refrained from joining small business in fighting organized labor had now shifted their position.

Not all of the Business Roundtable's efforts in the 1970s were defensive. In 1978 the Business Roundtable was instrumental in turning a mildly progressive tax reform bill into one that was a business wish list, including a reduction in the top tax rate on capital gains from a proposed 48% to 28%. In the same year, criticisms of "excessive government regulation" by the Business Roundtable as well as by other business organizations and in the mass media pushed President Carter to issue an executive order requiring regulatory agencies to conduct economic impact studies of proposed regulations (Ferguson and Rogers, 1986, 106). This was the beginning of the shift away from the original rationale for social regulation—that business practices should be stopped if they cause harm—to the cost-benefit approach of comparing the projected harm to the difficult-to-measure costs of the regulations.

After Ronald Reagan took office in January 1981, his administration quickly put together a program aimed at implementing the key components of neoliberal restructuring. In March 1981 the Business Roundtable publicly endorsed his entire economic program. A Business Roundtable statement on the Reagan administration's economic plan said, "The business community feels strongly that all four parts of the economic recovery plan [decreases in social spending, tax cuts, regulatory reduction, and tight monetary policy] are essential, interrelated, and must be acted upon". Two months later the Business Roundtable issued a report stating, "An economic crisis confronts the American people and requires far-reaching changes in economic policy" (McQuaid, 1982, 320). Thus, the Business Roundtable gave up its earlier support of the institutions of regulated capitalism to first oppose any further extension of them and then to work toward reversing some of the key institutions of regulated capitalism.

The actions of the Business Roundtable, representing many of the same corporations that had played key roles in the CED's endorsement of regulated capitalism in the 1940s, in support of what came to be called neoliberal restructuring during the 1970s through 1981 is one piece of evidence that a broad, and decisive, section of big business shifted its position in those years. Big business deserted its previous coalition with organized labor, allying with small business instead.

However, there are other types of evidence of this shift on the part of big business in this period as well.

The CED remained an active policy institution in the 1970s, and in 1980 its board of trustees still included representatives of a broad cross-section of U.S. big business, both financial and nonfinancial (CED, 1980), although the CED did not play the same role as the main representative of big business in the policy arena that it had played in the 1940s. Policy statements by the CED from the early 1970s through 1980 show a gradual evolution from its earlier positions in favor of regulated capitalism to the endorsement of key elements of neoliberal transformation. A 1972 CED report, *High Employment without Inflation,* sounded a Keynesian note, endorsing "sound management of total demand through appropriate fiscal and monetary policies" (CED, 1972, 16). It went even further in the direction of state intervention by endorsing wage-price regulations (17). In 1976 the CED issued a report on inflation and economic growth that withdrew support from highly interventionist wage-price regulations but stuck with the traditional Keynesian policies. It recommended expansionary fiscal and monetary policy aimed at a 6% per year growth rate over the following two years to bring down unemployment while pursuing longer-run efforts to reduce structural unemployment and increase business investment (CED, 1976). However, by 1980 the CED issued a report that endorsed "firm restraint in fiscal and monetary policies" to bring inflation under control, despite the recession in that year (CED, 1980, 2–4). The report called for tax and regulatory reform to spur saving and investment (5).[37]

In 1979 the CED issued a broad policy statement entitled *Redefining Government's Role in the Market System,* which indicated the organization's shift in policy orientation. The report criticized "the largely unguided growth of government involvement in the economic system," warning that the government was "placing increasingly excessive demands on the private sector" (CED, 1979, 9–10). It called for cutting back the state's regulation of business, stating that "the country would be well served by freeing markets from ill-designed government constraints" (14). Thus, the change in the CED's policy statements over the course of the 1970s provides further evidence that U.S. big business abandoned regulated capitalism to support neoliberal transformation over the course of that decade.

Another kind of evidence of this shift involves public policy think tanks. In the 1950s and 1960s a number of influential think tanks had issued policy analyses framed within the Keynesian consensus of that period. Big corporations provided financial support for these think tanks, of which the Brookings Institution was the most important. Such think tanks play an important role in the United States by providing policy analyses not just to Congress and the executive branch of government but also to the mass media. Their influence is not limited to individual policy issues, but extends to affecting the dominant framework for assessing public policy. Brookings was a pillar of the dominant "mixed economy" view of public policy in the postwar decades.

During the 1970s several new, or revived, think tanks emerged that aggressively supported neoliberal restructuring. The most influential was the American Enterprise Institute. The American Enterprise Institute had its origins in the 1940s and had remained a small, modestly funded conservative think tank through the end of the 1960s. In 1970 the American Enterprise Institute's annual budget was less than one million dollars. In the following decade its annual budget rose more than ten-fold. By 1980 the American Enterprise Institute's trustees included officials of Shell Oil, Chase Manhattan Bank, Citicorp, Hewlett-Packard, Standard Oil of California, and Texas Instruments, and General Electric had become a donor (Peschek, 1987, 28; Phillips-Fein, 2009, 211). Another important neoliberal think tank, the Heritage Foundation, founded by longtime supporter of right-wing causes Joseph Coors, in 1973 had trustees from Chase Manhattan Bank, Dow Chemical, General Motors, Pfizer, Sears Roebuck, and Mobil (Edwards, 1997, 227–229; Phillips-Fein, 2009, 171–172). One study found that while in 1970 the three top "conservative" think tanks—the American Enterprise Institute, Heritage, and the Hoover Institution—had combined annual budgets amounting to only 45% of that of the Brookings Institution, by 1980 their combined budgets were two-and-a-quarter times as large as that of Brookings. The American Enterprise Institute alone had a budget surpassing that of Brookings by 1980. At the same time, the studies published by Brookings shifted in the direction of the neoliberal think tanks (Clawson and Clawson, 1987, 207).

The rapid rise of corporate-funded think tanks promoting neoliberal ideas and policies in the 1970s, along with an increasingly favorable treatment of neoliberal policy ideas in the mass media in that decade, was a major reason for the rapid increase in the influence of neoliberal ideas and theories in the U.S. economics profession. Suddenly young academic economists could easily obtain funding for research aimed at demonstrating the virtues of free markets and the dangers of government regulation. However, another factor was the intellectual appeal to academic economists of the purity of the free-market theory, by comparison to the mixed message of the Keynesian version of economics, which claimed to find virtues and flaws in both markets and states with no simple "optimal" combination of the two.[38]

A final piece of evidence of the big business shift from support of regulated capitalism to endorsement of neoliberalism comes from support of candidates for national office. In 1964 Senator Barry Goldwater of Arizona won the Republican presidential nomination on a platform that foreshadowed the neoliberal agenda, including opposition to state regulation of business, social welfare programs, and trade unions.[39] However, the 1964 election came at the high point of regulated capitalism and of big business support for it. Goldwater was trounced in a landslide by the incumbent, President Lyndon Johnson. The Johnson campaign was able to gain endorsements from a long list of big corporate officials, including from Ford, Morgan Guarantee Trust, Eastman Kodak, Federated Department Stores, Xerox, and Phillips Petroleum. Even more telling was the shift in campaign donations by members of the elite Business Council, a big business organization that had helped create the CED in the 1940s. In the 1956 and 1960 presidential elections, Business Council members' donations had gone overwhelmingly to the Republican candidate.[40] However, in the 1964 race this reversed, as Business Council members' donations to the Johnson campaign exceeded those to the Goldwater campaign by more than 50% (McQuaid, 1982, 232).

The 1980 presidential campaign turned out differently. As in 1964, one candidate, this time Ronald Reagan, clearly represented a platform of abandoning regulated capitalism in favor of neoliberalism. Initially Reagan's presidential aspirations relied for financial backing primarily on self-made entrepreneurs from the South and West. After winning the Republican presidential nomination, Reagan jettisoned or played down some of his problematic positions, such as his call for recognizing Taiwan in place of China and his support of trade protectionism. He then got overwhelming support from big business in the final round of the campaign. Carter retained only "a few investment bankers and a handful of multinational business figures" (Ferguson and Rogers, 1986, 112–113). The growing assertiveness of big business in politics was reflected in the abandonment in the 1980 election of the previous pragmatic approach of support for incumbents of either party by corporate political action committees. Unlike in previous elections, in 1980 about 40% of corporate PACs ended up "supporting ideological conservative challengers, even where they were running against powerful moderate incumbents" (Clawson and Clawson, 1987, 213). Thus, in 1980 big business helped not only to put an avowed neoliberal in the White House but also sought to provide a like-minded Congress.

The casual observer might view Reagan's election in 1980 as the cause of the neoliberal revolution, which would seem to point toward changing views on the part of the electorate as the explanation. However, the evidence strongly supports the different interpretation proposed here: that over the course of the 1970s big business shifted from support of regulated capitalism to endorsement of neoliberal restructuring. This led to a beginning of neoliberal restructuring in the United States several years before Reagan's election. Even after Reagan's election, the success of his neoliberal program would be difficult to explain based on popular political views. Public opinion surveys show that during the first two years of his presidency—the period when his neoliberal program was enacted—Reagan had the lowest level of popularity of any president (during the first two years of the term) in the fifty-five years of surveys on that question, well below the ratings of Eisenhower, Kennedy, Nixon, or Carter in their first two years. In 1981 the Reagan administration faced a Democratic majority in the House of Representatives, and in the Senate the Republicans had a majority of fifty-three to forty-six that was far short of the number needed to end a filibuster. Despite lagging public support and large obstacles in Congress, Reagan was able to push his neoliberal program through Congress with only minor modifications. Clawson and Clawson (1987, 214–215) conclude that "Reagan's success is . . . to be explained by the fact that his program was supported by a virtually unanimous business community"—an outcome made possible by big business's desertion of its previous coalition with organized labor to ally with smaller business.[41]

Why Did Big Business Shift to Support for Neoliberal Restructuring?

Several factors explain the surprising shift of big business from support for regulated capitalism to promotion of neoliberal restructuring. The first stems from the economic crisis of the 1970s as it was experienced by big business. Previously it was shown that, after the mid-1960s, the rate of profit in the United States fell significantly. The founding document of the Business Roundtable showed awareness of and concern with this trend as of 1973, complaining, "After-tax profits peaked in 1966 . . . but declined sharply in the ensuing period of cost-squeeze," adding that "profits as a percentage of national output were lower in the early Seventies than in any year in the entire postwar period [sic]." As for the cause of this cost-squeeze on profits, the document left no doubt: "Starting in 1966 . . . unit labor costs accelerated sharply, and the aftermath was excessive inflation and a severe profit squeeze" (Business Roundtable, 1973, slides 18–20). As early as 1973 the Business Roundtable was concerned that rising wages and stagnating productivity (also mentioned in the document) had led to the years of declining profitability.

A second factor was the expansion of social regulation—that is, regulation of the environment, job safety and health, and consumer product safety—in the 1960s and early 1970s. This was a product of a combination of new popular movements and a politically strengthened labor movement, which came together in the late 1960s to pass new social regulation laws.[42] When big business had accepted the key institutions of regulated capitalism in the late 1940s, a high degree of social regulation was not part of the deal. Unlike the original main features of regulated capitalism, social regulation entailed constraints on the profit-seeking behavior of most sectors of business. Hence, it tended to unite business in opposition. A number of studies of business political behavior in the 1970s, such as Vogel (1989) and Clawson and Clawson (1987), argue that the expansion of social regulation was a significant factor in the political mobilization of big business against an active government role in the economy. Following Bowles et al. (1990), this factor can be interpreted as a response by business to the extension of regulated capitalism occasioned by the empowerment of labor and citizen organizations, which in turn was due to the operation of regulated capitalism

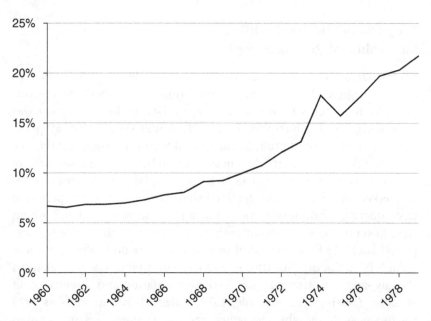

Figure 3.4   Goods imports as a percentage of goods-only gross domestic product, 1960–1979.

Source: U.S. Bureau of Economic Analysis, 2013, NIPA Tables 1.1.5, 1.2.5.

over several decades. That is, this is an example of a way in which an initially effectively working social structure of accumulation eventually gives rise to developments that undermine its further effectiveness in promoting profit-making and economic expansion.

It was noted above that in the mid-1970s labor and public interest groups were on the political offensive, seeking to further advance their interests within the system of regulated capitalism. This was a threat to the balance of regulated capitalism from the perspective of big business. At the same time, as Bowles et al. (1990) have argued, U.S. big business was facing other threats as well, such as that from newly empowered oil-exporting-country governments in the Middle East and Latin America. With a whole set of seemingly intractable problems besetting big business, it is not surprising that they would start to question whether the existing arrangements were any longer to their advantage. There is evidence from the Business Roundtable's founding document that, even in 1973, they were considering whether big changes might be needed, suggesting that solutions might "involve changes in the law, or its administration or interpretation. Some may involve a new philosophy" (Business Roundtable, 1973, 6).[43] However, in 1973 the Business Roundtable did not seem to know yet what the required new direction would be.

A third factor was the impact of intensifying international competition faced by U.S. big business in the 1970s. In Chapter 2 it was noted that U.S. imports began to rise relative to GDP in the late 1960s (Figure 2.9). From the mid-1960s through 1980 imports of goods and services rose from about 4% of GDP to about 10%. However, this understates the rapidly growing competitive threat that U.S. business faced from foreign competition in this period, since a large part of the goods and services in the GDP are not traded across national boundaries. Goods imports relative to goods output in the GDP was 6% to 7% in the early 1960s, as Figure 3.4 shows. In the late 1960s it began to rise, reaching 13.1% in 1973 and 21.8% in 1979. It had tripled over the period. Major manufacturing industries that had little or no foreign competition in the 1950s and early 1960s now faced growing inroads by companies based in Japan and Western Europe.[44]

The increasing market share of foreign companies that entered core U.S. industries put pressure on the co-respective form of competition that had been followed in those industries. Establishing and maintaining co-respective competition is feasible only in an industry dominated by a small number of companies that are able to build the stable relationships necessary to avoid price wars. Entry into such industries by foreign companies undermined the old order, and industries once governed by stable price leadership became increasingly competitive. Price wars returned to the world of the large corporation. This had the effect of transforming the world of big business into a form well known to small business. Instead of stable prices and dependable profits, big corporations suddenly faced intense price competition and even the threat of bankruptcy.

The importance of the establishment of co-respective competition by big business—or of its demise—has not been sufficiently appreciated. Big companies located in industries that practice co-respective competition, relieved of concern about short-term survival, can take a long-run view. They can appreciate arrangements that entail short-run costs if they promise long-run benefits.

In the 1970s, following a quarter-century of a highly developed form of regulated capitalism in the United States, co-respective competition was breaking down, largely due to the impact of growing import competition. Simply put, this turned big business into small business. Big business, no longer having the luxury of a stable existence undisturbed by the prospect of bankruptcy, became determined to find ways to cut labor costs, reduce tax obligations, and avoid regulatory restraints on their freedom of action. This made neoliberal ideas and policies, which stressed just such aims, appealing to big business. This was an important reason for the shift on the part of big business away from support for regulated capitalism and toward support for neoliberal restructuring.

What explains the relatively sudden invasion of U.S. markets by foreign companies starting in the late 1960s? On one level, this was a product of the ever-present tendency in capitalism for companies to break down boundaries to their profit-seeking activities, including national boundaries. One can observe this tendency throughout the history of capitalism. In this particular case, the process in the late 1960s was the result of twenty years of operation of the Bretton Woods system. That system supported relatively free trade in goods, which became freer over time. At first U.S. industry, left unscathed by the war, dominated both domestic and world markets. However, the effective operation of the system of regulated capitalism on a global level led to rapid recovery and economic advance in Western Europe and Japan. The Bretton Woods system, which had been a key institution promoting stability and economic growth, by the late 1960s was starting to contribute to the destabilization of another key institution of regulated capitalism, co-respective competition.[45] By so doing, it helped to undermine the class coalition that had underpinned regulated capitalism in the U.S.

A fourth factor pushing big business away from regulated capitalism and toward neoliberalism was the receding of the Great Depression of the 1930s into the dimly remembered past. As the 1948 Business Roundtable document cited earlier showed, that searing experience, and fear of its return after World War II, had undermined free-market economic thought and pushed big business toward acceptance of Keynesian policy. The Great Depression had also played a role in getting big business to accept the welfare state. However, by the 1970s the Great Depression began to appear as a long-ago historical accident that was best forgotten. For decades Milton Friedman had promoted the claim that the Great Depression was a result, not of any flaw in the private sector that the government must correct, but of misguided government monetary policy in the early years of the depression (Friedman and Schwartz, 1963). By the 1970s this view had become influential among academic economists. If a big interventionist state was not needed to prevent depressions, then why should big business continue to support it and foot the bill for it in taxes?

The forces moving big business to abandon the existing regulated form of capitalism in the 1970s were overwhelming. Some of the factors discussed above tended not only to push big business to turn against regulated capitalism but to support neoliberal restructuring as well. However, neoliberal restructuring was not the only alternative to regulated capitalism. As was mentioned earlier, some big capitalists proposed a more highly regulated form of capitalism, based on tripartite bodies representing business, labor, and government, to resolve the problems facing business. However, it appears that big business saw the central problem to be the strength of labor and its allies, a view which was reflected in the Business Roundtable statements cited above. Only nationalization is more threatening to business than declining profitability, and the big business diagnosis of declining profitability focused on labor costs. A form of capitalism based on tripartite bodies would grant labor increased power, so it is not surprising that that proposal found almost no support among business.

Neoliberal transformation represented a viable type of regime change that would restore the power of big business over labor, as well as achieving the other goals of big business in the 1970s cited above. That direction of change could draw upon long-established values embedded in American culture, such as individual freedom and autonomy and limited government. While neoliberal transformation is couched in the language of free markets and individual liberty, it serves to empower capital and weaken labor, as was noted in Chapter 2. Neoliberal transformation promised to reverse the long decline in profitability that was the central concern of big business.

Ideas and Economic Continuity and Change

The rise of neoliberal capitalism, viewed against the background of the earlier rise and demise of regulated capitalism, offers lessons about the role of ideas in economic continuity and economic change. We have seen that in the 1940s big business moved to support regulated capitalism due to a conviction that it was in their best interest. Keynesian ideas and economic theories provided a rationale by arguing that everyone, including both business and labor, would benefit from the institutions of regulated capitalism, which were supposed to bring high employment, high production, and high profits.

In the 1970s, neoliberal ideas and economic theories were remarkably well suited to advance the interests and solve the problems faced by big business at that time. Consider the following examples:

- How can unions be weakened so that labor costs can be driven down? It would not be effective to demand that workers sacrifice so that wealthy capitalists can have more, but it is effective to denounce the union bosses for violating the right of individual workers to act on their own, as neoliberal ideology insists they do.
- How can the welfare state be cut back? It would not be effective to argue that poor people are too well off and so social welfare programs must be cut back to leave more money in the hands of high income taxpayers. However, it is effective to argue that welfare programs destroy work incentives and make people dependent on handouts, so that cutting them will benefit the poor.
- How can the costs and intrusion of social regulation be reduced? It is not effective to defend environmental destruction, unsafe jobs, or dangerous consumer products, but it is effective to denounce meddling Washington bureaucrats who have hamstrung American business, making it impossible for them to compete and destroying jobs.
- How can the cost to business of long-term job security and secure pensions for workers be eliminated? It would not be effective to suggest that workers should be without any job security or retirement security, but it is effective to insist that "flexible labor markets" are necessary to create jobs and compete in the market while workers would be better off if they could invest their own retirement accounts in the stock market.
- How can the taxes paid by business be reduced? It would not be effective to argue that the tax burden should be shifted from those with the most financial resources to those with the least, but it is effective to argue that tax cuts for job-creating businesses will

benefit workers while individual responsibility and fiscal rectitude require that (regressive) payroll taxes must be increased to cover retirement costs projected to rise decades in the future.

Neoliberal ideas and theories offered arguments that every single institution of regulated capitalism was misconceived, that they are based on collectivist ideas that undermine individual initiative, efficiency, and economic progress. At the same time, neoliberal ideas and theories offered support for every goal of big business in the 1970s. It is not surprising that big business adopted neoliberal ideas in that context. Ideas are indeed important in the demise of an existing form of capitalism and in the construction of a new form.

This is not to suggest that big business leaders were hypocritical, saying one thing while meaning another. Most people, of every station in life, have ideas about what is just and right, and while everyone admits to occasional transgressions, there is a powerful need to believe that one's own actions are just and not merely self-seeking. Coherent sets of ideas have a reality of their own. They motivate and justify a program of action. While big business leaders must have been aware that the neoliberal restructuring they began to endorse in the 1970s would have rewards for them, there is no reason to doubt their simultaneous belief that it represented the best way forward for the U.S. economy and would benefit society as a whole, at least in the long run, as neoliberal theory claimed. The trickle-down effect, recently so often lampooned by comedians and cartoonists, appeared to be a plausible result of neoliberal restructuring at the beginning of the process.

To be effective, a set of ideas must be followed with some degree of consistency. Ideas are an important part of the glue that holds an institutional form of capitalism together and renders it viable. This explains why some developments in the neoliberal era have been contrary to the interests of all or part of big business. For example, a high level of investment in and maintenance of infrastructure is essential to profit-making activity in the long run. However, infrastructure investment is necessarily public investment, and that runs contrary to the way that neoliberal capitalism works—and so that essential form of expenditure has languished in the neoliberal era, as was demonstrated in Chapter 2. Deregulation was opposed by the airlines, railroads, the telephone monopoly, and power companies, but their resistance was overcome by a combination of neoliberal ideology and lobbying by corporate users of such services. Neoliberal ideology is not a perfect fit for all of the interests of big business—and on some issues big companies are divided—but it has been remarkably effective at promoting the core interests of big business as a whole.

As we will see in the next chapter, neoliberal transformation in the United States succeeded in resolving, or ameliorating, all of the major problems faced by big business in the 1970s. However, the "success" of neoliberal transformation had two flaws. First, while neoliberal capitalism restored the rate of profit and stable economic expansion, the benefits were concentrated, and over time increasingly so, among those at the top. While this provoked some protest in the United States and in most of the rest of the world, neoliberal capitalism was able to withstand the protest, and inequality continued to rise. Second, the manner in which neoliberal capitalism restored the profit rate and stable economic expansion turned out to be quite different from the process that had been promised by neoliberal economic ideas and theories. The actual way in which neoliberal capitalism brought economic expansion, in which growing economic inequality played an important part, over time generated financial and economic problems that were bound to eventually derail the system. This derailment occurred in 2008, when the specter of economic depression and financial collapse, which had supposedly been banished from the realm of the possible, suddenly made their return.

4

How Has Neoliberal Capitalism Worked?

By the early 1980s the main institutions of the neoliberal form of capitalism had been constructed in the United States. All eight of the changes in the role of government listed in Table 2.1, including deregulation, privatization/contracting out, and renunciation of Keynesian aggregate demand management, had been launched. The removal of barriers to global trade and investment was well underway. Neoliberal economic ideas had achieved dominance.

As in the case of regulated capitalism, the neoliberal social structure of accumulation continued to develop over time after its initial construction. For example, while two new laws passed in 1980 and 1982 represented the major launch of financial deregulation, it was deepened at the end of the 1990s, as was noted earlier. Some institutions of neoliberal capitalism, such as casualization of jobs and penetration of market principles inside corporations, emerged after the early 1980s. The shift toward new activities by financial institutions developed gradually. However, the neoliberal form of capitalism was sufficiently well established by the early 1980s to treat that date as the starting point of the neoliberal era.

In this chapter, first we will consider how neoliberal capitalism was supposed to perform, according to its advocates. Second, we will examine the actual record of performance of the U.S. economy, and to some extent the global economy, during 1979–2007, with comparisons to economic performance under the previous regulated capitalism.[1] Third, we will offer explanations for both the positive and negative aspects of economic performance during this period. Fourth, we will provide evidence of the continuity of economic policy over the neoliberal era in the

United States, despite alternations between Republican and Democratic control of the White House. We conclude with an explanation of the remarkable resistance of neoliberal capitalism to any significant change in direction prior to 2008, despite the problems it produced.

How Neoliberal Capitalism Was Supposed to Work

Neoliberal restructuring was supposed to bring optimal economic performance by removing the conscious hand of government, as well as that of trade unions, from economic decision-making, replacing them with the "invisible hand" of the free market. Lower taxes on business and the wealthy were expected to increase incentives to save and invest. A higher rate of investment in new plant and equipment would increase the growth rates of output and labor productivity while also bringing faster job growth. Financial deregulation would unleash market incentives in that previously "repressed" sector, assuring that financial institutions would provide the funds for a growing level of productive investment.

Neoliberal economic theory holds that in a free market every participant receives a level of income that reflects the individual's economic contribution to the satisfaction of consumer wants, through supplying labor or capital to production.[2] While neoliberal theory makes no specific prediction about the trend in economic inequality in a free-market system, any increase in inequality that might emerge is assumed to simply reflect inequalities in economic contribution and hence would be justified.

Furthermore, if the incentive system of the free market, including the low taxes for business and the rich, swell corporate profits and the incomes of already rich households, this would ultimately benefit those in the middle and at the bottom through faster growth in output, productivity, and jobs. The average person's share of the pie might decline, but the faster growth of the whole pie would mean that everyone's income would rise faster. That is, some of the benefits to the rich would "trickle down" to the rest.

Finally, neoliberal economic theory holds that a capitalist economy, including its financial sector, is inherently stable. The elimination of the misguided Keynesian attempts to stabilize the macroeconomy should not cause any problem, given the presumed natural stability of the free market. If an external "shock" to the economy should cause a recession, the natural corrective mechanism of the free market will quickly bring the economy back to full employment. Deregulation of the financial sector removes unneeded restrictions on financial institutions, and the rational actions of individual lenders and borrowers should assure the stability of the financial system—banks would be constrained from taking on undue risk since doing so would cause them to lose depositors or even court bankruptcy.

Starting in the early 1980s, a great experiment based on these theories was begun, in the United States, the United Kingdom, and many other parts of the world.[3] Of course, it was not really a new experiment. In the United States a free-market form of capitalism had prevailed in the late nineteenth century and in the 1920s (discussed in Chapter 6). However, the claims of the neoliberal advocates were based on strongly held theoretical beliefs rather than an examination of historical evidence. In any event, we now have more than thirty years of experience with neoliberal capitalism, and we are in a position to compare the promises of its advocates with the economic record.

The economic record shows that in most respects the U.S. economy did not perform as well in the neoliberal era as it had in the period of regulated capitalism. However, one indicator, macroeconomic stability, showed relatively good economic performance through 2007. That is, during 1979 to 2007 the U.S. economy had long economic expansions punctuated by relatively mild and brief recessions, and the rate of inflation remained low. However, the underlying reasons for that element of good performance were quite different from the scenario laid out by neoliberal theory. When the actual reasons for the twenty-five years of relative macroeconomic stability are examined, one finds that a disaster was lurking under the surface of stability, a disaster that emerged in 2008.

Economic Performance in the Neoliberal Era

Figure 4.1 extends Figure 3.1 to show the rate of profit of the nonfinancial corporate business sector in the United States through 2007. It shows that after 1982 the profit rate recovered from the long decline that had set in after the mid-1960s. The profit rate, which fluctuates sharply over the business cycle, had cyclical peak levels that rose steadily from 9.2% in 1981 to 12.6% in 1997 before falling somewhat in the next profit rate peak to 11.7% in 2006. While the profit rate decline from the mid-1960s to the early 1980s was arrested and reversed in the neoliberal

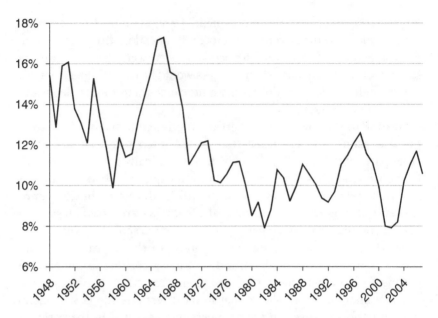

Figure 4.1. Rate of profit of the U.S. nonfinancial corporate business sector, 1948–2007.

Source: U.S. Bureau of Economic Analysis, 2013, NIPA Table 1.14 and Fixed Assets Table 4.1.

Note: The rate of profit is pre-tax profit plus net interest and miscellaneous payments divided by fixed assets.

era, it did not reach the levels of the regulated capitalist era. Dumenil and Levy (2004, 24) found that a composite profit rate for three major Western European countries showed the same pattern, of a sharp decline after the mid-1960s and a recovery starting in the early 1980s, although they found that by the late 1990s the European profit rate had surpassed that of the mid-1960s.[4]

An analysis of the determinants of the profit rate in the United States in the neoliberal era shows that wage stagnation has been the main contributor to the recovery of the profit rate after the early 1980s, with the reduction in taxes on corporate profit playing a secondary role (for the methodology of this analysis, see the appendix to this chapter). From 1979 to 2007, the after-tax rate of profit in the nonfinancial corporate business sector increased by 20.4%.[5] That increase in the after-tax profit rate was entirely due to an increase in the *share* of after-tax profit in net income.[6] A declining wage share in net income contributed just over 84% of the increase in the after-tax profit share, while a reduction in corporate profit taxes contributed 16% of the increase in the after-tax profit share. The reduced wage share resulted from the very slow rate of increase in total employee compensation over the period, of 0.25% per year, while output per labor hour rose at the rate of 1.72% per year.[7] Thus, the efforts by big business to hold down wages and reduce their taxes via neoliberal restructuring bore fruit, in a recovery of the rate of profit.

The volume of corporate profit, including the profit of financial as well as nonfinancial corporations, also resumed a rapid growth rate in the neoliberal era.[8] From 1948 to 1966 corporate profits corrected for inflation grew at 4.5% per year. It was noted above that the rate of profit fell during 1966 to 1979, and during that same period the volume of corporate profit barely increased, at 0.1% per year. In the neoliberal era the volume of profit resumed growth, increasing at the rate of 3.3% per year in 1979–2007. Neoliberal capitalism did bring a recovery of profit growth by this measure, as expected for a new social structure of accumulation.

Three long economic expansions followed the opening of the neoliberal era in the United States, in 1982–1990, 1991–2000, and 2001–07. The long expansions were interrupted by relatively mild and short recessions, until 2008. The average length of those three cyclical expansions was ninety-five months, compared to fifty months each for the five cyclical expansions in 1948–73. This suggests a relatively stable macroeconomy. Once the rapid inflation of the 1970s had been tamed in 1982, the average consumer price index inflation rate was only 3.1% per year during 1982–2007. The long expansions, brief and mild recessions, and low and stable inflation rate led Princeton economist Ben Bernanke, later named chairman of the Federal Reserve, to proclaim the arrival of a "Great Moderation" in the economy. This record seemed to substantiate the view that free-market capitalism would be more stable than its predecessor, regulated capitalism.

However, economic growth has not been rapid in the neoliberal era. Figure 4.2 compares the U.S. GDP growth rate in the neoliberal era with growth during the period when regulated capitalism was working well as well as the crisis period of regulated capitalism. The GDP growth rate during 1979–2007 was only 3.0% per year, compared to the 4.0% GDP growth rate of 1948–73.[9] The GDP growth rate in 1979–2007 did

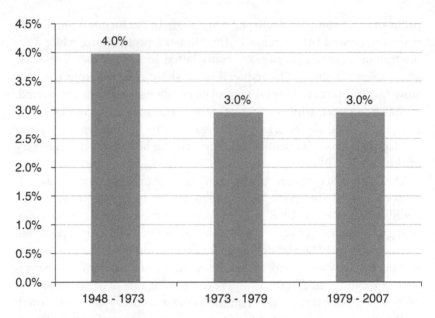

Figure 4.2. Annual growth rate of U.S. gross domestic product in chained 2005 dollars.

Source: U.S. Bureau of Economic Analysis, 2013, NIPA Table 1.1.6.

not even exceed that of 1973–79, the structural crisis phase of regulated capitalism. Even the fastest peak-to-peak GDP growth rate of the neoliberal era—3.4% per year during 1990–2000—was significantly below the 4.0% growth rate for the whole regulated capitalist era.

The economist Angus Maddison produced well-respected estimates of long-run growth rates for the world economy and various parts of it.[10] Figure 4.3 shows Maddison's estimates of world GDP growth rates for the three periods we have been considering, except the data for the first period start in 1950 rather than 1948. This estimate finds much slower GDP growth in the neoliberal era than in the period of regulated capitalism. It finds the neoliberal era growth rate was even slightly below that of the crisis period of regulated capitalism.

Figure 4.4 gives the Maddison estimates of the GDP growth rate for Western Europe in the three periods, which omit the effect of China's very rapid growth in recent decades, a growth process that has been based on an economic model more like regulated capitalism than

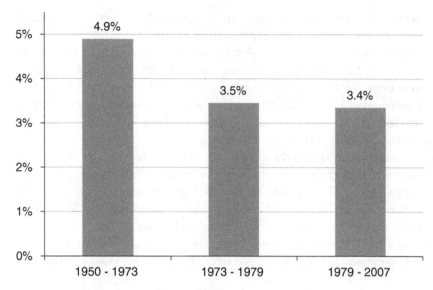

Figure 4.3. Annual growth rate of world gross domestic product.
Source: Maddison, 2010.

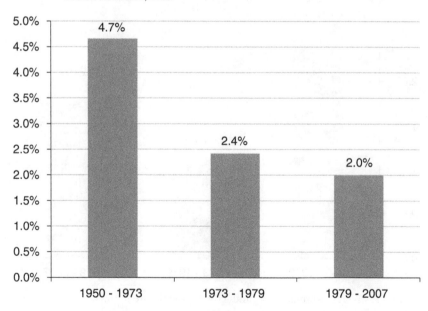

Figure 4.4. Annual growth rate of Western European gross domestic product.
Source: Maddison, 2010.

neoliberal capitalism. The Western European GDP growth rate estimate for the neoliberal era is far below that of the regulated capitalist era and significantly below that of the crisis phase of regulated capitalism. However, the implications of that estimate for the economic success of neoliberal restructuring is ambiguous. While the countries of Western Europe have had to function within a world economy dominated by neoliberal institutions, internally some of them undertook neoliberal restructuring only to a limited extent.

Figure 4.5 compares the growth rate of labor productivity (output per labor hour) in the United States in the three periods. While labor productivity growth improved in the neoliberal era over its very low rate in the crisis of the 1970s, the 2.0% productivity growth rate is substantially slower than the 2.8% of the regulated capitalist era.

The high level of business investment that neoliberal restructuring was supposed to promote should have brought rapid labor productivity

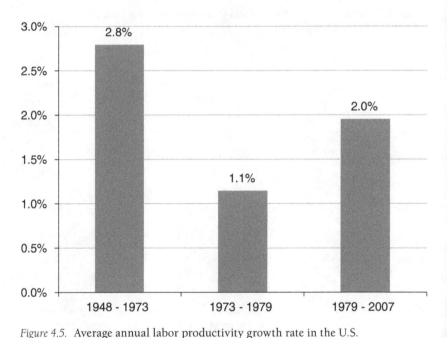

Figure 4.5. Average annual labor productivity growth rate in the U.S.
Source: U.S. Bureau of Labor Statistics, 2013.
Note: Annual average growth rate in output per hour in the nonfarm business sector.

growth. However, the disappointing productivity growth rate is not surprising since, contrary to that expectation, business investment has not been vigorous in the neoliberal era. Figure 4.6 provides two measures of private investment in the neoliberal era and the regulated era. One measure, the rate of capital accumulation, is the annual percentage increase in the value of the stock of private capital goods per year. The second is net private investment as a percentage of net domestic product, averaged over the periods.[11] Both show less vigorous investment in the neoliberal era than in the preceding period.[12]

The expected increase in saving as a result of the incentives provided by neoliberal restructuring was not forthcoming. As Figure 4.7 shows, the personal saving rate out of disposable (after-tax) income rose over

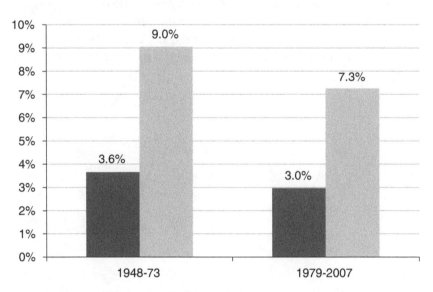

Figure 4.6. Investment performance in the U.S. in two periods.

> *Sources:* U.S. Bureau of Economic Analysis, 2013, NIPA Tables 1.1.9, 1.7.5, 5.2.5, Fixed Assets Table 4.1.

> *Note:* The rate of capital accumulation is net private nonresidential fixed investment divided by net private nonresidential fixed assets, both corrected for inflation.

the regulated capitalist era, reaching 10% of disposable income in 1971. The saving rate showed no trend in the 1970s, and then after the early 1980s the saving rate trended steeply downward, to a low of only 1.5% in 2005. Rather than increasing, personal saving practically disappeared over the course of the neoliberal era. As a result, personal saving made little contribution to investment growth in the neoliberal era.

How did neoliberal capitalism in the United States bring long economic expansions, if not by stimulating saving and investment as had been promised? Neoliberal capitalism turned out to stimulate, not business investment in plant and equipment, but consumer spending. During 1979–2007, Figures 4.8 and 4.9 show that consumer spending rose as a percentage of GDP, from 63.0% to 69.7%, while the share of business fixed investment declined from 13.0% to 11.7%. In the 1990s business fixed investment did contribute significantly to the expansion, as Figure 4.9 suggests, as large investments were made in new information-processing equipment, but this did not extend into the 2000s. All the other components of GDP—residential investment, government

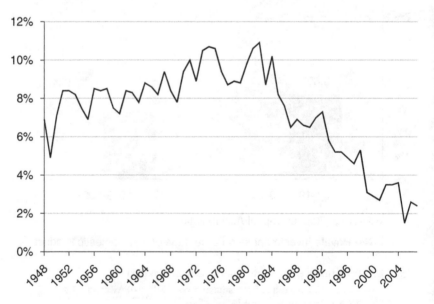

Figure 4.7. Personal saving as a percentage of disposable personal income, 1948–2007.

Source: U.S. Bureau of Economic Analysis, 2013, NIPA Table 2.1.

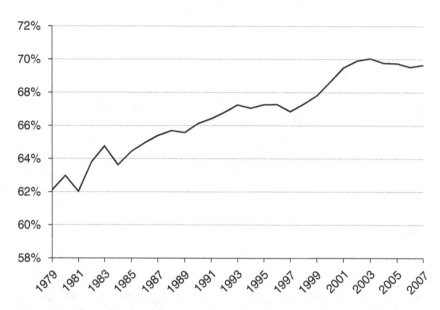

Figure 4.8. Consumer spending as a percentage of gross domestic product, 1979–2007.

Source: U.S. Bureau of Economic Analysis, 2013, NIPA Table 1.1.5.

consumption and investment, and net exports—also declined relative to GDP over the period 1979–2007, leaving only consumer spending as a rising share of GDP over the neoliberal era as a whole.[13]

Income inequality increased dramatically in the United States over the neoliberal era. Figure 4.10 shows the shares of total income received by the richest 5% and the poorest 20% of families in the United States, indicating that, following a reduction in income inequality over the regulated capitalist era, inequality increased substantially in the neoliberal era, more than canceling out the reduction during the previous era. The share of income going to the richest 1% and 0.1% increased dramatically over the neoliberal era. As Figure 4.11 shows, the share of the richest 1%, which had reached a high of 23.9% of total income in 1928, declined significantly to about 10% of income in the post-World War II decades. After 1981 it began a long climb, reaching 23.5% in 2007, nearly equaling the previous high on the eve of the Great Depression. The share of the richest 0.1% rose even higher than its previous 1928 high.[14] The average pay of the CEO of a large corporation rose from 29.0 times

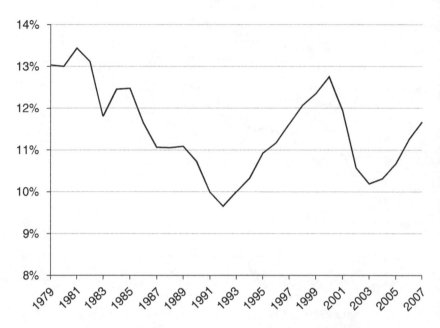

Figure 4.9. Business fixed investment as a percentage of gross domestic product, 1979–2007.

Source: U.S. Bureau of Economic Analysis, 2013, NIPA Table 1.1.5.

as great as that of the average worker in 1978 to 351.7 times as great in 2007, a twelve-fold increase in that ratio (Mishel et al., 2012, 289).[15]

A second form of inequality is found in the growing gap between profits and wages in the neoliberal era. Figure 4.12 shows the annual growth rates of wages and salaries and of corporate profit, corrected for inflation, over various subperiods from 1948 to 2007. It shows that wages and profits grew at similar rates in 1948–66, before the profit rate decline that set in after 1966 (discussed in Chapter 3).[16] From 1966 to 1979 wage growth slowed while profits barely grew at all. From 1979 to 2007 profit growth resumed at a much higher rate than that of wages and salaries. In 2000–07, the last full business cycle prior to the 2008 crisis, profits grew more than thirteen times faster than labor income.

Those in the middle and at the bottom have not fared well in the neoliberal era. From 1948 to 1973 the average hourly earnings of nonsupervisory workers rose at a 2.3% rate per year, for an increase of 74.6% over the period (Figure 4.13).[17] However, in 2007 the average hourly earnings

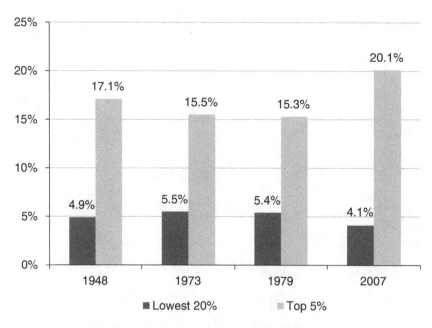

Figure 4.10. Share of aggregate income received by lowest 20% and top 5% of families.

Source: U.S. Bureau of the Census, 2013, Table F-2.

of nonsupervisory workers were 3.7% *below* the 1979 rate, a decrease over twenty-eight years. Real median family income, which more than doubled during 1948–73, rose by only 17.7% during the longer period 1979–2007, despite the entry of many married women into the labor force in the neoliberal era which boosted family median income (U.S. Bureau of the Census, 2013).

Figure 4.14 shows the percentage increase in the average real income of each fifth of the families in the United States, from poorest to richest, along with that of the top 5%, over the two periods. It shows that during 1948–73 the average income of the poorest 20% rose the fastest, while the income of the three middle quintiles also more than doubled. Both the poor and the "middle class" did very well during 1948–73. However, in 1979–2007 the poorest quintile had almost no increase, while the average income of the three middle quintiles increased only modestly over the twenty-eight-year period. From 2000–07 (not shown in Figure 4.14), the average real income of the lowest 40% declined while that of the middle quintile rose by only 0.6%. This suggests that in the years

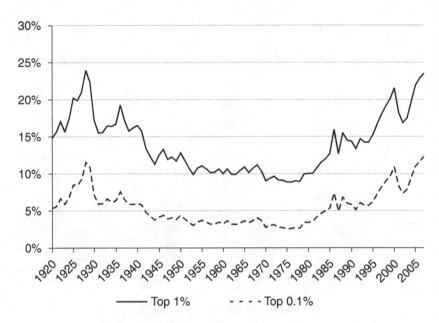

Figure 4.11. Income shares of richest 1% and richest 0.1% as a percentage of total income, 1920–2007.
Source: Piketty and Saez, 2010.

leading up to the 2008 crisis, many families in the bottom 40% of the income distribution had declining real income.

Thus, the rapidly rising share of income going to the rich did not trickle down as had been promised. Those at the middle and bottom not only received a shrinking share of a total pie that was growing more slowly than previously but their real income rose far more slowly than before, while after 2000 real income actually was declining for many in the bottom 40%. This was a major reversal of the trends in the regulated capitalist era, which had showed a lessening of inequality along with rapidly growing income of those at the middle and bottom.

The large shift in income to those sometimes called "job creators" did not produce an increased rate of job creation. Figure 4.15 shows the average unemployment rate in 1949–73, 1974–79, and 1980–2007.[18] The average unemployment rate was significantly higher in 1980–2007 than in 1948–73. In the earlier period, an unemployment rate over 6% was associated with recessions. The number of full-time equivalent jobs in the U.S. economy grew at the average annual rate of 1.9% per year in

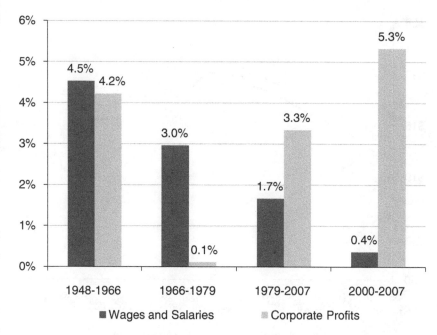

Figure 4.12. Annual growth rates of wages and salaries and corporate profit.
Source: U.S. Bureau of Economic Analysis, 2013, NIPA Tables 1.14, 1.1.4; U.S.
Bureau of Labor Statistics, 2013.

Notes: Profit is deflated by the gross domestic product price index and wages
and salaries by the consumer price index. Wages and salaries are for all
employees of the corporate business sector.

1948–73, while from 1979 to 2007 the growth rate was only 1.4% per
year despite the structural changes that were supposed to bring faster
job growth (U.S. Bureau of Economic Analysis, 2013, NIPA Tables 6.5A,
B, and C).[19]

It is not surprising that, after 1979, the poverty rate jumped upward.
Figure 4.16 shows that the poverty rate for families fell steadily from
20.3% in 1961 to 10.4% in 1969, after which it showed no trend up or
down through 1979. After 1979 the poverty rate rose again, remaining
above its 1979 rate, except for 2000 and 2001 after a decade-long economic expansion.

Homelessness was not a topic of major public concern before the end
of the 1970s in the United States. Suddenly in 1980 there was an explo-
sion of homelessness on the streets of America's cities. The U.S. Department of Housing and Urban Development estimated between 250,000

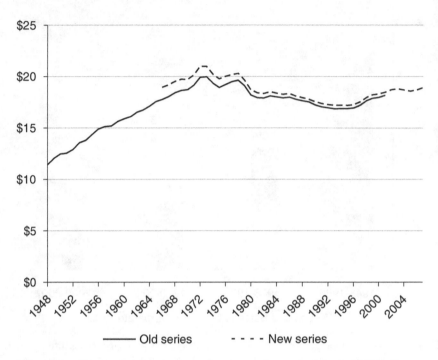

Figure 4.13. Average hourly earnings of nonsupervisory workers in 2011 Dollars, 1948–2007.

Source: Economic Report of the President, 1990, 2003, and 2010.

Note: See note 17 of this chapter.

and 350,000 homeless people in the United States in 1983. Much of the commentary on this development emphasized the deinstitutionalization of people with mental illness. However, it was also a result of the combination of trends in poverty and in low-cost housing units. A study by Freeman and Hall (1998, 22) noted that the number of families living below the poverty line grew by 45% during 1979–83, while the number of low-cost rental housing units grew by only 0.1% over that period as a result of cutbacks in public programs that provide or subsidize housing for the poor. Both trends resulted from neoliberal restructuring.

Despite a transformation that was supposed to strengthen the U.S. economy, over this period the competitive strength of U.S. industry sank steadily. Figure 4.17 shows the U.S. trade balance as a percentage

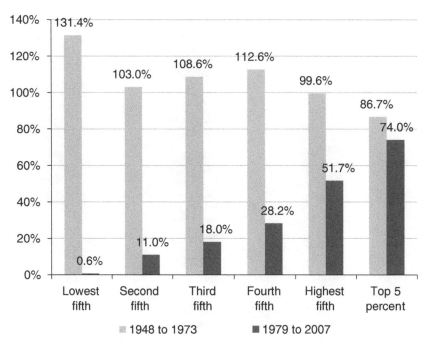

Figure 4.14. Percentage increase in the average real family income of quintiles and the top 5%.
Source: U.S. Bureau of the Census, 2013, Table F-3.

of GDP from 1948 to 2007. In 1971 the U.S. trade balance went into negative territory for the first time since 1893. After the mid-1970s the trade deficit grew, from a modest 1.1% of GDP in 1979 to a highly problematic 6.0% of GDP in 2007, causing a rapid buildup of foreign debt to cover the imbalance.

Explaining Economic Performance under Neoliberal Capitalism

Both the successes and failures of neoliberal capitalism are rooted in the same processes set in motion after 1979. How can the successes—long economic expansions, brief and mild recessions, and a low rate of inflation—be explained? The claims of neoliberal advocates of an expected burst of saving and investment did not happen, yet neoliberalism did

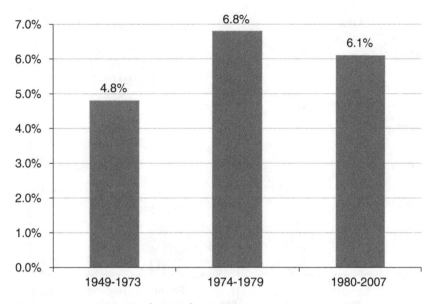

Figure 4.15.   Average annual unemployment rate.
Source: U.S. Bureau of Labor Statistics, 2013.

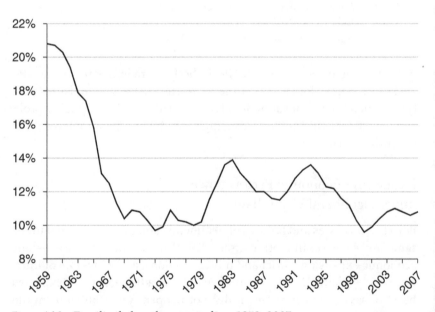

Figure 4.16.   Families below the poverty line, 1959–2007.
Source: U.S. Bureau of the Census, 2013 historical poverty tables, Table 2.

Figure 4.17. U.S. trade balance as a percentage of gross domestic product, 1948–2007.

Source: U.S. Bureau of Economic Analysis, 2013, NIPA Tables 1.5, 4.1.

function as a social structure of accumulation that promoted a long period of rising profit and relatively stable, if not rapid, capital accumulation. The manner in which neoliberal capitalism brought these outcomes was radically different from the predictions.

Neoliberal capitalism gave rise to three developments that, in combination, produced the economic successes noted above, yet also led to the severe economic crisis that began in 2008. These three developments were rising inequality between profits and wages and among households, a series of large asset bubbles, and a financial sector that engaged in speculative and increasingly risky activities. These three developments were not planned by anyone to achieve some purpose but rather arose from the working of neoliberal capitalism. First we will examine how neoliberal capitalism gave rise to each of these three developments, then show how they were responsible for the macroeconomic successes of the neoliberal era. Those three developments eventually led to the financial and economic crisis that broke out in 2008, a process to be explained in Chapter 5.

Neoliberal Capitalism and the Rise of Inequality,
Asset Bubbles, and Speculative Finance

The rising inequality of the post-1979 period has been of two types, a growing gap between profits and wages and increasing income inequality among households. Growing inequality among households results from rising inequality among wage earners as well as from the growing gap between profits and wages.[20] These two growing forms of inequality were fostered by many of the institutions of neoliberal capitalism. Consider the effects of the following institutional changes from Table 2.1:

- Removal of barriers in the global economy put workers in every country in competition with one another. As U.S. industry moved to low-wage countries, many previously high-wage industrial jobs disappeared, while the remaining high-wage jobs in tradable goods experienced severe downward wage pressure.
- The renunciation of Keynesian policies contributed to the higher average unemployment rate that was documented above, which reduced the bargaining power of workers.
- Deregulation of basic industries, such as airlines, communication, and power, put competitive pressure on what had been relatively high-paid unionized jobs in those industries, resulting in large pay cuts over time.
- Privatization and contracting out of public services often replaced relatively well-paid public sector jobs with much lower-paid private sector jobs.
- Cutbacks in and elimination of social welfare programs directly increased household income inequality, while also reducing the bargaining power of workers as a whole, since their fallback position if unemployed grew worse. Of particular importance has been the big decline in the real value of the minimum wage, which affects the pay rate for a broad swath of low-wage jobs.
- Tax cuts for business and the rich increased the after-tax income of big corporations and wealthy households.
- Marginalization of collective bargaining (along with the near-disappearance of unions' most effective weapon, the strike) left workers with little bargaining power over their wages.

- Casualization of jobs replaced relatively high-paying long-term jobs with low-wage temporary jobs.
- Unrestrained competition among large corporations put pressure on them to reduce wages, although such competition can also put downward pressure on profits.
- Hiring corporate CEOs from the outside led to the escalation of CEO pay referred to above, which also pulled up the pay of other high-level corporate managers.[21]

Asset bubbles have played an important role in the economy in the neoliberal era. A common definition of an asset bubble is "When the prices of securities or other assets rise so sharply and at such a sustained rate that they exceed valuations justified by fundamentals, making a sudden collapse likely—at which point the bubble 'bursts'" (*Financial Times* Lexicon, 2013). However, it is not a simple matter to determine what asset price would be justified by "fundamentals."

Bubbles occur in assets that have two characteristics: their economic value derives entirely or largely from unknown future developments, and they do not have a normal "production cost," such as for land or securities. Perishable food does not undergo bubble pricing. Machines might derive their value partly from future use, but their production cost sets a limit on the price. Land and securities have no production cost to set a limit on the price, and the economic benefit that will be derived in the future from owning them is difficult to predict—and so they are potentially subject to the bubble process in a market economy in which such assets are bought and sold.

The best way to understand an asset bubble is by reference to the process that creates and sustains it. An asset bubble occurs when the price of an asset—such as real estate or corporate stocks—rises due to growing demand for the asset stemming from an expectation of capital gains from future price rises, where the expectation of future price rises is based on the recent past price increase. Thus, an asset bubble is a self-sustaining rise in an asset price, where past increases in the asset price generate capital gains for those holding the asset, which draws more investors, which in turn raises the asset price further, which in turn draws in still more demand, and so on in an upward spiral. Not every case of a rising asset price indicates a bubble. An asset price can rise for reasons considered to be "fundamentals," such as rising real estate prices in a city experiencing a big influx of residents (or residents with rising income), or stock prices rising based on reasonable evidence of a near future increase in corporate profits.

It is easy to identify an asset bubble after it has deflated. Every asset bubble must eventually deflate, since at some point there will be no additional buyers to be found, whereupon the asset price stops rising. Once the asset price stops rising, the incentive that had led investors to hold the asset disappears, and the owners start to sell, driving the process into reverse. It is sometimes said that an asset bubble cannot be identified until after it is over, but that is an overstatement. While it is impossible to directly know the motivations of all of the people who invest in an asset, if an asset price rises for a period of at least several years without any identifiable reason stemming from the own-use-demand for the asset (real estate) or the economic value of the asset (corporate profit for corporate stocks or rental values for real estate), then one can reasonably conclude that an asset bubble is under way.

Neoliberal capitalism tends to produce big asset bubbles. There were no significant asset bubbles in the U.S. economy from 1948 to 1973. However, a series of large asset bubbles arose in the United States after 1979. In the mid-1980s an asset bubble arose in southwestern commercial real estate, in the 1990s a bubble emerged in the New York stock market, and in the 2000s there was a giant nationwide real estate bubble. From 1994 to 1999 the Standard and Poor's 500 stock price index rose at the rate of 23.6% per year while corporate profit after taxes in current dollars rose at only 5.9% per year. This constitutes strong evidence of a stock market bubble in that period. After the stock market peak in 2000, the index fell by 30.3% over the next two years. Figure 4.18 provides evidence, which was available at the time, that a housing bubble was underway in the early to mid-2000s. That figure shows the ratio of the house price index to the homeowner's equivalent rent, where the latter is a measure of the economic value of owning a home. In the 1980s and 1990s that ratio rose in expansions and fell in recessions. However, in the 2001 recession the ratio rose instead of falling, continuing to rise and at an accelerating rate after 2002. At its peak in 2006 the index was 43% above its 1995 level. As expected the ratio fell sharply after the bubble began to deflate in 2007.

Why has neoliberal capitalism produced large asset bubbles? The high and rising degree of inequality in neoliberal capitalism, reflected in profits rising rapidly compared to wages and the concentration of

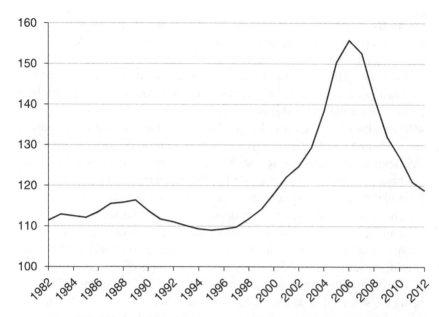

Figure 4.18.   The house price index relative to homeowner's equivalent rent, 1982–2012.

Source: Federal Housing Finance Agency, 2013; U.S. Bureau of Labor Statistics, 2013.

Note: Owner's equivalent rent of primary residence.

household income among the rich, generated more investable funds than could be used for productive investments. Some of these funds tended to find their way into buying assets, such as real estate or corporate stock. This started the price of the asset rising. However, to be sustained, a big asset bubble requires financial institutions that are ready to lend for speculative investment in the asset. Neoliberal restructuring transformed financial institutions from a sector that focused on lending for productive purposes into a sector eager to lend for speculative and risky purposes, such as in support of investment in an inflating asset. (The reasons for the turn toward speculative activities on the part of financial institutions will be considered below.) Thus the series of big asset bubbles was a result of increasing inequality and the rise of speculatively oriented, risk-seeking financial institutions.[22]

In Chapter 5 we will examine the various types of new and highly risky financial instruments that were introduced in this period. Here we address the question of why neoliberal restructuring give rise to a speculatively oriented, risk-seeking financial sector. There are three main reasons for this development. First, financial deregulation, which was a major part of neoliberal restructuring, released financial institutions to pursue whatever activities were expected to gain the highest profit. Financial institutions can gain greater profit from speculative activity than from lending for productive purposes, and deregulation freed them to shift their activities in this manner.[23] The customers of financial institutions are at a serious disadvantage in knowledge about the products and services provided by financial institutions. The staff of financial institutions specialize in analyzing the products that they create and trade, which gives them opportunities for large and quick profits from speculative activities, gained in various forms such as trading profits, markups on securities purchased and then repackaged or just resold, various kinds of fees, and speculative bets of various types.[24]

The increasingly speculative behavior of the financial sector did indeed bring outsize profits, at least until the financial crisis of 2008. We saw in Chapter 2 (Figure 2.8) that the share of financial sector profit in total corporate profit doubled over the neoliberal era. Financial profit began growing rapidly after 1990, reaching its peak in 2005. During 1990–2005 nonfinancial corporate profit in 2005 dollars grew at the healthy clip of 5.0% per year but financial corporate profit grew at 9.1% per year (U.S. Bureau of Economic Analysis, 2013, NIPA Table 1.14 and 1.1.4).

Financial deregulation is not the only feature of neoliberal capitalism that has promoted speculative, high-risk behavior by the financial sector. Two other features also promoted such a shift. One is the unrestrained competition of neoliberal capitalism. Some old-line financial institutions resisted a descent into highly risky activities, but the growing competitive pressure from rivals that had already moved in that direction eventually compelled them to follow suit.[25] Second, the penetration of market principles inside large corporations also played a role. Trading groups within big banks were often treated as independent profit centers and were allowed to function with little oversight from top management, as long as they gained high profits. Both growing competitive pressure and the penetration of market principles inside corporations fostered a short-run time horizon, which also favored speculative over long-run productive uses of funds. For a full analysis of this process, see Crotty (2008).

How the Three Developments Explain the Macroeconomic
Successes of Neoliberal Capitalism

The rising rate of profit after neoliberal restructuring encouraged firms to expand. However, the institutions of neoliberal capitalism created an obstacle to sustained economic expansion. A high rate of profit is not enough by itself to bring a sustained economic expansion, since sustained expansion also requires growing demand for output. Wages were stagnating, while profits were rising rapidly. Government spending growth was limited compared to the previous era. A rising trade deficit meant a reduction in demand from foreign trade. From what quarter could growing demand emerge? Neoliberal theory assumes that demand is never a problem—that "supply creates its own demand," as Say's Law asserts. However, Keynes clearly showed that Say's Law does not hold in the real world.[26]

Growing business investment can, for a time, provide the growing demand necessary for economic expansion. Investment constitutes demand for current output in the form of purchases of structures, equipment, and software while also creating additional productive capacity. However, growing investment cannot continue to be the sole source of growing demand, without creating an imbalance between productive capacity and final demand from households, government, and the foreign sector—and in any event we saw that investment did not grow rapidly in the neoliberal era. The data show that, despite stagnating wages in the neoliberal era, household consumer spending rose rapidly, and increased as a percentage of GDP, over the neoliberal era (Figure 4.8).

How can consumer spending rise significantly over time when wages are stagnating? High income households tend to save a larger percentage of their income, and consume a lower percentage, than those at the middle and bottom, so the growing inequality should have depressed consumer spending (and increased the saving rate)—yet instead consumer spending kept rising relative to GDP. The answer to this riddle is found by examining the trend in consumer spending relative to disposable (after-tax) income and the growth of household borrowing. Figure 4.19 shows that in the regulated capitalist era consumer spending declined as a percentage of disposable income over time, reaching 87.1% of income in 1973. It hit a low of 86.0% in 1982, and thereafter trended upward to 94.9% in 2005. The apparent paradox of stagnating wages and increasing inequality on the one hand and rising consumer spending

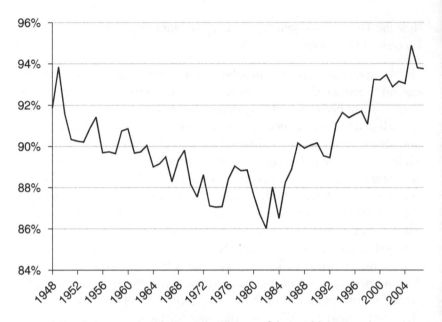

Figure 4.19. Consumer spending as a percentage of disposable personal income, 1948–2007.

Source: U.S. Bureau of Economic Analysis, 2013, NIPA Table 2.1.

on the other is explained by consumer spending that rose independent of income, fueled by growing household borrowing.

Household debt, made up primarily of mortgage debt and secondarily consumer debt, rose gradually relative to income from 1948 to the mid-1960s as home mortgage debt grew along with the rising home ownership rate of that period. After the mid-1960s it stabilized through the early 1980s (see Figure 5.1 in Chapter 5). However, after the early 1980s the trend of household debt relative to income changed, rising over time and more than doubling from 59.2% of income in 1982 to 126.7% in 2007, as Figure 4.20 shows. One study found that, in 2004–06, U.S. households withdrew funds from their home equity via mortgages amounting to between 9% and 10% of their disposable income (Greenspan and Kennedy, 2007).

The long-term rise in household debt implies not only that households sought to borrow at a growing rate but also that financial institutions were ready to extend more and more credit to them, despite rising debt ratios. It is difficult to determine with any certainty the reasons why households sought to borrow at a growing rate, but the decline in nonsupervisory workers' wages, the marked slowdown in the growth of household median income, and the very slow growth of average income for lower income families are likely to have played a significant role. In the neoliberal era, the prices of some essential goods and services have risen rapidly, including out-of-pocket health care costs, the cost of a college education, energy costs, and in some regions housing costs including local property taxes. It is likely that many hard-pressed families resorted to credit to maintain an acceptable living standard.[27]

However, that is only half of the story. Why were financial institutions willing to lend growing sums to millions of middle and low income households to finance consumer spending? The answer lies in the two other developments cited above, the series of asset bubbles and the turn to speculative, risky activities by the financial sector. An asset bubble brings rising wealth to those who own the asset, which can serve as security for obtaining a loan. In addition, the speculatively oriented financial institutions proved adept at developing new and very

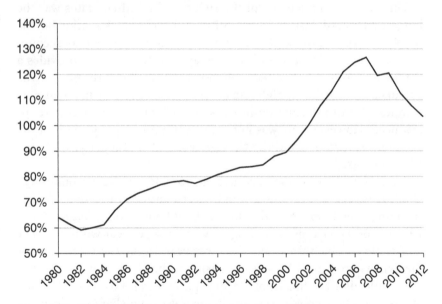

Figure 4.20. Household debt as a percentage of disposable personal income, 1980–2012.

Source: Board of Governors of the Federal Reserve System, 2013, *Flow of Funds Accounts,* Table B.100; U.S. Bureau of Economic Analysis, 2013, NIPA Table 2.1.

profitable ways to lend money to middle and low income households, despite the risk of doing so.

Normally lenders will not lend without the prospect of likely repayment including interest. That requires some combination of adequate income and assets on the part of borrowers. Although the income of most of the population was lagging, the series of large asset bubbles that arose in the United States after 1979 provided assets against which households could borrow money. The first asset bubble of the neoliberal era, in the mid-1980s, was mainly a regional bubble, and it affected only commercial real estate. One study concluded that the collapse of that bubble was one factor that led to the 1990–91 recession but that it was not a major cause of the recession (Geltner, 2012). However, the collapse of that bubble caused the bankruptcy of a large number of small to medium-sized savings and loan institutions in the Southwest. It cost the federal government an estimated $123.8 billion to clean up the mess that resulted from the savings and loan crisis of the late 1980s (Curry and Shibut, 2000, 33).

The economic expansion of the 1990s in the United States was the longest on record, lasting from 1991 to 2000. The stock market bubble of 1995 to 2000 can explain why it lasted so long as well as account for some unusual features of that expansion. Kotz (2003) provides a detailed analysis of that economic expansion. The early part of the expansion was led by a high rate of business fixed investment, as new technologies in information-processing and communication were introduced. However, this was not enough to bring rapid growth in the economy as a whole, and the GDP grew at only 3.2% per year during 1991–95.

After 1995 GDP growth accelerated, to 4.3% per year from 1995–2000. This acceleration was driven by accelerating growth in consumer spending after 1995, when the stock market bubble was inflating. From 1995 to 2000 consumer spending grew at 4.6% per year while after-tax household income rose at only 3.5% per year. In the last three years of the expansion, from 1997–2000, consumer spending grew at 5.3% per year while after-tax household income growth was 4.0% per year. This implies that households were financing a growing share of consumer spending through borrowing. Figure 4.20 shows that household debt rose rapidly at the end of the 1990s. It appears that the stock market bubble of 1995–2000 enabled upper income households, whose stock portfolios were rapidly inflated by the bubble, to borrow to finance a consumer spending binge in the late 1990s. This accelerated and prolonged the expansion despite the fact that the profit rate declined steeply after 1997 (as Figure 4.1 showed), which normally would lead to an end to an expansion. The expansion finally ended in 2000 when the stock market bubble deflated.

In the last pre-crisis expansion of the neoliberal era in 2001–07, the real estate bubble played the central role. A much larger share of the population owns real estate than corporate stock. The total market value of the U.S. housing stock was about $20 trillion in 2007, and one analyst estimated that by that year about $8 trillion of that total, or 40%, represented bubble-inflated value (Baker, 2007, 8). Economists estimate that for every dollar of increase in household wealth, consumer spending increases by about five cents. Hence, the estimated $8 trillion in bubble-inflated wealth would have directly generated about $400 billion in additional consumer demand. The effect of rising housing wealth on consumer spending operates primarily through household borrowing made possible by rising home values.

A large asset bubble affects business fixed investment directly as well as affecting consumer spending. It tends to produce an atmosphere of euphoria among investors, as the bubble generates large profits year after year, and the 2000s real estate bubble was no exception. Thus, it is likely that the real estate bubble directly stimulated business fixed investment as well as consumer spending.

Kotz (2008) examined the 2001–07 expansion in the U.S. economy in detail, finding that it was driven primarily by the real estate bubble, which enabled households to spend beyond their means while also stimulating residential investment which grew rapidly through 2005.[28] The real estate bubble grew most rapidly from 2002 to 2005 (Figure 4.18), before housing prices stopped rising in 2006.[29] During 2002–05 after-tax household income grew at 2.2% per year while consumer spending rose at 3.2% per year. In the last two years of the expansion, 2005–07, as housing prices stopped rising and then began to fall, the growth rate of consumer spending declined and with it GDP growth, which fell to 1.9% in the last year of the expansion in 2007. While the expansion of 2000–07 was not as long, or as robust, as that of the 1990s, it was relatively long-lasting, and like that of the 2000s, it was sustained by the effects of a large asset bubble.

As was noted above, the neoliberal era saw a low rate of inflation. From 1982, when the inflation of the 1970s was finally stopped, through 2007, the consumer price index rose at an average rate of only 3.1% per year. The decade-long expansion of the 1990s eventually drove the unemployment rate down to 4.0% in 2000, yet in that last year of the expansion inflation remained subdued at 3.4% per year for the consumer price index and 2.2% for the GDP price index. At the end of the 2000s expansion in 2007, the unemployment rate fell to 4.6% while the CPI inflation rate was only 2.8% and the GDP price index inflation rate was only 2.9%. The features of neoliberal capitalism discussed in Chapter 2 explain why inflation remained moderate even at low unemployment rates. First, workers' bargaining power remained low even at a 4.0% unemployment rate. In the last three years of the 1990s expansion, average real employee compensation rose at 3.1% per year, only slightly faster than output per labor hour growth of 2.8% per year, so there was little real wage pressure on prices. In the last three years of the 2000s expansion, real employee compensation declined while productivity grew at 0.8% per year (see sources given in appendix).[30] Second, the intensified competition of neoliberal capitalism acted as a restraint on inflation.

Thus, the long economic expansions of the neoliberal era did not result from rapid growth of saving and investment as had been predicted by neoliberal advocates. The cause is found in the interaction among growing inequality, large asset bubbles, and speculatively oriented financial institutions, which together propelled consumption-led growth financed by consumer borrowing.[31] The low inflation rate was primarily due to the lack of bargaining power on the part of workers and the resulting wage stagnation of neoliberal capitalism.

Federal Reserve chairman Alan Greenspan had warned of the danger of possible "irrational exuberance" early in the stock market bubble of 1995–2000, suggesting that he was aware of the bubble process underway at that time.[32] However, had he used the Federal Reserve's power to reign in the stock market bubble, or later the real estate bubble, he would have disabled the only mechanism that could promote economic expansion in neoliberal capitalism. Perhaps he was aware of this when he quickly pulled back from his "irrational exuberance" warning and proceeded to give his blessing to the bubble-driven expansions of the 1990s and 2001–07.

The Continuity of Neoliberal Policies
in the Face of Political Change

An outstanding feature of the neoliberal form of capitalism has been its continuity in the face of change in the political party in power. Many associate the origins of neoliberalism with Ronald Reagan and Margaret Thatcher, both political figures well to the right of center politically. Both were true believers in neoliberal ideas and both were backed by big business in their countries. We saw in Chapter 3 that neoliberal restructuring began in the United States before Reagan took office, during the Democratic administration of President Jimmy Carter with a Congress controlled by the Democratic Party. This is so despite the association of the Democratic Party with organized labor, which was one of the main targets of neoliberal restructuring.

However, the important role in neoliberal transformation played by a Democratic Party administration, despite the Democratic Party's ties to the labor movement, is not an anomaly. Over time leaders of left-of-center political parties in many countries, whose main base has been the working class, have run campaigns for office on a platform criticizing neoliberalism, yet once in office, have instead accepted neoliberal institutions, pursued neoliberal policies, and even on occasion deepened neoliberal transformation. This has occurred in Western Europe, in Latin America, and in countries in Eastern and Central Europe formerly ruled by Communist parties. Here we look into two cases, that of the Clinton administration in the United States during 1993–2001 and the Blair government in the United Kingdom from 1997 to 2007.

Bill Clinton came from the centrist "New Democrat" wing of the Democratic Party, but in his campaign against President George H. Bush he sounded traditional Democratic Party themes from before the neoliberal era. These included an assertion of the positive role that government can play in the economy and society. He even used the slogan "people first," which suggested the slogan "people before profits" from left-wing movements. Popular discontent with rising inequality and slow job creation since the early 1980s following neoliberal restructuring contributed to Clinton's victory over a sitting president. While the recession of 1991 was relatively brief, the recovery from it was slow, and unemployment remained stubbornly high in the 7.3% to 7.6% range during the fall 1992 presidential campaign. Candidate Clinton argued strongly for a government jobs program, which was high on the agenda of the labor union supporters of the Democratic Party.

In Clinton's first year in office, he introduced a jobs bill as promised. The measure called for investing $19 billion in infrastructure, the environment, and education to create one million jobs. Such a bill, which would use the federal government to create jobs, was contrary to what had been the dominant policy approach in the neoliberal era. Despite large Democratic majorities in both houses of Congress, Clinton failed to get the bill through Congress in April 1993. While Clinton supporters attributed this to Republican opposition in the Senate, knowledgeable observers told a different story, believing that Clinton was unwilling to expend political capital to fight for the bill. As early as the December 1992 post-election summit meeting in Little Rock, labor representatives found that Clinton was backing away from serious support for the jobs bill.[33]

While there were some government actions that ran contrary to neoliberalism in the Clinton years, such as the expansion of the Earned Income Tax Credit which provided significant income supplementation to low-wage working families, the main thrust of the Clinton administration's economic and social policies was well within the neoliberal framework. Early in his administration, he encountered enormous pressure against any departure from neoliberal priorities. At a meeting with his top advisors in April of 1993, he surprised the group by blurting out the following sarcastic remark:

> Where are all the Democrats? I hope you're all aware we're all Eisenhower Republicans. . . . We stand for lower deficits and free trade and the bond market. Isn't that great? (Woodward, 1994, 165)

Clinton actually misrepresented the Eisenhower era, when the federal government undertook a massive public investment program to build the Interstate Highway System and presided over a heavily regulated financial sector. The Clinton administration ended up following contemporary neoliberal policies rather than imagined 1950s Republican policies.

The economic strategy of the Clinton administration centered around reducing the budget deficit, signing free trade agreements, and reforming welfare programs. President Clinton's first budget bill, the Omnibus Budget Reconciliation Act of 1993, popularly known as the Deficit Reduction Act, called for a 12% reduction in federal discretionary spending over five years (*Economic Report of the President*, 1994, 3). The *Economic Report of the President* to Congress of February 1994 began with the aim of reducing the budget deficit so as to increase private investment (*Economic Report of the President*, 1994, 3).

In 1995 Clinton signed a bill that eliminated the principal welfare program that had served low income people since 1935, Aid to Families with Dependent Children (AFDC). The bill replaced AFDC with Temporary Assistance for Needy Families (TANF). TANF substituted a state block grant for the federal program, set a limit of five years for receiving assistance, added a work requirement that even applied to the disabled, and ended automatic Medicaid coverage. A number of administration officials resigned in protest, including longtime Clinton friend Peter Edelman, an assistant secretary in the Department of Health and Human Services. In departing, Edelman stated, "I have devoted the last 30-plus years to doing whatever I could to help in reducing poverty in America. I believe the recently enacted welfare bill goes in the opposite direction" (Mitchell, 1995).

Over time the Clinton administration's focus on deficit reduction intensified. The early aim of increasing public investment was never realized, as we saw in Chapter 2, but deficit reduction was a "success." The federal budget, which had a deficit of 4.8% of GDP in fiscal year 1992, went into surplus by fiscal year 1998. By fiscal year 2000 the surplus rose to $236 billion, which was 2.4% of GDP. The administration spoke of the aim of entirely paying off the federal debt. The administration's final economic report to Congress said the following:

> Our strategy has been based, first and foremost, on a commitment to fiscal discipline. By first cutting and then eliminating the deficit, we have helped to create a virtuous cycle of lower interest rates, greater investment, more jobs, higher productivity, and higher wages. (*Economic Report of the President*, 2001, 3)

While deficit reduction might seem like a common-sense aim, a single-minded pursuit of a balanced budget, and more so a surplus, is not good economic policy in general. The federal government is not like an individual household. Cutting the federal deficit reduces demand for the output of the economy, which is not undesirable when the economy is expanding rapidly, but under conditions of stagnation or economic contraction, deficit reduction turns stagnation into contraction or worsens a contraction. Fortunately for the Clinton administration, the gradual reduction in the deficit in the early 1990s coincided with rapidly rising private investment, due not to falling interest rates but to a technological revolution in computers and communications.[34] As we noted earlier in this chapter, in the late 1990s the stock market bubble drove the economy forward by stimulating consumer spending as well as prolonging the growth in private investment after the profit rate had begun to fall. Actually paying off the entire federal debt would be a disaster for the economy, since it would retire the U.S. treasury bonds that the Federal Reserve buys and sells to conduct traditional monetary policy as well as depriving private savers of the only totally safe marketable domestic financial asset.

The Clinton administration's increasing focus on deficit reduction represented an acceptance of neoliberal economic policy and the economic theories that justify it. As we will see in Chapter 5, some six months after the crisis of 2008 a belief in deficit reduction, now dubbed austerity policy, emerged as the main counterattack against any alternative to neoliberal economics.

Clinton's 1993 outburst about standing for free trade was borne out in the case of the North American Free Trade Agreement (NAFTA). On January 1, 1994, President Clinton signed NAFTA into law, despite opposition from labor, environmental, and consumer product safety organizations. The treaty was not popular with the public, but it was high on the corporate legislative agenda. The treaty had been signed by President George H. W. Bush, but it was not ratified by Congress until late in 1993.

To mollify opponents among the Democratic Party's base, Clinton introduced labor and environmental supplements to NAFTA. However, the supplements were weak and did little to assuage the concerns that lower labor and environmental standards in Mexico would result in job flight that would not have occurred had strong standards been in place. Critics of NAFTA claim that it undermined U.S. manufacturing, contributed to rising inequality in the United States, allowed unsafe food produced abroad to enter the U.S. market, and blocked regulation of environmentally dangerous products (Public Citizen, 2013). While NAFTA was advertised as a free trade bill that would reduce barriers to exports and imports, it had key provisions affecting foreign investment as well. It established unique tribunals, with private sector attorneys serving as the judges, to which foreign investors could bring claims against the signatory governments, providing investors with remarkable new privileges. Through such a tribunal, in the late 1990s the U.S. Ethyl Corporation was able to overturn a Canadian ban on MMT, a carcinogenic gasoline additive, as well as winning $23 million in compensation from the Canadian government (Public Citizen, 2013, 7).

Near the end of Clinton's presidency, top administration officials played a key role in pushing through the final stages of financial deregulation, as was noted in Chapter 2. The financial deregulation bills of 1999 and 2000 banned regulation of financial derivatives and overturned key provisions of the Depression-era Glass-Steagall Act that had forbidden banks from expanding into non-banking activities. Top Clinton administration officials gave strong support to those measures, accepting the prevailing view that little regulation of the financial sector was necessary. This set the stage for the rapid spread of speculative, high-risk practices in the financial sector that were to play a large role in bringing a financial meltdown in 2008. Deregulation also enabled the leading banks to grow rapidly and expand their share of the banking sector, making them "too big to fail."

In the United Kingdom, Tony Blair led the Labor Party back to power in 1997 after eighteen years in opposition. Like Clinton, Blair was viewed as a representative of the centrist wing of his party, called "New Labour," which wanted to distance the party from its traditional policies of public ownership and a generous welfare state. Once in power the Blair government did pass some measures aimed at benefiting workers, such as a windfall profits tax on privatized utilities for retraining displaced workers. However, the thrust of the new government's first budget was in keeping with the neoliberal agenda, including a reduction in taxes for big business to the lowest rates of any Western industrial country. It was reported that the budget's emphasis differed little from those passed under the previous Conservative government and that the reaction of Britain's financial center was "triumphant."[35]

Like the Clinton administration, the Blair government undertook "welfare reform," which included cuts in support for unemployed single mothers and introduction of means testing for benefits to the sick and disabled (Hoge, 1998). Blair's workfare scheme was modeled closely on Clinton's welfare reform. In June 1999 *The Times* of London reported

that Blair had joined with Gerhard Schroeder, then the Social Democratic Party leader and chancellor of Germany, to issue an economic
program document that called for flexible labor markets, tax cuts, and
a pro-business policy-making stance (Webster, 1999).

When Blair was in opposition prior to 1997, he had condemned the
Tories' privatization of British Rail. However, once in office he pushed
through a partial privatization of the London Underground in April
2003, despite strong opposition from the labor base of the Labor Party.
The privatization turned over the operation and maintenance of the
integrated metro system to two separate private companies. A House
of Commons report two years later found that the cost to the taxpayers
had risen twenty-fold under partial privatization with no improvement
in performance. Punctuality declined on many lines and the number of
derailments quadrupled since the privatization. The two private companies made sizeable profits from the arrangement, including bonus
payments, despite the failure to improve service (Webster, 2005).

Blair also enacted a partial privatization of the air traffic control system in July 2001, despite reluctance about the plan from the usually
privatization-supporting Conservative Party and warnings from the
Civil Aviation Authority of fiscal risk in the plan. As critics had warned,
the partially privatized system required a government bailout the following year.[36]

Why Neoliberal Capitalism Has Proved Difficult to Challenge

The neoliberal form of capitalism consistently failed to deliver on its
promises over some twenty-five years, through 2007. Inequality kept
increasing, with none of the promised benefits from unleashing the free
market and from providing generous incentives to big business and the
rich. The economy and the number of jobs expanded, but more slowly
than they had under regulated capitalism. Investment performance
was lackluster, except for the early and mid-1990s during the rapid introduction of new computer technologies. Saving almost disappeared.
What growth resulted was due to rising consumption fueled by growing debt. The majority has not fared well, and this sometimes has had
an impact at election time. However, neoliberal policies remained in
place around the world regardless of election outcomes, and neoliberal
restructuring was deepened in many countries over time. It seemed as

if the operative principle was "If it isn't working, double down." Trying something different could not make it onto the agenda.

The explanation for the remarkable tenacity of an approach that lacked any success stories for some twenty-five years has several levels. First, neoliberalism, like other social structures of accumulation, has been a coherent, mutually reinforcing system of ideas, theories, and institutions, which makes it resistant to significant change. Since the institutions and ideas fit in with one another, it is difficult to change or replace one or a few of them. Significant and workable change would require replacing the entire social structure of accumulation. A social structure of accumulation has great staying power as long as it promotes high profits and relatively stable capital accumulation. Neoliberal capitalism did indeed bring high profits, as we have seen, and it did bring relatively stable, if not rapid, capital accumulation. That it did so by means other than what was promised by neoliberal advocates did not matter much, as long as profits rose and stable accumulation continued.

Second, big business and small business, which formed the base of support for neoliberal restructuring, had no reason for complaint as long as neoliberalism was delivering the goods that they valued most. That powerful alliance has had great power to shape the policy agenda of governments regardless of election outcomes. Working class-based political parties and trade unions continued to criticize neoliberalism but without effect in the face of the enormous power of a unified business class.

Third, neoliberal ideology is very strong. It is essentially a contemporary version of the original ideology of early capitalism, when a young bourgeoisie and its allies were fighting against the remains of a dying feudal order. The battle cries of individual liberty, freedom from arbitrary state power, and elimination of special privileges based on birth, which helped to batter down the remains of the preceding system centuries ago, still has great appeal beyond the small part of society that actually owns means of production.[37]

Keynesian ideology never achieved the same legitimacy or power in the period of its ascendance after World War II. While neoliberal ideology is clear and consistent, claiming the unlimited virtues of individual choice, free markets, and private property, Keynesian ideology has no such clarity or consistency. Keynesian ideology mixes the benefits of the market and private ownership with the advantages of government regulation and planning and even some public ownership. Neoliberal ideology makes a clear distinction between capitalism and socialism and explains why capitalism is superior. Keynesian ideology gives no clear reason why capitalism should be superior to socialism, beyond an endorsement of a middle ground between the two systems. In capitalist society, an ideology that presents capitalism in a way that demonstrates its superiority to socialism has a great advantage.

Fourth, the demise of the Communist Party-run state socialist systems in Eastern and Central Europe during 1989–91, followed by a rapid transition to capitalism, gave a powerful boost to neoliberalism. In China, the only remaining large Communist-ruled state, the "reform and opening" of the 1980s, initially described as an experiment in market socialism, by the 1990s had initiated large-scale privatization, with billionaires soon emerging and inequality reaching U.S. levels.

In the 1990s neoliberal advocates produced what became the dominant interpretation of the demise of state socialism, asserting that socialism had to fail since a state-run economy cannot work.[38] This major historical event was interpreted as proving not just that socialism could not work, but that an active state role in the economy was bound to lead to economic collapse. The regulated form of capitalism after World War II had long been viewed by free-market thinkers as either a kind of socialism or a slippery slope leading to it. Now regulated capitalism and socialism were merged in the neoliberal account into the general category of a state-run economy, which, it was proclaimed, had been proved by events to be doomed to failure.

The acronym TINA arose, standing for "There is no alternative." Those who pointed out the worsened conditions of the majority under neoliberal capitalism were told that it was the only "possible" approach since there is no alternative. In the postwar decades capitalism had offered working people steadily improving economic conditions. Neoliberal capitalism lacked the ability to do the same, but its advocates insisted that anything else would be worse. Political leaders who represented working class constituencies were generally unable to stand up to this line of attack against any departure from neoliberalism. When in office, economic experts informed them that their election promises were all well and good, but now they had to be realistic. President Bill Clinton's outburst cited earlier was probably not the only one of its kind. Socialist and Communist parties found they no longer had an alternative program, and center-left parties such as the Democratic Party in the United States gave up its earlier Keynesian policy approach.

This juggernaut could not be dislodged by suffering among the majority, as long as profits rose and stable economic expansion continued. Only a structural crisis of the neoliberal form of capitalism could create conditions in which the only possible kind of effective challenge to neoliberalism could be mounted, one that sought to replace it with a different set of institutions. A structural crisis of a social structure of accumulation weakens and demoralizes its supporters and strengthens its critics, setting the stage for major change.

Although neoliberal capitalism continued to function "normally" through 2007 in the developed capitalist countries, it gave rise to severe economic crises in some countries in Latin America toward the end of that period. That led to breaks with neoliberalism in several Latin American countries. This occurred in Venezuela starting in the late 1990s, in Argentina in 2001, and in Bolivia in 2006. While each of the three had unique features, in all three cases state efforts to enforce neoliberal policies were followed by severe economic collapse, which destabilized the existing system and led to the rise of political leaders who pushed beyond neoliberalism. In Venezuela the new leadership has sought to move beyond capitalism as well as neoliberalism, pursuing "Twenty-First Century Socialism" that is supposed to be a bottom-up, participatory version of socialism, in contrast to the top-down authoritarian socialist systems of the twentieth century.

The economic crisis that began in 2008 appears to mark the end of the ability of the neoliberal social structure of accumulation to promote profit-making and stable capital accumulation. That suggests that the long-lasting immunity of neoliberal capitalism to any challenge may have ended. That crisis is the subject of Chapter 5.

Appendix: Analyzing the Recovery of the Rate of Profit in the Neoliberal Era

After a long decline in the rate of profit in the United States from the mid-1960s to the early 1980s, neoliberal restructuring was followed by a long recovery of the profit rate. There are various ways to measure the average rate of profit. We define the profit rate as

$$r = \frac{P}{K} \tag{1}$$

where r is the rate of profit, P is the flow of profit over a year, and K is the value of the capital stock at the beginning of the year. For the purpose of analyzing the determinants of an increase in the rate of profit, the best version of the rate of profit is the broad after-tax rate of profit for the nonfinancial corporate business sector. The broad profit measure is constructed by adding corporate profit and net interest paid by that sector, then subtracting corporate profit taxes paid. We include net interest since we need a definition of profit that can be viewed as a return to the total fixed capital, and a substantial part of the fixed capital is purchased with borrowed funds in the nonfinancial corporate business sector. Here we measure profit after corporate taxes, since one goal of neoliberal restructuring was a reduction in profit taxes (the figures showing the rate of profit in the text are for the pre-tax rate of profit). The capital stock is the value of structures and equipment and software, at replacement cost on December 31 of the preceding year.

Our profit rate measure excludes the financial sector because of conceptual problems encountered in constructing such a combined profit rate measure. It is conceptually difficult to construct a broad rate of profit on the reproducible capital stock for the financial sector, since the physical capital of the financial sector is a very small part of the assets of that sector. The profit generated by the financial sector derives not primarily from its physical capital but from its financial capital, most of which belongs to depositors or lenders. If the profit rate is constructed based on total assets rather than reproducible capital, that introduces a problem of double-counting, since a significant part of the financial assets of the financial sector represents the value of the tangible capital in the nonfinancial business sector. Because of such considerations, most profit rate studies focus on the nonfinancial sector of the economy.

Equation (1) can be decomposed into

$$r = \frac{P}{K} = \frac{P}{Y} \times \frac{Y}{K} \tag{2}$$

where Y is net output (which is the same as net income). Thus, $\frac{P}{Y}$ is the profit share of income and $\frac{Y}{K}$ is the output-capital ratio. Thus, the profit rate can rise due to a rising profit share in total income and/or due to a rising output-capital ratio. Equation (2) can be used to determine the percentage of a change in the profit rate over a period that is "accounted for" by the change in the profit share and by the change in the output-capital ratio.

The profit share can be additively decomposed by using the following identity:

$$P = Y - W - T - TR \qquad (3)$$

where W = employee compensation ("wages"), T = taxes (corporate profit tax plus taxes on production), and TR is the small category of net business transfer payments. Dividing equation (3) by Y and rearranging terms, we get

$$\frac{P}{Y} = 1 - \frac{W}{Y} - \frac{T}{Y} - \frac{TR}{Y} \qquad (4)$$

Equation (4) can be used to determine the "contributions" of the changes in each of the three right-side variables to the change in the profit share over a period.

By multiplying numerator and denominator by the same factors, the wage share of income can be expressed as

$$\frac{W}{Y} = \frac{W}{Y} \times \frac{Py}{Py} \times \frac{CPI}{CPI} \times \frac{N}{N} = \frac{\dfrac{W}{CPI \times N} \times \dfrac{CPI}{Py}}{\dfrac{Y}{Py \times N}} = \frac{wr \times \dfrac{CPI}{Py}}{PR} \qquad (5)$$

where Py is the output price index, CPI is the consumer price index, N is the number of labor hours per period, wr is the real wage per hour, and PR is real output per labor hour, or labor productivity. If the price ratio $\frac{CPI}{Py}$ in equation (5) does not change, then the rate of change in the wage share of income is equal to the rate change in the real wage minus the rate of change in labor productivity.[39]

Data for the above variables were obtained from the following sources: For the variables in equations (1) and (4), the U.S. Bureau of Economic Analysis, National Data: National Income and Product Accounts Tables, NIPA Table 1.14 (http://www.bea.gov/iTable/index_nipa.cfm) and Fixed Assets Table 4.1 (http://www.bea.gov/iTable/index_FA.cfm).

For the variables in equation (5), the additional sources were the U.S. Bureau of Economic Analysis, NIPA Tables 6.9B, 6.9C, and 6.9D (http://www.bea.gov/iTable/index_nipa.cfm), and the U.S. Bureau of Labor Statistics. All data were downloaded in 2013.

Equations (2), (4), and (5) were applied to the relevant data series for 1979–2007. For equation (2), we found that $\frac{Y}{K}$ declined over the period, so that the rising profit share $\frac{P}{Y}$ accounted for all of the increase in the profit rate over the period. For equation (4), we found that the wage share and the corporate profit tax share declined (increasing the profit share), while the production tax share and transfer share increased (reducing the profit share). The falling wage share contributed 84% and the falling profit tax share contributed 16% of the joint contribution of those two variables to the increase in the profit share over the period. For equation (5), we found that the real wage grew at only 0.25% per year while output per hour rose at the rate of 1.72% per year over the period, which means that the falling wage share over the period was accounted for by the slow growth rate in the real wage compared to the growth rate of labor productivity. However, the effect of this large discrepancy between wage and productivity growth on the wage share was reduced by a rising ratio $\frac{CPI}{Py}$, which rose at the rate of 1.27% per year over the period. An economic interpretation of the rapidly rising ratio $\frac{CPI}{Py}$ in the neoliberal era—the ratio did not rise rapidly before 1973—is offered in Kotz (2009).

5

Crisis

Many observers view the crisis that began in 2008 as essentially a financial crisis. The public was given a riveting show by the sudden collapse of major financial institutions and the Federal Reserve's rescue of America's largest banks, a bailout first rejected by Congress and then reluctantly endorsed by it. However, this crisis does not involve only the financial sector, and it has less dramatic aspects that are no less important. The roots of the crisis that began in 2008 lie in the entire neoliberal form of capitalism, as it operated over the preceding period. As the crisis broke out, it engulfed both financial and real sectors of the economy.

This chapter first analyzes the roots of the crisis, arguing that the three developments cited in Chapter 4—growing inequality, large asset bubbles, and a speculative and risk-seeking financial sector—gave rise to long-term trends that led to the crisis. Second, we trace the emergence and evolution of the crisis in the financial and real sectors during its initial stage in 2007–09. Third, we examine the early Keynesian response to the crisis by economists and the state, in the United States and in most of the rest of the world. Fourth, we analyze the sluggish economic recovery since 2009. Fifth, we examine the sudden shift to austerity policy in mid-2009 and the following debate over the advisability of austerity. We conclude with consideration of the implications of viewing the crisis as a structural crisis, including a brief comparison to the structural crisis of the 1930s.

Roots of the Crisis

In Chapter 4 we analyzed three developments in the U.S. economy in the neoliberal era that together explain how neoliberal institutions were able to promote long economic expansions. One was growing inequality between wages and profits and among households, which reached historically high levels in the 2000s. We saw that growing inequality was the product of most of the institutions of neoliberal capitalism. The second development was a series of three large asset bubbles of increasing magnitude over time, culminating in the huge real estate bubble in the 2000s. This development was a product of growing inequality and the transformation of the financial sector in the neoliberal era. The transformed financial sector, whose institutions engaged in speculative and increasingly risky activities, was the third development. This was the result of bank deregulation, unrestrained competition, and the penetration of market principles inside corporations.

While these three developments explain the long economic expansions, they also led to three unsustainable trends over the course of the neoliberal era: growing household and financial sector debt ratios, the spread of new toxic financial instruments throughout the financial sector, and increasing excess productive capacity in the real sector of the economy. Taken together, these three trends were unsustainable over the long run. These trends explain the crisis that emerged in 2008.

Growing Debt Ratios

Figure 4.20 in Chapter 4 showed the steep rise in household debt relative to household income, which more than doubled during 1982–2007.[1] The growing rate of household borrowing played a positive role in the macroeconomy, solving the demand problem caused by stagnating wages that otherwise would have prevented long economic expansions. Of course, households did not borrow in order to solve a problem of the economy. For millions of low and middle income families in the 2000s, borrowing was the only way to pay their bills given the decline or stagnation of their incomes. As we shall see below, financial institutions found new ways to make high profits by lending to low and middle income households in the 2000s.

Given the profitability of the new methods of lending money to low and middle income households, financial institutions sought to do more of it by borrowing themselves to finance such activities. That is, they wanted to increase their leverage. If the profit rate on an investment exceeds the interest rate paid on funds borrowed to finance it, then the firm comes out ahead on each dollar borrowed, although increased leverage also brings greater risk. However, despite financial deregulation there remained constraints on the leverage ratios of financial institutions.

The big investment banks were making very high profits in the early 2000s, and in April 2004 the top five investment banks asked the Securities and Exchange Commission to grant an exemption, for institutions with over $5 billion in assets, from a rule that limited investment banks' borrowing. In the Securities and Exchange Commission hearing on this request, one commissioner, Harvey J. Goldschmid, presciently worried that "these are the big guys . . . but that means if anything goes wrong, it's going to be an awfully big mess." After cursory discussion, the commissioners voted unanimously to grant the exemption and allow the banks themselves to monitor their own degree of risk. The only dissenting testimony had come by mail from a computer consultant and risk management expert in Indiana, who warned that the investment banks' computer models for risk assessment would not be reliable if an episode of severe turbulence arose in the markets. From 2004 to 2007 the leverage ratio rose sharply for each of the top five investment banks, to over 30-to-1 for four of the five.[2]

The growing borrowing by financial institutions was not limited to investment banks. One thinks of financial institutions as lenders rather than borrowers, but over the neoliberal era financial institutions became the biggest debtors in the economy. Figure 5.1 shows the debt of major sectors of the economy as a percentage of GDP. The debt of nonfinancial corporate business rose gradually over the neoliberal era, from 1979 to 2007, from 32.9% to 49.1% of GDP. However, the debt of the financial sector grew from 19.7% of GDP in 1979 to 117.9% of GDP in 2007, increasing just under six-fold over the period. The United Kingdom had a similar run-up of financial sector debt, reaching almost 250% of GDP (Wolf, 2009).

A high level of debt by households and businesses is not a problem as long as the debtors are receiving sufficient revenue to enable them to make the payments on the debt—and as long as the assets backing up the loans retain their value. For households, default may loom if required debt payments rise high enough relative to income. If a home's market value falls below the outstanding mortgage debt—a condition referred to as an "underwater mortgage"—a household may be motivated to default

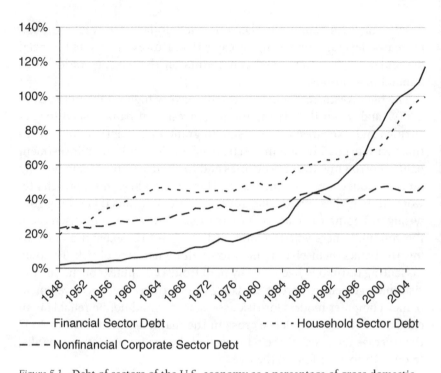

Figure 5.1. Debt of sectors of the U.S. economy as a percentage of gross domestic product, 1948–2007.

Source: Board of Governors of the Federal Reserve System, 2010; U.S. Bureau of Economic Analysis, 2010, NIPA Table 1.1.5.

rather than continuing to make payments. For a business, if the gross profit rate falls below the interest rate it pays, a debtor firm encounters a net loss on borrowed funds after payment of interest. Even worse, if profits turn negative, leverage works in reverse, magnifying the loss. Apart from the rate of profit, if the value of the assets that back up the debt declines sufficiently, debtor firms can face bankruptcy.

The Spread of Toxic Financial Instruments

The second threatening trend was the spread of highly risky financial instruments throughout the financial system.[3] As noted in Chapter 2, during the postwar decades before 1980 the regulatory system had compelled banks and other financial institutions to limit their activities to providing traditional financial services. Commercial banks made loans to businesses, holding them until they were paid off and making a profit from the difference between the interest rate on the loan and the interest paid on deposits. Investment banks and other securities firms floated new securities at a markup and traded securities, activities that are more risky than those permitted for commercial banks, but investment banks gambled with their own funds rather than the government-insured deposits held by commercial banks. The Depression-era Glass Steagall Act forbade depository institutions from engaging in the risky business of securities dealing. Insurance companies sold conventional insurance policies, keeping reserves against expected payouts. Financial deregulation removed the constraints on financial institutions, freeing them to move beyond their traditional activities.

The advocates of financial deregulation had promised greater efficiency and a wave of innovation. Starting in the 1990s, a succession of so-called "financial innovations" emerged, to great hoopla from the media. These involved the creation of increasingly complex financial instruments. Much has been written about this topic. We will single out five "financial innovations" that came to play important roles in the financial crisis: securitization of home mortgages, adjustable rate mortgages, subprime mortgages, collateralized debt obligations, and credit default swaps.

A home mortgage is a debt contract between a homeowner and a lender. Long before bank deregulation many home mortgages were resold by the issuing bank to another institution, such as the originally government-owned Fannie Mae.[4] In 1970 the practice arose of creating securities based on a number of home mortgages, for sale to investors.[5] Such mortgage-backed securities make payments from the interest and principal payments on the underlying mortgages, and unlike individual mortgages, mortgage-backed securities can be readily bought and sold in markets. The outstanding value of mortgage-backed securities rose gradually in the 1980s and 1990s, reaching $3.6 trillion in 2000. Then it rose rapidly to $8.2 trillion by 2007, making up 25% of all U.S. bond market debt outstanding in 2007, up from 4% in 1980 (SIFMA, 2013). The leading role in creating mortgage-backed securities was played by the big Wall Street investment banks, which were able to extract high profits from the process.

The advocates of mortgage-backed securities argued that they benefited both home buyers and lenders and reduced risk to lenders, investors, and the financial system as a whole. The belief in risk reduction was based on two questionable assumptions. One was that the likelihood of default on any one mortgage was independent of the probability of default on other mortgages, so that combining them into securities represented diversification that would reduce the risk of loss.[6] The second was that the risks associated with the underlying mortgages would be accurately known by potential buyers of mortgage-backed securities.

Another "innovation," adjustable rate mortgages, which were first permitted by the Garn-St. Germain Depository Institutions Act of 1982, carry an interest rate that is adjusted over the life of the mortgage, unlike for the traditional long-term fixed-rate home mortgage. In standard adjustable rate mortgages the rate is adjusted when interest rates rise or fall. An adjustable rate mortgage can enable a homeowner to initially get a lower interest rate on a mortgage, but it increases the risk borne by the borrower. Various specialized forms of adjustable rate mortgages arose, including the "option ARM" (for "option adjustable rate mortgage"), for which the initial payments can be interest-only payments as low as 1%. Such a "teaser rate" lasts for a few years, at which point the monthly payment can increase by 100% or more.

Subprime mortgages are designed for households whose credit rating is too low to qualify for a standard ("prime") mortgage, due to low income, limited assets, or other factors. Subprime mortgages were first permitted by the 1980 bank deregulation act, but few were created before the late 1990s. In 1994 subprime mortgages represented 4.5% of total mortgage originations, rising to 13.2% in 2000. After declining in the 2001 recession and its aftermath, the share rose to 21.3% of mortgage originations in 2005. During 2004–06 between 75 and 81% of subprime mortgages originated were packaged into mortgage-backed securities (Barth et al., 2008, 6).[7]

A 1999 study found that more than half of subprime mortgage refinances had been in predominantly African-American census tracts (Chomsisengphet and Pennington-Cross, 2006, 36–37).[8] In June 2009 the city of Baltimore filed a lawsuit charging Wells Fargo Bank with targeting the black community for subprime mortgage loans, even pushing them on customers who would have qualified for lower rate prime loans. A former Wells Fargo employee stated that employees referred to subprime lending as "ghetto loans" and sought to get black churches to promote them.[9] Subprime mortgages were promoted as a way to enable families who would otherwise be unable to get a mortgage at all to do so at a suitably higher interest rate to cover the increased risk of default. As subprime mortgages were bundled into mortgage-backed securities, often combined with prime mortgages, it was claimed that the resulting mortgage-backed securities were safe assets.

The fourth "financial innovation," collateralized debt obligations, involved securities backed by other securities (the collateral), such as corporate bonds and mortgage-backed securities. The collateralized debt obligation makes payments from the payments on the collateralized securities. Collateralized debt obligations first appeared in 1987, issued by Drexel Burnham Lambert based on low-quality corporate "junk bonds." Combining many different risky securities into one collateralized debt obligation (along with some less risky ones) was expected to grant access to the high returns on risky securities at reduced risk due to diversification. Collateralized debt obligations are created by securities firms and investment banks, and they are typically divided into "tranches" (slices) that are priced and sold separately, with the more senior tranches having first call on the income of the underlying securities in case some of them default.[10] Collateralized debt obligations became significant only in the 2000s, as Figure 5.2 shows. The outstanding value of collateralized debt obligations worldwide rose from $2.9 billion in 1995 to $1.34 trillion in 2007 (SIFMA, 2013).

Credit default swaps were the fifth new type of financial instrument. A credit default swap is not a security but rather an insurance contract between two parties. The seller of the credit default swap agrees to pay a sum of money to the buyer if a certain event occurs, such as a default on a bond. In return, the buyer makes regular payments to the seller over the life of the contract. Thus, a buyer of corporate bonds can purchase a credit default swap as insurance against default on the bonds. If the bond defaults, the credit default swap seller is obligated to pay the buyer. The risk of default is transferred from the security holder to the credit default swap seller in return for regular payments. Credit default swaps were invented by an employee of J.P. Morgan in the mid-1990s. Advocates argue that credit default swaps enable lenders to hedge against the risk of default as well as other risks of doing business.

From 2000 to 2008 the value of credit default swaps in the U.S. ballooned from $900 billion to $45 trillion according to one estimate. The top twenty-five commercial banks held $14 trillion in credit default

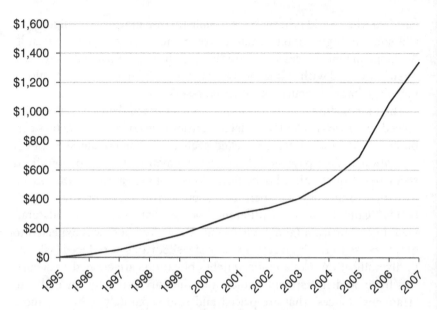

Figure 5.2. Outstanding value of collateralized debt obligations in the global
economy, billions of U.S. dollars, 1995–2007.
   Source: SIFMA, 2013.

swaps at the end of the third quarter of 2007, with JPMorgan Chase the
biggest holder.[11] The value of credit default swaps outstanding has been
estimated at more than ten times as great as the value of the assets insured by credit default swaps—it is possible to buy a credit default swap
without owning the security being insured. This indicates that they are
created primarily to gamble rather than hedge against risks.

The term "derivatives" arose to refer to assets whose value is derived
from other assets. Mortgage-backed securities and collateralized debt
obligations are examples of derivative securities. Credit default swaps
are also derivatives although they are not securities. Over time derivatives became increasingly complex. For example, collateralized debt obligations were created by bundling large numbers of other collateralized
debt obligations. Setting a value on such derivatives could be done only
by complex computer models.

We have argued that financial institutions in this period engaged in
speculative and highly risky activities, yet all of the above "financial
innovations" were supposed to reduce risk, not increase it. A neoliberal

theory of financial markets, known as the efficient markets hypothesis, provided assurance that the spread of all of the foregoing new financial products did not pose any risk to the financial system. This theory asserted that unregulated financial markets would necessarily price all securities accurately based on all relevant information about their risk and return, without the need for costly, cumbersome, and efficiency-destroying government oversight. In the now deregulated environment, these new types of securities were believed to be reducing the risk in the financial system, not increasing it. However, the neoliberal claims rested on assumptions that were out of touch with reality—as was dramatically demonstrated in 2008.

Why were these new financial products risky? The underlying reasons have to do with information and incentive problems that were overlooked in the efficient markets hypothesis. First, how were the buyers of these new financial products supposed to know the actual risk of these complex entities? Individual investors, even big ones such as major pension funds and mutual funds, do not have the means to accurately evaluate all of the securities they might purchase. Investors depend on a small group of credit rating agencies, led by Moody's Investors Service, Standard & Poor's, and Fitch Ratings. These agencies study new securities and issue ratings, from AAA (safest) to C (riskiest). Some institutional investors are required to hold a minimum percentage of their assets in securities rated AAA by one of the agencies.[12]

However, the credit rating agencies came to be paid by the financial institutions that issue securities. That had not always been the case. Prior to the 1970s Moody's had not been paid by bond issuers but obtained its income from investors who bought its publications. In 1957 a Moody's vice-president wrote, "We obviously cannot ask payment for rating a bond" since then "we could not escape the charge . . . that our ratings are for sale." However, in the early 1970s Moody's and other rating agencies, facing securities of growing complexity, began to do just that, charging bond issuers for ratings (Morgenson, 2008).

In 1975 the Securities and Exchange Commission, in an act of deregulation, decided to allow banks to base their capital requirements on the ratings of the securities they held. In the 2000s fierce competition among the rating agencies for the business of the big security issuers led to pressure on employees of the rating agencies to give AAA ratings regardless of the information uncovered by the rating experts. In

2005 Moody's reportedly several times raised its rating on securities underwritten by the mortgage company Countrywide Financial after the company complained of low ratings (Morgenson, 2008). Many low-quality securities were given AAA ratings in the 2000s, as became apparent in the financial crisis.

Five years after the financial crash investors filed a lawsuit against all three rating agencies, charging that they had assigned undeserved high credit ratings to mortgage-backed securities sold by the investment bank Bear Stearns prior to the financial crash of 2008. The lawsuit claimed the overstated ratings had caused the investors to lose more than $1 billion when the bonds later collapsed in value. The suit cited an internal email message from a Moody's employee saying, "We sold our soul to the devil for revenue" and another from a Standard & Poor's employee calling the company's rating procedures a "scam." Representatives of the three rating agencies denied the charges.[13]

A second reason why the derivative securities were highly risky is that they were inherently very difficult to evaluate, and this problem grew more severe as the products became more complex over time. The investment banks made high profits from the fees and markups on the derivative securities they created, and they had a strong incentive to maximize the perceived safety of these products in order to persuade customers to buy them at a high price. The specialists at the investment bank who created the products had far more knowledge about them than did their customers.

Third, the efficient markets hypothesis claim that financial markets price securities accurately in light of all risk and return information does not even apply to derivatives that are sold in private deals rather than markets. Some 80% of the world's derivatives were sold via private deals, according to one estimate (Crotty, 2009, 566). In such private deals, there are no competing offers to reveal information about the product, and the buyer has to rely on the information provided by the seller, which is a recipe for ripoffs.

In times past the leading investment banks sought to maintain good long-term relations with their customers. However, in the neoliberal era the big investment banks changed their behavior. In March 2012 Gregory Smith, a retiring executive director at Goldman Sachs, claimed that the firm's culture had changed to one of taking advantage of customers to benefit the firm. He revealed that traders referred to customers as "muppets" and "bobbleheads," and that the way to move up in the firm was to persuade clients to buy securities that Goldman wanted to unload because of low profit potential (Smith, 2012).

Smith's claims gained support from a Securities and Exchange Commission civil suit against Goldman Sachs, which charged that the firm, together with hedge fund manager John A. Paulson, had designed a complex housing market-related collateralized debt obligation that was intended to fail so that Goldman and Paulson could bet against it. The unwitting clients, including pension funds and insurance companies, lost hundreds of millions of dollars when it failed as had been intended. Goldman settled the suit for $550 million without admitting any wrongdoing.[14] A factor that promoted a turn toward pursuit of short-run profit is that the big investment banks over time had shifted from partnership form to corporate form, in line with the neoliberal trend toward marketizing. Their top officials no longer had their own wealth tied up in the company over the long run.

Decision-makers in the big investment banks gained huge pay packages in this period. Bonuses were handed out to employees based on how much profit they generated for the firm each year, regardless of how the products they created would fare over time. Bonuses in the securities industry went from about $3 billion in 1990 to about $36 billion in 2006.[15] Bonuses are not returned if the activities that generate them later cause losses for customers, or even for the employing firm. This created a strong incentive for employees at investment banks to take advantage of customers.

Pay in the financial sector as a whole rose over the neoliberal era compared to pay in the rest of the economy. One study found that pay in the financial sector was only slightly higher than the private sector average from the mid-1950s through 1980, falling to less than 5% above the average in 1980. After 1980 financial sector pay gradually climbed relative to the average, and starting in the mid-1990s it climbed steeply, reaching more than 60% above the average in the 2000s. The pay ratio for the financial sector had previously been almost as high in the late 1920s (Philippon and Reshef, 2009, fig. 10). In the early 2000s a large percentage of the graduates of the leading U.S. colleges were drawn to Wall Street by the money as well as the prestige it offered.

Seattle-based Washington Mutual provides an example of the way the financial system created incentives to engage in highly risky behavior for commercial banks as well as investment banks. Washington Mutual grew rapidly during 1996–2002 through aggressive acquisitions, becoming the sixth largest bank in the United States. CEO Kerry Killinger turned the bank into a loan factory that specialized in adjustable rate mortgages, which grew to 70% of its new home mortgage loans in 2006. Washington Mutual reportedly pressed its sales agents to make as many mortgage loans as possible without checking financial information about borrowers, which generated big fees for the bank. It focused on option ARMs with their low teaser rates. Between 2001 and 2007 Killinger received compensation of $88 million. On September 25, 2008, buried under a mountain of bad loans, Washington Mutual failed and was taken over by the Federal Deposit Insurance Corporation.[16]

However, most of the mortgage originations in this period were not done by banks. Mortgage brokers played the major role. In 1987 mortgage brokers had accounted for only 20% of mortgage originations. However, from 2002 to 2006 their share of mortgage originations varied between 58% and 68% (Chomsisengphet and Pennington-Cross, 2006, 39). Mortgage companies such as Countrywide Financial of California aggressively originated subprime mortgages, which were passed on to investment banks for securitization and then sale to institutional investors. The mortgage companies, banks, and investment banks were presumed to be safe since the mortgages were quickly passed along to investors. Credit default swaps enabled all of the actors in the financial system to take out insurance against possible defaults.

Countrywide Financial came to symbolize mortgage companies that knowingly originated unsound mortgage loans in the 2000s. Once one of the biggest originators of mortgages in the United States, its aggressive promotion of subprime mortgages and other high-risk loans led to its failure in 2008, when it was taken over by Bank of America. In June 2010 the Countrywide Financial unit of Bank of America agreed to pay $108 million to settle a federal lawsuit claiming it had overcharged more than 200,000 struggling homeowners prior to its takeover by Bank of America. That same year former Countrywide CEO Angelo R. Mozilo paid a fine of $67.5 million to settle fraud charges lodged by the SEC. In October 2013 a former mid-level executive of Countrywide, Rebecca S. Mairone, was found liable in a civil fraud case for having unloaded bad mortgages on Fannie Mae and Freddie Mac (another government-sponsored enterprise), resulting in over $1 billion in losses.[17] In a

Countrywide program nicknamed "the Hustle," bonuses were based on how quickly loans could be originated.[18]

Such practices were not restricted to mortgage companies and medium-sized banks. The largest U.S. banks could not resist the lure of high profits from these highly risky and sometimes legally questionable activities. In October 2013 JPMorgan Chase reached a record $13 billion tentative settlement with the Justice Department over its mortgage practices during 2005–07. The investigation had "raised questions about whether JPMorgan had failed to fully warn investors about the risks of the deals" it had promoted to them. The $13 billion fine was more than half of the bank's profit in the previous year.[19]

The increasingly speculative behavior of the financial institutions depended for its viability on the real estate bubble of the 2000s. As we saw earlier in Figure 4.18, housing prices rose rapidly in the U.S. during 2002–06 without any relation to the economic value of owning a home. Rising real estate values made the most implausible mortgage loans seem safe. Why would anyone think loans to homeowners who were not required to show anything about their ability to make the payments would be safe? Why would a teaser rate loan whose payments would become unaffordable in two years be safe? As long as real estate prices kept rising, an eventual default would give the creditor an asset—the home—that, it was assumed, would have appreciated in value, thus covering the amount of the loan.

The claim that real estate prices only rise and never fall was repeated again and again during the real estate bubble, and many people believed it. However, some sophisticated players knew it had to end—but no one knew when. As long as the bubble kept inflating, the dynamics of the intense competition of the system compelled even the savvy to press on and gain the huge profits that could be made. This was stated most clearly by Charles O. Prince, CEO of Citigroup, in an interview with the *Financial Times* in July 2007:

> When the music stops, in terms of liquidity, things will be complicated. But as long as the music is playing, you've got to get up and dance. We're still dancing.[20]

The combination of a real estate bubble and inequality also played a key role in enabling the financial institutions to succeed in their effort to generate more and more high-risk mortgage loans. Mortgage companies sent their sales agents into low and moderate income neighborhoods to knock on doors peddling second mortgages. The pitch is easy to imagine in the following hypothetical example: "Why are you worrying about how to pay your electric bill, or your medical bill, when you have $50,000 of equity in your home?" Millions of people hard pressed by falling or stagnating wages would be interested in such a proposition. If the suspicious homeowner asked what the interest rate would be, a low teaser rate could be cited. If the homeowner asked what would happen to the rate in two years, the agent could admit that it would jump up to a much higher level, adding that, however, the homeowner would never have to pay the higher rate. The homeowner would be assured that, after two years had passed, the home would be still more valuable, enabling the homeowner to refinance again at a low initial rate. The asset bubble and inequality interacted to create a pool of ready borrowers who could not afford to borrow, if one takes account of the reality that the music was indeed going to stop at some point.

Every bubble eventually deflates, and the U.S. real estate bubble was no exception. Once the bubble stopped inflating, a wave of mortgage defaults would follow, which in turn would assure that the entire web of derivatives erected on the inflating housing market would plummet in value. The financial institutions that had borrowed heavily to create the new financial products would find the value of their assets falling sharply, and their high leverage would go into reverse. The nearly six-fold increase in financial sector debt during 1979–2007 was bound to cause a severe crunch for financial institutions once the real estate bubble deflated. As early as 2003, the savvy investor Warren Buffet had warned that derivatives were "financial weapons of mass destruction," adding, "Large amounts of risk have become concentrated in the hands of relatively few derivatives dealers . . . which can trigger serious systemic problems" (BBC News, 2003).

As was noted above, it was widely believed that the institutions participating in this process—mortgage companies, commercial banks, investment banks—would escape harm since they passed the new products along to the final investors. However, it turned out that all three types of institutions kept large inventories of the toxic products they had created. The most obvious reason is that it takes time for newly created mortgage-backed securities and other derivatives to be sold to the next level, resulting in a sizeable inventory in all three types of institutions at any time. In addition, there were other reasons why the institutions (and their shadow affiliates) kept large amounts of the derivative securities, which are discussed in Crotty (2009).

The credit default swaps that were assumed to be the last line of defense against financial disaster instead turned out to heighten the systemic risk. Unlike for the issue of conventional insurance policies, credit default swaps do not require the issuer to hold reserves to pay off expected future claims. When widespread defaults began, the credit default swaps were time bombs that either sank the credit default swap sellers who had to come up with funds to make good on the contracts or provided no assistance to the credit default swap buyers if the seller could not make the payments. As we shall see below, this problem came to light in the case of the bankruptcy and bailout of the giant insurance company AIG in 2008.

The end of the real estate bubble would also cause a big problem for households. The buildup of household debt, dating to the early 1980s, was driven on in the 2000s by the real estate bubble. When the real estate bubble eventually came to an end and home prices fell, households would no longer be able to continue borrowing and expanding their debt and instead would have to start paying down their debt. This was bound to have a substantial downward impact on consumer demand.

Excess Capacity

The third threatening long-term trend in the U.S. economy in the neoliberal era was the development of excess productive capacity, or overcapacity. It is difficult to measure the percentage of total productive capacity that is in use accurately except in a few sectors of the economy, such as manufacturing, mining, and electric power. The Federal Reserve publishes series on the capacity utilization rate in manufacturing and in the broader category of industry, which includes mining and electric power as well as manufacturing. Since capacity utilization varies greatly over the business cycle, long-term trends can be seen by comparing business cycle peak years. Figure 5.3 shows the manufacturing capacity utilization ratio in the last three peak years during 1948–73 and the last three peak years during 1979–2007.[21] As Figure 5.3 shows, in the regulated capitalist era the rate rose in each successive peak year, reaching 87.7% in the last peak in 1973. By contrast, in the neoliberal era the rate was lower in each successive peak year, reaching only 78.6%

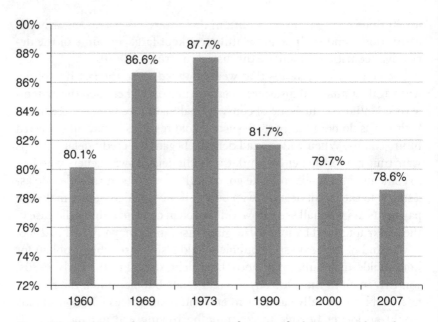

Figure 5.3. Capacity utilization rate in manufacturing for business cycle peak
years.
Source: Board of Governors of the Federal Reserve System, 2013.

in 2007. This strongly suggests that, despite the relatively modest pace
of capital accumulation in the neoliberal era compared to that of the
regulated capitalist era, firms in the industrial sector were building too
much productive capacity relative to demand over the long run.[22]

This suggests that the series of asset bubbles did produce the effect
cited in Chapter 4, of promoting exaggerated expectations about the
future on the part of corporate decision-makers, leading to excessive
expansion of productive capacity relative to actual output.[23] This is one
more factor that tended to keep inflationary pressures at bay, while it
also depressed the rate of profit below what it would have been had capacity been more fully utilized.[24] Neoliberal capitalism also gave rise to
a problem with what can be called the "sustainable" capacity utilization
rate as well the actual rate. As we saw in Chapter 4, in the 2000s households borrowed heavily to support consumer spending. Firms respond
to rising consumer spending by investing in additional productive capacity so as to be able to meet the rising demand and to profit from it.

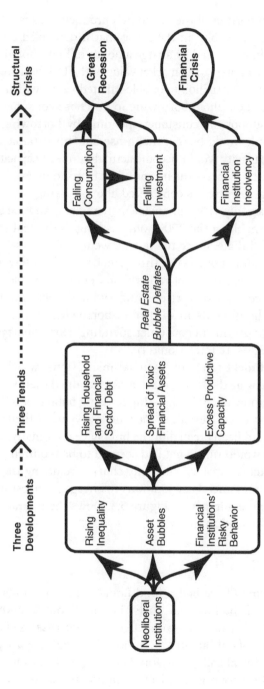

Figure 5.4. Causes of the economic crisis.

By 2007 some portion of the economy's productive capacity that was in use was "unsustainable" in the sense that it depended on a level of consumer spending elevated by a large amount of household borrowing. As was noted in Chapter 4, the market value of the U.S. housing stock included an estimated $8 trillion in bubble-inflated value, which supported a large volume of household borrowing to purchase consumer goods. If the process of supporting consumer spending by borrowing suddenly stopped, the result would be that the in-use but "unsustainable" part of the productive capacity would become actually unused capacity. That in turn would severely depress the incentive for firms to invest.[25]

All three long-term trends considered above—rising debt ratios, the spread of increasingly risky financial instruments, and excess capacity—were sustainable in the 2000s only as long as the real estate bubble continued to inflate. Once the bubble went into reverse—as it was bound to do at some point—the three trends would interact to bring a major crisis. Household debt ratios that were sustainable as long as housing prices continued to rise would suddenly became unsustainable, requiring households to shift from borrowing to repaying debt, causing a sudden decline in consumer spending. Home mortgage delinquency and foreclosure rates would rise.

The very high debt ratios of financial institutions, which had been sustainable as long as the institutions' assets retained their value, would threaten bankruptcy once the deflating housing bubble rapidly reduced the value of their assets, revealing the true low value of the toxic financial assets that had been created in the bubble years. Finally, a deflating housing bubble would turn what had seemed to be required productive capacity into excess capacity, suddenly sharply reducing the incentive on the part of nonfinancial corporations to engage in investment in additional plant and equipment.[26] Figure 5.4 shows the interaction of the various factors that led to the crisis.

Emergence of the Crisis

In 1998 the bailout of the hedge fund Long-Term Capital Management had foreshadowed the financial crisis that broke out in 2008.[27] Long-Term Capital Management, a giant hedge fund with assets of about $90 billion but capital of only about $2.3 billion, faced failure partly from the fallout of the financial collapse in Russia in August 1998. On September 23 the Federal Reserve organized a $3.5 billion rescue by a consortium of banks and brokerage houses, despite the absence of any regulatory responsibility for the unregulated hedge fund on the part of any government agency. Federal Reserve chairman Alan Greenspan defended his action by warning that a failure by Long-Term Capital Management would have harmed the financial markets and economic growth.[28]

This event seemed to teach three lessons: 1) in the new deregulated financial environment, large institutions could face failure, even those with a record of high profits; 2) any failure by a large financial institution posed a risk of contagion to the financial system as a whole; and 3) the Federal Reserve could be counted on to come to the rescue of any large financial institution that got into difficulty, including those not officially backed by government guarantees. These three lessons suggested that all types of large financial institutions were free to plunge into speculative activities, since success would bring high profits while, in the worst case of institutional failure, the Federal Reserve would ride to the rescue.[29]

In 2006 housing prices finally stopped rising, as Figure 5.5 shows. In the third quarter of 2006 the average house price hit its maximum, then changed little for nine months before starting a downward plunge

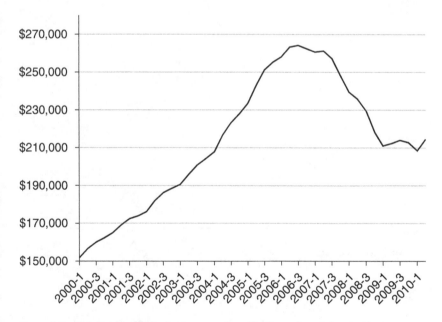

Figure 5.5. Estimated average house price by calendar quarter, 2000–2010.
Source: Federal Housing Finance Agency, 2013.

in the third quarter of 2007. In 2006 the interest rates on a large number of subprime adjustable rate mortgages reset upward. After late 2006 mortgage delinquency and foreclosure rates, which had been at historic lows, began to rise at an accelerating pace, largely involving subprime mortgages. Figure 5.6 shows the rapid rise in the percentage of home mortgages that were delinquent. By March 2008 about one in eleven home mortgages were either past due or in foreclosure.[30] In addition, as home values fell, the percentage of homes that were underwater (with a mortgage exceeding the home value), which had been under 5% in 2006, began to rise in early 2007, reaching 10.3% in February 2008.[31]

In 2007 signs of financial distress began to appear. On April 2 a leading subprime lender, New Century Financial, filed for bankruptcy protection. In August Fitch Ratings downgraded a major subprime lender, Countrywide Financial, to BBB+, its third-lowest rating. That same

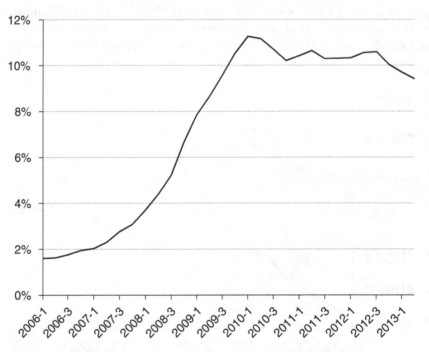

Figure 5.6. Delinquency rate on single-family residential mortgages, quarterly rates, 2006–2013.

Source: Federal Reserve Bank of St. Louis Economic Research, 2013.

month the Federal Reserve, the European Central Bank, and the Bank of Japan engaged in a coordinated injection of more than $100 billion into the global financial system. In September Citibank borrowed $3.4 billion from the Federal Reserve. In October Merrill Lynch announced an $8.4 billion loss from involvement in the subprime mortgage market.

The financial distress intensified over the course of 2008. On January 11 Bank of America acquired failing Countrywide Financial. On March 14 the Federal Reserve provided a loan of $30 billion to assist JP-Morgan Chase to take over Wall Street's fifth-largest investment bank, Bear Stearns, which had incurred large losses on ALT-A mortgages, a type of mortgage better than subprime but below prime. This marked the first failure of a major institution. Ironically, in 1998 Bear Stearns had declined to join in the Federal Reserve-organized rescue of Long-Term Capital Management.[32] On July 11 the Federal Deposit Insurance Corporation placed Indymac Bank, a major mortgage originator, into receivership, marking the fourth-largest bank failure in U.S. history.

In September 2008 the financial crisis suddenly broke out. On September 7 the government took over the giant government-sponsored mortgage market enterprises, Fannie Mae and Freddie Mac. On September 14 the venerable Merrill Lynch was forced to sell itself to Bank of America. On September 15 Lehman Brothers, a major investment bank whose origins dated back to the nineteenth century, was allowed to go bankrupt by the Federal Reserve. On September 17 the Federal Reserve bailed out AIG, an insurance company, with $85 billion, taking an 80% share of its stock. AIG, which as an insurance company had no legal call on government support, was sunk by its huge holdings of credit default swaps, lacking the funds to make good on them. On September 25 the giant mortgage lender Washington Mutual, with assets valued at $307 billion, was closed and sold to JPMorgan Chase. In the week of October 6–10 the Dow Jones Industrial average fell by 18.2%.

The financial crisis quickly spread to Europe, including the U.K., Ireland, France, Belgium, and Iceland. Big housing bubbles had arisen in the U.K., Spain, and Ireland in the 2000s, and they deflated along with the U.S. housing bubble. The increasingly integrated global financial and economic system that had developed in the neoliberal era assured that the crisis would rapidly spread to the global economy. No country could entirely escape the powerful downward impulse coming from the sharp recession that quickly emerged in the U.S. economy, although those countries that did not allow their financial institutions to fully integrate into the global financial system, such as China, escaped the financial dimension of the crisis.

The recession in the United States started before the financial crisis broke out in September 2008. Shortly after the housing bubble began to contract in the third quarter of 2007, the economy reached a peak in the fourth quarter of that year, as Figure 5.7 shows. As Table 5.1 shows, the recession began in the first quarter of 2008 with a decline in GDP at a -1.8% annual rate.[33] While recessions usually are led by a decline in business investment, in the first quarter of 2008 consumer spending turned from positive growth to decline at an annual rate of -1.0%, while smaller business fixed investment declined at the slower rate of -0.8%. Consumer spending on services is difficult to reduce, and the more easily reducible consumer spending on goods fell at a -5.6% rate while durable goods consumption fell at a -9.6% rate in that quarter. Business

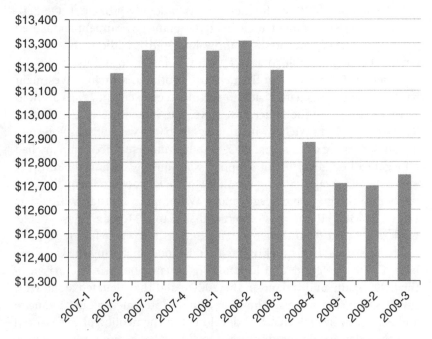

Figure 5.7. Gross domestic product, first quarter of 2007 to third quarter of 2009, billions of chained 2005 dollars.

Source: U.S. Bureau of Economic Analysis, 2013, NIPA Table 1.1.6.

Table 5.1. Quarterly Changes in Gross Domestic Product, Consumer Spending, and Business Fixed Investment (Annual Percentage Rate of Change)

	2007				2008				2009		
	I	II	III	IV	I	II	III	IV	I	II	III
Gross Domestic Product	0.5	3.6	3.0	1.7	**-1.8**	1.3	-3.7	-8.9	-5.3	-0.3	1.4
Consumer Spending	2.2	1.5	1.8	1.2	**-1.0**	-0.1	-3.8	-5.1	-1.6	-1.8	2.1
Goods Consumption	2.6	1.9	3.0	1.0	**-5.6**	0.5	-7.7	-12.6	0.2	-2.1	7.5
Consumer Durables Consumption	5.1	5.7	5.2	2.3	**-9.6**	-2.9	-12.3	-25.4	1.3	-2.0	20.9
Business Fixed Investment	6.5	10.8	9.1	5.4	**-0.8**	-2.3	-9.9	-22.9	-28.9	-17.5	-7.8

Source: U.S. Bureau of Economic Analysis, 2013, NIPA Table 1.1.1.
Note: Boldface entries show growth rates in the first quarter of 2008, when the recession started.

fixed investment started declining rapidly in the third quarter of 2008, shrinking at an accelerating rate of decline through the first quarter of 2009 when it reached a record annual rate of decline of -28.9%.[34]

This sequence is consistent with the bubble-deflation scenario for the real sector, in which the deflating bubble drives down household borrowing, which in turn causes consumer spending to fall, which in turn reveals excess productive capacity that soon causes business investment to drop rapidly. The start of the rapid decline in business fixed investment, in the July-to-September third quarter of 2008, occurred before the financial crisis had fully emerged. In the second quarter of 2008, the economy grew slightly, propelled by a one-quarter-long large increase in exports (at a 12.7% rate). Thereafter the economy returned to contraction through the second quarter of 2009.

Starting in the last quarter of 2008, the financial crisis undoubtedly contributed to the accelerating decline in investment, as expectations about the economic future crashed downward. However, the common view that the crisis is essentially a financial crisis, from which all the other features of the crisis are derived, is not convincing. It is often assumed that the real sector part of the crisis—often called the "Great Recession"—stemmed from the financial crisis undermining the ability of banks to lend to nonfinancial corporations. However, had that occurred, there would be evidence that demand for credit by the nonfinancial sector exceeded the supply, but none can be found. Interest rates fell to historically low levels. The Federal Reserve kept the federal funds rate below 1% after September 2008, and the AAA corporate bond yield, after rising from 5.64% to only 6.28% from August to October 2008, fell to 5.05% by December and remained low for years after that.

The Federal Reserve's unprecedented monetary actions pumped a huge amount of reserves into U.S. banks starting in September 2008. Reserves are the basis for banks to make loans and investments. Figure 5.8 shows the very rapid growth in excess reserves after August 2008, which is the amount of reserves the banks could have made loans against but had not.[35] By January 2009 the banks held just under $800 billion in excess reserves, rising to more than $1 trillion by November of that year. The banks made few loans, not because they were unable to do so, but because they evidently did not find desirable borrowers due to the real sector recession, making lending to businesses appear risky.

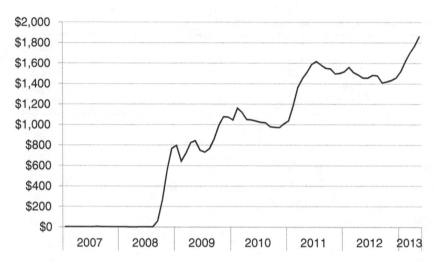

Figure 5.8. Monthly excess reserves of depository institutions in billions of dollars, 2007–2013.

Source: Federal Reserve Bank of St. Louis Economic Research, 2013.

Note: Through May 2013.

The real sector recession, which started in January 2008, continued through June 2009, with a recovery starting in the third quarter of 2009. It was the most severe of any since the Great Depression, apart from the brief but severe postwar readjustment in 1945–46.[36] During the first twelve months of the recession, both global output and global trade contracted more rapidly than they had during the first twelve months of the Great Depression of the 1930s (Eichengreen and O'Rourke, 2009). However, after one year big state interventions moderated the course of the crisis in 2009.

Table 5.2 compares the 2008–09 recession to the ten preceding post-World War II recessions. Measured by GDP decline, duration, or increase in the unemployment rate, the 2008–09 recession is the most severe. The unemployment rate hit a high of 10.0% in October 2009. The capacity utilization rate in manufacturing fell to 64.0% in June 2009, which was almost 4.5 percentage points lower than its previous low since 1948 (reached in December 1982). The Great Recession was the only postwar recession that the government combated with a large stimulus program, without which the recession would have been significantly deeper and longer lasting.

Table 5.2. The Eleven Recessions since 1948

Recession	(1) Decline in GDP	(2) Duration in Months	(3) Rise in Unemployment Rate (Percentage Points)
1948–49	–1.6%	11	4.5
1953–54	–2.5%	10	3.6
1957–58	–3.1%	8	3.8
1960–61	–0.5%	10	2.3
1969–70	–0.2%	11	2.7
1973–75	–3.2%	16	4.2
1980	–2.2%	6	2.2
1981–82	–2.6%	16	3.6
1990–91	–1.4%	8	2.6
2001	0.7%	8	2.5
2008–09	–4.7%	18	5.6
Average through 2001	–1.7%	10.4	3.2

Source: U.S. Bureau of Economic Analysis, 2013, NIPA Table 1.1.1; National Bureau of Economic Research, 2013; U.S. Bureau of Labor Statistics, 2013.

The crisis spread rapidly from the United States to much of the rest of the world. Table 5.3 shows the GDP growth rate and unemployment rate for fourteen major countries. Measured by GDP decline, the crisis was most severe in Russia, Iceland, Ireland, Italy, and Japan. China's growth slowed from a blistering pace in 2008 but remained robust, a performance to be discussed below. Brazil suffered only a slight contraction. The crisis was mainly one of the developed economies. The biggest increases in unemployment in 2009 were in Spain, Ireland, Iceland, and the United States. After 2009 the impact on various countries shifted, as we shall see in the next section of this chapter. We will comment below on Germany's declining trend in unemployment.

Some analysts had expected the large imbalances in the U.S. external accounts to eventually trigger a big crisis. As Figure 4.17 showed, the United States had a rapidly growing trade deficit in the 2000s, rising ıble 5.3. Gross Domestic Product Change and Unemployment Rate in Fourteen Countries

	2007	2008	2009	2010	2011	2012
ercentage Change in Gross Domestic Product						
Brazil	6.1	5.2	−0.3	7.5	2.7	0.9
Canada	2.1	1.1	−2.8	3.2	2.6	1.8
China	14.2	9.6	9.2	10.4	9.3	7.8
France	2.3	−0.1	−3.1	1.7	1.7	0.0
Germany	3.4	0.8	−5.1	4.0	3.1	0.9
Greece	3.5	−0.2	−3.1	−4.9	−7.1	−6.4
Iceland	6.0	1.2	−6.6	−4.1	2.9	1.6
Ireland	5.4	−2.1	−5.5	−0.8	1.4	0.9
Italy	1.7	−1.2	−5.5	1.7	0.4	−2.4
Japan	2.2	−1.0	−5.5	4.7	−0.6	2.0
Russia	8.5	5.2	−7.8	4.5	4.3	3.4
Spain	3.5	0.9	−3.7	−0.3	0.4	−1.4
United Kingdom	3.6	−1.0	−4.0	1.8	0.9	0.2
United States	1.9	−0.3	−3.1	2.4	1.8	2.2
nemployment Rate						
Brazil	9.3	7.9	8.1	6.7	6.0	5.5
Canada	6.1	6.2	8.3	8.0	7.5	7.3
China	4.0	4.2	4.3	4.1	4.1	4.1
France	8.4	7.8	9.5	9.7	9.6	10.2
Germany	8.8	7.6	7.7	7.1	6.0	5.5
Greece	8.3	7.7	9.4	12.5	17.5	24.2
Iceland	1.0	1.6	8.0	8.1	7.4	5.8
Ireland	4.7	6.4	12.0	13.9	14.6	14.7
Italy	6.1	6.8	7.8	8.4	8.4	10.6
Japan	3.8	4.0	5.1	5.1	4.6	4.4
Russia	6.1	6.4	8.4	7.5	6.6	6.0
Spain	8.3	11.3	18.0	20.1	21.7	25.0
United Kingdom	5.4	5.6	7.5	7.9	8.0	8.0
United States	4.6	5.8	9.3	9.6	8.9	8.1

Source: International Monetary Fund, 2013a.

above 6% of GDP in 2005–07. This deficit was financed by large inflows of capital from around the world. Some analysts believed this process was unsustainable. However, when the crisis emerged in 2008, the value of the U.S. dollar rose rather than falling. If the trade (or current account) deficit had brought the crisis, the value of the dollar should have plummeted. From July to November 2008, as the crisis entered its acute stage, the trade-weighted value of the U.S. dollar rose rather than falling, afterward remaining relatively stable through April 2009 when it began to gradually decline through the summer of 2011, then trending upward again. While the huge U.S. trade deficit is undesirable—it means that the richest country in the world borrows from poorer countries to enable it to spend more than it produces—public and private investors in the rest of the world have continued to willingly finance the U.S. trade deficit. The main reason is that the dollar has been seen by investors as a safe haven in time of instability.

Immediate Response to the Crisis

As the largest banks in the United States approached insolvency, the government sprang into action. On September 19, 2008, President Bush's treasury secretary, Henry M. Paulson, began negotiations with Congress over a huge bank bailout. The $700 billion Troubled Assets Relief Program (TARP) was introduced in Congress, but a rebellion by both Republican and Democratic members led to its defeat in the House on September 29, by a vote of 228–205. After enormous pressure was applied, including warnings that the financial system would collapse without it, the measure passed and became law on October 3. It authorized an initial government investment of $250 billion in endangered banks along with extension of Federal Deposit Insurance Corporation guarantees to the senior debt of all insured banks as well as to previously uninsured non-interest-bearing bank deposits of businesses. It also authorized the Federal Reserve to buy unsecured commercial paper issued by companies with good credit ratings.[37]

On October 13, Treasury Secretary Paulson, re-enacting a famous event when J. P. Morgan locked the top bankers of his day in his private library during the Panic of 1907, brought the CEOs of the nine largest U.S. banks into his gilded conference room. Paulson handed them prepared statements, telling them they must sign before they left. All nine signed, agreeing to accept a government bailout of their institutions including a (non-controlling) government stake in them.[38] At the same time, the Federal Reserve actively intervened by lending freely to banks and buying various types of financial sector securities. By late November the U.S. government had committed an estimated $7.8 trillion to the financial sector in the form of grants, loans, investments, and guarantees.[39] The amount committed rose to an estimated $14 trillion in 2009.

The bailouts of big institutions extended beyond the financial sector. As General Motors Corporation, America's largest manufacturing company, veered toward bankruptcy in December of 2008, the Bush administration extended more than $13 billion in loans to the company. After President Obama took office, the government pumped still more funds into GM and acquired a 61% stake in the company, effectively nationalizing it.[40]

The astonishing near-collapse of the major financial institutions and one of the most famous industrial giants, followed by an unprecedented government bailout, had a profound effect on society. This was reinforced by the rapid decline in the real sector. The unemployment rate rose precipitously, illustrated in Figure 5.9. As Figure 5.10 shows, during September and October 2008 more than 450,000 jobs disappeared each month, and in November and December more than 700,000 were lost monthly, numbers that were regularly announced in the media. The economy seemed to be falling off a cliff.

For decades the public had been told that free-market capitalism was a self-regulating system that delivered the goods. The old days of government intervention in the economy were over. Firms and households alike were supposed to sink or swim based on their own efforts. Now the economy seemed to be collapsing, and the government was rescuing the largest banks and other financial institutions. Pundits noted that the name of the financial sector bailout—the "Troubled Assets Relief Program"—left the question hanging of why only troubled corporate assets were rescued while no such dramatic rescue was forthcoming for troubled low and middle income households.

Keynes, or rather the policy ideas associated with his name, suddenly returned from the grave. A clamor arose for the government to do something. Some leading economists who had previously advocated neoliberal policies began to sound like Keynesians. Harvard economics professor Martin Feldstein was known for his research supporting

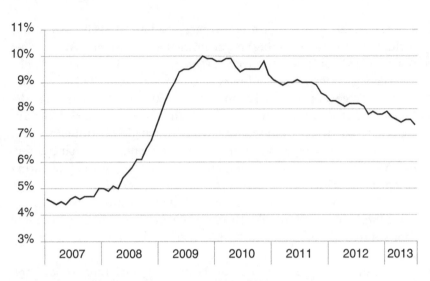

Figure 5.9. Monthly unemployment Rate, 2007–2013.
Source: U.S. Bureau of Labor Statistics, 2013. Through July 2013.

the neoliberal "crowding out" hypothesis, which holds that increased public spending simply reduces ("crowds out") an equal value of private spending, with no stimulative effect on GDP. That is, expansionary fiscal policy does not expand the economy. In the grim month of January 2009 Feldstein, speaking to an overflow audience at the main annual conference of North American economists in San Francisco, asserted that the only way to counter the gathering recession was expansionary fiscal policy. He called for a stimulus of $300 to $400 billion per year aimed at increasing aggregate demand, with the "heavy lifting" to be done by increased government spending rather than tax cuts.[41] He offered no explanation for why he was abandoning his long-held position on the ineffectiveness of fiscal policy. One wag remarked, "In a crisis we are all Keynesians."

Not all of the leading neoliberal economists advocated Keynesian measures. Some hewed to long-held theories despite their seeming contradiction by events, denouncing the revival of what they insisted was a false Keynesian theory and bemoaning the desertion of neoliberal economics by some of their colleagues. An op-ed column on October 10, 2008, by Casey Mulligan of the University of Chicago Department of Economics insisted that banking was of marginal importance to the

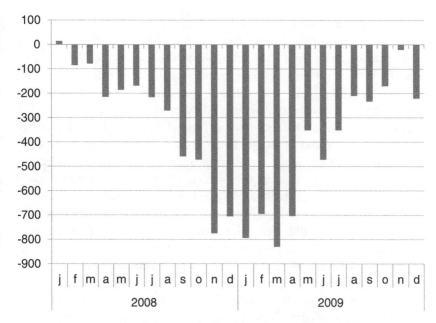

Figure 5.10. Monthly job gain or loss, hundreds of thousands, 2008 and 2009.
Source: U.S. Bureau of Labor Statistics, 2013.

economy and that the financial system "is more resilient today than it has been in the past." The economy "doesn't really need saving" by the government since "the fundamentals of the economy are strong" (Mulligan, 2008).[42] However, such views were swept aside as established opinion suddenly swung toward Keynesian economics in late 2008 and early 2009. A modest revival of interest in the works of the left-wing Keynesian Hyman Minsky arose, as some began to refer to a "Minsky moment" having arrived. Minsky had written articles starting in the 1960s warning of the inherent instability and crisis-prone nature of the financial system in a market economy. Suggestions even appeared in the mainstream media that the economic crisis showed Karl Marx had been right after all about capitalism's self-destructive tendencies, although coupled with the observation that of course Marx had long ago been proven wrong about socialism.

Perhaps the most poignant moment came when Alan Greenspan appeared before a congressional committee on October 23, 2008. Greenspan, Federal Reserve chairman from 1987 to 2006, had a reputation as a profound analyst and wise overseer of the financial system. He had enthusiastically promoted the deregulation of finance. The devotee of conservative author Ayn Rand admitted to the committee, "Those of us who have looked to the self-interest of lending institutions to protect shareholders' equity, myself included, are in a state of shocked disbelief." Asked by a committee member whether his long-held individualist ideology had led to bad decisions as Federal Reserve chairman, he replied, "Yes, I've found a flaw. . . . I've been very distressed by that fact."[43]

In early 2009 economic stimulus programs—that is, expansionary fiscal policies—were adopted in nineteen of the Group of Twenty major economies.[44] In the United States President Obama and the Democrats in Congress pushed through Congress the American Recovery and Reinvestment Act of 2009, signed into law on February 17. This stimulus plan called for $787 billion in spending and tax cuts, with a focus on infrastructure, education, health care, and green technologies, along with funds for extending unemployment benefits. The funding was for two years, so that the annual stimulus was half the total, or $393.5 billion per year. The administration forecast that 3.5 million jobs would be created by the bill.

Some economists thought the stimulus was too small. The unemployment rate had jumped to 8.3% by February 2009, which amounted to 12.9 million officially unemployed workers. Each month the economy was shedding more than 600,000 jobs without government stimulus. At the time Nobel Laureate Paul Krugman estimated that the stimulus plan had only about $600 billion in "real stimulus," which, spread over two years, would average $300 billion per year. He argued that the amount was far too small to replace the drop in private spending (Krugman, 2009b).[45] Stimulus spending of $300 billion per year may seem large, but it was only about 2.1% of GDP, while the decline in real consumer and investment spending from their previous peaks by the second quarter of 2009 was about 8.4% of GDP.[46]

The effectiveness of the Chinese government's response to the crisis, compared to that of the U.S. stimulus program, suggests that Krugman's critique was correct. In late 2008 China's GDP growth rate, which had been in the double digits, began plummeting as its exports to the United States and Europe dropped sharply. China's rapid growth had relied heavily on fast growing exports since 2001 (Zhu and Kotz, 2011). The authorities responded earlier than in other countries, announcing a $586 billion infrastructure investment program in November 2008. This program amounted to about 7% of China's GDP each year over two years.[47] By comparison, the U.S. stimulus program, using Krugman's estimate of $600 billion of actual stimulus spent over two years, was less than one-third of China's program relative to U.S. GDP. China's economy quickly resumed growth at 9 to 10% per year.[48]

The undersized U.S. stimulus program undoubtedly reduced the severity of the recession and the sluggishness of the recovery. Estimates from government and leading private analysts of the effect of the stimulus on GDP by the second quarter of 2010 were in the range of 2.1% to 3.8% above what it would have been without the stimulus. For employment, such estimates ranged from 1.8 million to 2.5 million additional jobs by the second quarter of 2010 (Council of Economic Advisors, 2013, 13). However, it was not large enough to bring a vigorous recovery or lower the unemployment rate to an acceptable level.

This created an opportunity for opponents of the turn toward Keynesian policies. Big government spending programs always face a problem with the public in the United States. Surveys show that, while large majorities approve of most types of public spending, most nevertheless disapprove of government spending in general. Critics of the stimulus program pointed to the poor state of the economy and job market after it had gone into effect and claimed the stimulus had failed. The defenders were left in the uncomfortable position of saying the economy, although disappointingly bad, would have been even worse without the stimulus. This poor public relations outcome for the stimulus program was one factor, if not the most fundamental one, that promoted another surprising shift in the dominant economic policy paradigm: a return to neoliberal policy under the name "austerity." We will examine the austerity shift below.

Bank bailouts and a stimulus bill were two of the five major government responses to the crisis. The other three were a shift in the Federal Reserve's monetary policy, a financial regulatory bill, and a home mortgage relief plan. Right at the start of the crisis, the Federal Reserve shifted its policy stance toward expansionary and innovative monetary policy, under the leadership of Federal Reserve chairman Ben Bernanke. The Federal Reserve pushed short-term interest rates down to almost zero and held them there for years. In addition, the Federal Reserve moved beyond its traditional monetary policy instruments to engage in what has been called "quantitative easing," buying longer-term securities which can directly lower long-term interest rates. While these measures tend to stimulate spending by businesses and households, Keynesians argue that, in a severe recession such as that of 2008–09, expansionary monetary policy is likely to have only limited effectiveness. When demand is seriously depressed and business has a large amount of unused productive capacity, low interest rates by themselves are unlikely to lead to much new spending by business or households. Bernanke periodically stated that the Federal Reserve was doing its part but that Congress and the White House had to do theirs if the economy were to recover quickly.

The fourth major government response was a structural one. To prevent a recurrence of the financial crisis, the Democratic majority in Congress introduced the Dodd-Frank Wall Street Reform and Consumer Protection Act, which was finally signed into law on July 21, 2010. This bill rationalized and modestly increased government oversight of the financial sector. The bill included the "Volcker Rule," named after former Federal Reserve chairman Paul Volcker, forbidding federally insured banks from trading securities on their own account. Most of the new regulations in the bill were not clearly defined, leaving that to later rule-making by regulatory agencies. After passage, financial institution lobbyists descended on the agencies, and critics of the bill claim that the resulting new regulatory rules ended up weak and diluted.

The fifth major government response was intended to relieve mortgage-burdened homeowners as well as reviving the severely depressed residential construction industry. On February 17, 2009, the Obama administration introduced a $75 billion mortgage relief program, financed by the $700 billion TARP fund. It was intended to aid up to nine million homeowners facing unaffordable monthly payments on homes whose value had fallen drastically. However, while the program provided incentives to participate for the financial institutions that service mortgages, their participation was voluntary (Luhbi, 2009). Unlike with the bank bailout, the mortgage servicers were not called to a meeting in the Treasury Department and ordered to sign up. In December 2009 a House committee revealed that only 680,000 borrowers had obtained loan modification offers, representing only 7.6% of the target of nine million, despite a record 14% of homeowners with a mortgage either delinquent or in foreclosure.[49]

Sluggish Recovery

The U.S. economy hit bottom in June 2009 and a recovery officially began in July of that year. However, the recovery has been very sluggish. Normally a particularly deep recession is followed by a vigorous rebound in economic activity and, after a lag, solid growth in employment. This recovery has been far from normal.

Column (1) of Table 5.4 shows the annual growth rate of GDP and its main components from the low point of the recession in the second quarter of 2009 through the first quarter of 2013. The GDP growth rate of 2.1% per year is very slow for a recovery period.[50] Consumer spending has grown at the same lackluster rate. Business fixed investment normally grows very rapidly after a severe recession. For example, in the two previous severe recessions, in 1974–75 and 1981–82, business fixed investment over the three years following the trough grew at the rates of 10.3% and 7.4% per year, respectively (U.S. Bureau of Economic Analysis, 2013, NIPA Table 5.2.6). In the recovery following the 2009 trough, business fixed investment has grown at the rate of 5.2% per year, not low but well below the rate in the two previous recoveries from severe recessions. While federal consumption and investment rose significantly during the recession, during the recovery it declined while state and local numbers declined faster, which tended to slow the recovery.

Column (2) of Table 5.4 shows the state of the economy in the first quarter of 2013 compared to the pre-crisis peak in the fourth quarter of 2007. GDP was just 3.0% above its pre-crisis peak level after more than five years. The 5.2% per year growth rate of business fixed investment since the trough was not fast enough to bring it up to the previous peak—it was still 4.3% below its pre-crisis level. Despite claims of excessive federal spending, the federal component of GDP was only 6.5% above its level on the eve of the crisis, and the government component as a whole was below the late 2007 level due to decline in the larger state and local government consumption and investment.

The economy lost 8.7 million nonfarm jobs from the employment peak in January 2008 to the last month of employment decline in February 2010. This job loss had not been made up as of July 2013, by which month only 6.7 million jobs had been added.

The official unemployment rate leaves out those who are working part-time because they cannot find a full-time job and those who want

Table 5.4. U.S. Economic Recovery since the End of the Recession

	(1)	(2)
	Annual Growth Rate since Trough	Total Change since Previous Peak
GDP	2.1%	3.0%
Consumer Spending	2.1%	4.4%
Business Fixed Investment	5.2%	−4.3%
Residential Investment	4.9%	−23.7%
Exports	6.4%	13.0%
Imports	6.1%	1.5%
Government Consumption and Investment	−1.7%	−1.1%
Federal	−1.2%	6.5%
State and Local	−2.0%	−5.5%

Source: U.S. Bureau of Economic Analysis, 2013, NIPA Table 1.1.6.
Notes: Data go through the first quarter of 2013. In column 2, although federal consumption and investment rose faster than the decline in state and local, total government consumption and investment fell since state and local amounts are much larger than federal.

a job but have given up looking (considered "marginally attached to the labor force"). Figure 5.11 shows the "rate of underemployment," which includes both of the foregoing categories. That measure reached 17.1% in October 2009. The number of officially unemployed rose to 15.0 million in September 2009, declining to 14.4 million in December 2010 and 11.5 million in July 2013. The more inclusive "underemployed" numbered between 25 and 26 million for three years from 2009 to 2011, falling to 23.1 million in 2012 (U.S. Bureau of Labor Statistics, 2013).

The crisis period has also seen a large increase in the long-term unemployed, that is, those who have been out of work for more than twenty-six weeks. Figure 5.12 shows the percentage of the officially unemployed who are long-term unemployed, a figure which rose steeply starting in 2008 and has remained high. The slow employment growth has also produced a disturbing trend in the relation between employment and the working-age population. Figure 5.13 shows the large drop in that ratio during the recession and the absence of a rebound during

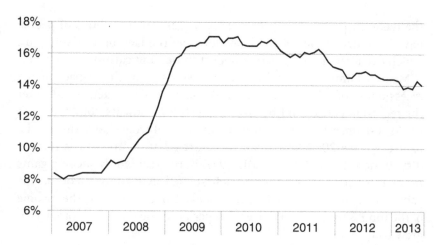

Figure 5.11. Monthly underemployment rate, 2007–2013.

Source: U.S. Bureau of Labor Statistics, 2013, Table A-15.

Notes: Includes officially unemployed, part-time workers for economic reasons, and those marginally attached to the labor force. Through July 2013.

Figure 5.12. Long-term unemployed as a percentage of all unemployed, monthly, 2007–2013.

Source: U.S. Bureau of Labor Statistics, 2013, Table A-15. Through July 2013.

the recovery period since 2009. This suggests that millions of people have been driven out of the labor force by the lack of available jobs, which can affect lifelong career opportunities and earnings potential.

Median family income had not recovered from the impact of the recession as of 2012, as Figure 5.14 shows. It continued to fall after the recession ended, and by 2012 it was 8.4% below its 2007 level and the lowest since 1995, seventeen years earlier. Income gains during the recovery since 2009 have been concentrated at the top of the income distribution. From 2009 to 2012, 95% of the real family income gains in the U.S. economy went to the richest 1%, leaving only 5% of income gains for the other 99% of families. Looked at another way, the income of the top 1% rose by 31.4% over that period while that of the other 99% grew by 0.4% (Saez, 2013, 1).[51]

Behind these dry statistics lies much human suffering, during recession and recovery. Early in the crisis, in November 2008, a farm couple in Colorado announced that anyone could come to take away vegetables

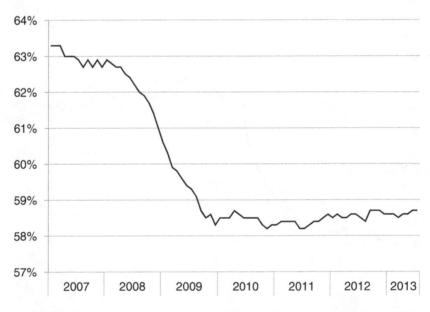

Figure 5.13. Employment as a percentage of the working age population, monthly, 2007–2013.

Source: U.S. Bureau of Labor Statistics, 2013. Through July 2013.

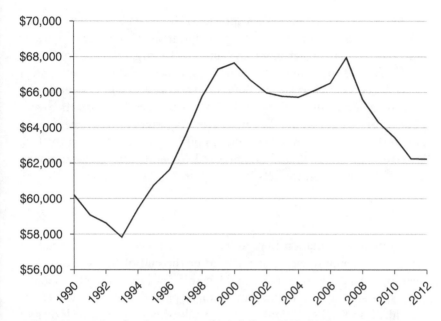

Figure 5.14.   Median family income in 2012 dollars, 1990–2012.

Source: U.S. Bureau of the Census, 2013, Historical Income Tables, Table F-8.

left over after the harvest. To their surprise, over 40,000 people showed up, picking their fields clean.[52] The large-scale presence of hunger in America was confirmed by a U.S. Department of Agriculture survey showing that in 2012 nearly forty-nine million people were living in "food insecure" households, meaning that some family members did not have "consistent access throughout the year to adequate food."[53]

Studies have found that the suicide rate rises and falls with the un-employment rate. One study estimated that in the United States 4,750 "excess suicides" occurred from 2007 to 2012 compared to previous trends, with the suicide rate higher in states with the greatest job loss (Stuckler and Basu, 2013). We have seen that long-term unemployment, of more than twenty-six weeks, has been stuck at record levels, and it has been reported that many employers prefer to hire new labor force entrants or those who already have a job. According to data from the Bureau of Labor Statistics as of July 2013, finding another job takes an average of forty-six weeks for workers aged fifty-five to sixty-four, and re-employment for that age group is at a median salary loss of 18%.[54]

The German government's response to the crisis was different from that of the United States, reflecting the far greater influence of workers and trade unions in Germany. Germany had a larger decline in GDP in 2009 than did the United States, of 5.1%. However, the unemployment rate fell rather than rising in 2008, and it rose by only one-tenth of a percentage point in 2009 as Table 5.3 has shown. This was the result of government programs that subsidized big employers to keep workers on the job rather than laying them off.[55] By contrast, when the U.S. government bailed out and nationalized General Motors, the company laid off 21,000 union workers.[56]

Austerity

The stubborn stagnation that afflicted the U.S. economy, and much of the global economy (see Table 5.3), after the end of the recession has been partly a result of another sudden shift in the dominant economic policy paradigm. The Keynesian moment passed quickly, and neoliberal ideas and policies came roaring back, this time in the clothes of "austerity." In the spring and summer of 2009, calls for cutbacks in government spending mounted, from economists, policy analysts, and public officials in the United States and Europe.

The new policy approach focused on the large government deficits and rising ratios of government debt to GDP in every country affected by the recession. While few countries in the G20 were running significant government deficits in the years immediately before the crisis, the sharp recessions brought large deficits, as tax collections declined with economic activity while spending on unemployment benefits and other social programs automatically grew. Then the stimulus programs further increased public deficits. Some policy analysts and officials had long viewed government deficits, and the growing public debt that results from them, as the most serious contemporary economic problem. Now they were joined by a growing chorus of influential people, and the mass media soon began to treat the austerity view as self-evident truth.

In some cases the same individuals and organizations that had vigorously supported government stimulus in late 2008 and early 2009 suddenly shifted their views toward austerity. In January 2010 Professor Martin Feldstein, while not renouncing his previous support for a stimulus expressed in January 2009, began warning of the dangers of the growing federal debt and calling for cutbacks in public spending.[57] In January 2009 Thomas J. Donohue, president of the U.S. Chamber of Commerce, had urged the government to pass a stimulus program including programs for the jobless and infrastructure investment. Immediately after the Republican victory in the House elections in November 2010, the Chamber issued the following statement: "Americans have sent a powerful message to Washington. . . . Voters have resoundingly rejected more government spending" (U.S. Chamber of Commerce, 2010).

The Republican takeover of the House of Representatives in the 2010 congressional election was to some extent the product of a reaction against government spending and taxes, with the new "Tea Party" movement pushing Republican candidates to renounce "big government." The mass media played a role in the shift in policy views, by regularly highlighting what was assumed to be dangerously large deficits and growing public debt. The belief that growing public spending and deficits had produced a "budget crisis" was treated as unquestionably true, contrary to the Keynesian view that growing public spending and deficits are the only effective medicine in a severe recession or a tepid recovery, as shown in the following samples of *New York Times* economic reporting:

- "[T]here is little doubt that the United States' long-term budget crisis is becoming too big to postpone. . . . [A]ll that new government debt is likely to put more upward pressure on interest rates. Even a small increase in interest rates has a big impact."
- "Europe can no longer afford its comfortable lifestyle [generous government-provided social benefits] without a period of austerity and significant changes."
- "[O]pposition is growing in Washington and abroad to *deficit-bloated* government spending" [emphasis added].[58]

The demand for austerity recalls the dominant economic policy beliefs before the New Deal, when "sound policy" in the face of recession-induced deficits was thought to be cutting spending and/or raising taxes while waiting for the "natural" corrective mechanism of the market to revive the economy. In the United States the Obama administration responded to the sudden change in mood by a dual and seemingly contradictory position, supporting continuing government stimulus measures while suggesting that cuts in major social programs, including popular ones like Social Security and Medicare, could be part of a "Grand Bargain" that included higher taxes on the rich. Such a combined approach could be consistent if the spending cuts and tax increases were postponed until after full economic recovery.

Congressional Republicans adopted a determined opposition to any tax increases and demanded immediate large cuts in public spending. After 2010 the administration's plans for further stimulus were blocked in the House. In 2011 the federal component of GDP in real terms turned from growth to decrease, at -2.2% in 2011 and -2.2% in 2012, while total federal spending in real terms stopped growing after 2009. In March 2013 a budget deadlock between Democratic and Republican members of Congress produced across-the-board reductions in federal spending under the "sequester" rule, followed by a sixteen-day-long partial shutdown of the federal government in October, bringing austerity policy to the United States, although in milder form than in some European countries.

Austerity has been severe in several European countries. Huge cuts in public spending were imposed on Greece, Ireland, and Spain by the European Central Bank and other EU institutions. The results can be seen in Table 5.3 (above). Greece entered its sixth consecutive year of contraction in 2013, with GDP in 2012 having fallen by about 20% from its 2007 level. Greece's unemployment rate hit 24.2% in 2012 and youth unemployment was reported at over 50%. Ireland sank into stagnation, with unemployment reaching 14.7% in 2012. In Spain unemployment was 25.0% in 2012.[59]

The Arguments for Austerity

The pro-austerity position was accompanied by a reinterpretation of the causes of the crisis by neoliberal economists. To most observers it appeared that the private sector had self-destructed. However, this was contrary to neoliberal theory, which insists that a capitalist economy is inherently stable and that serious problems can originate only from mistaken state actions. Neoliberal economists came up with three ways in which the state, not the private sector, had caused the crisis.

First, and most prominently, it was argued that the Federal Reserve had mistakenly kept interest rates too low in the 2000s, and the resulting cheap money caused the real estate bubble whose deflation led to the crisis. Of course, in the relevant period the chairman of the Federal Reserve was Alan Greenspan, a devotee of neoliberal thought, but that was overlooked since the Federal Reserve is a state institution. If the crisis could be pinned on the Federal Reserve, the private sector would be off the hook.

The evidence does not support this explanation. Bosworth and Flaaen (2009) provide a convincing argument on this point. Expansionary monetary policy has been the normal policy in response to a recession since the 1950s. When the economy was recovering from the 2001 recession in 2002–03, the Federal Reserve kept short-term interest rates very low but began raising them in 2004 as economic growth picked up, following traditional monetary policy. Short-term interest rates were steadily raised through 2007, and long-term rates remained relatively high during the whole period 2001–07. Also, there were earlier periods in which short-term rates were just as low as the early 2000s, such as the early to mid-1950s, but no asset bubble arose. While low interest rates are favorable for the development of an asset bubble, the evidence supports the view that they are not the underlying cause, which is found in structural conditions in the economy.

A second explanation for the crisis offered by neoliberals is that two "government institutions," Fannie Mae and Freddie Mac, caused the crisis by creating all those high-risk subprime mortgage-backed securities. Such actions by them are attributed to their presumed status as government enterprises, which need not worry about the risk of failure. This explanation is based on a misunderstanding of the nature of the two large government-sponsored home mortgage institutions as well as ignorance of the facts concerning the rapid increase in subprime mortgage-backed securities. Fannie Mae was privatized in 1968 and thereafter was owned by private shareholders.

Before 2005 the two largely stayed out of the business of securitizing subprime mortgages, but in 2005 they came under pressure from mortgage companies and their own shareholders. Because Fannie was avoiding significant involvement in subprime mortgage securitization, in 2004 it lost 56% of its loan-reselling business to Wall Street institutions and other competitors. In response, a hedge fund manager who had a stake in Fannie phoned Daniel Mudd, the CEO of Fannie, saying, "Are you stupid or blind? Your job is to make me money." Angelo R. Mozilo, the head of major subprime originator Countrywide Financial, reportedly threatened Mudd by warning that he would end his relationship with Fannie and bypass it, going directly to Wall Street for securitization, if Fannie did not start taking Countrywide's high-risk mortgages. Mozilo reportedly said, "You're becoming irrelevant. . . . You need us more than we need you and if you don't take these loans, you'll find you can lose much more." Mudd gave in to the shareholder and market pressure, purchasing or guaranteeing at least $270 billion in high-risk loans from 2005 to 2008, more than three times as much as in all previous years combined.[60]

The third neoliberal explanation of the crisis targets the 1977 Community Reinvestment Act, which requires commercial banks and savings banks to take steps to service the credit needs of the communities where they are located. It is argued that this misguided piece of legislation required banks to make unsafe loans to low income people, resulting in the financial crisis. However, this explanation ignores the facts. About 75% of the higher-priced loans during the peak years of the subprime boom were not issued by institutions covered by the Community Reinvestment Act but by mortgage firms and bank affiliates not covered by the law (Barr and Sperling, 2008).

Despite the weakness of the neoliberal accounts of the cause of the financial crisis, they became the accepted explanations among neoliberal economists. More importantly for public policy than their explanations for the crisis have been the arguments put forward by neoliberal economists to explain the necessity of austerity. There are three economic arguments for austerity, all based on the economic harm believed to result from either a large current year government budget deficit or a high ratio of debt to GDP that can result from a period of high deficits.[61] The most frequently cited of the three economic arguments is the crowding out hypothesis. This asserts that if the government raises spending above its tax revenues, it must borrow the difference, which in turn raises interest rates. The higher interest rates reduce private investment, by an amount equal to the increase in government spending. Hence, a deficit-financed government spending increase simply crowds out an equal value of private investment, with no net effect on GDP but just a shift in the composition of GDP from private to public spending.

Critics point out that, in the presence of large numbers of unemployed workers and idle productive capacity, crowding out will not occur. The Federal Reserve can keep interest rates from rising via expansionary monetary policy, and the increased deficit-financed government spending will increase total demand in the economy. Private investment is likely to increase, not decrease, as those whose incomes rise due to the government spending spend their increased income on consumer purchases. According to the critics of the crowding out theory, only at full employment is deficit-financed government spending ineffective, since then GDP cannot increase further. The experience of the period since 2008 appears to support the critics. As government deficit spending increased, interest rates were pushed to historic lows by the Federal Reserve and business fixed investment increased over time as we noted above.[62]

The second claim of austerity advocates is that deficit-financed spending causes inflation. There are several versions of the underlying basis of this claim, which critics dispute as unfounded except when the economy is operating at or near full employment. As for the crowding out theory, the evidence for the period since 2008 is not favorable to this thesis. Despite frequent warnings of the approach of rapid inflation, the predicted inflation has stubbornly refused to show up, in spite of the large deficits. Since the Great Recession ended in June 2009 and the economy began to recover, the consumer price index has risen at the historically low rate of only 2.0% per year through September 2013 despite the large federal deficits during that period (U.S. Bureau of Labor Statistics, 2013).

The third claim centers around the effect of high debt ratios on GDP growth. Austerity advocates warn that if the ratio of government debt to GDP rises above some level, long-run economic growth will slow down or even turn negative. The simple idea is that in the future payments on the debt will eat up resources that could otherwise go for investment, which is essential for economic growth (the "we should not burden our grandchildren" argument). However, there are arguments that suggest the opposite—if deficit spending does stimulate economic growth, then high debt may be associated with faster growth. Also, to the extent that the public debt is held by a country's residents, then payments on the debt redistribute income among residents without affecting the resources available for investment.

It is difficult to obtain reliable evidence about the relationship between public debt ratios and long-run growth performance. Some debt critics have simply warned that the U.S. public debt ratio is approaching the level reached at the end of World War II, which was financed by borrowing. While this danger is assumed to be self-evident, the very high

U.S. public debt ratio in 1946 of 98.0% of GDP was followed by some twenty-five years of the fastest, most equally shared economic growth in U.S. history, as we saw above. Thus, the danger that such a high debt ratio poses is not obvious. As Figure 5.15 shows, during 1946–73 the U.S. federal debt ratio declined from 98.0% to 20.4%—but this resulted not from repaying the debt but because the GDP grew faster than the debt. Despite the big decline in the debt ratio over the period, in 1973 the debt outstanding was 22% greater than it had been in 1946.

Two Harvard professors, Carmen Reinhart and Kenneth Rogoff, published a paper in 2010 that claimed, based on a statistical analysis of a large number of countries, that a public debt ratio of over 90% of GDP led to significantly slower long-term economic growth.[63] They concluded that "this would suggest that traditional debt management issues should be at the forefront of public policy concerns" (Reinhart and Rogoff, 2010, 575, 578). This study was widely cited by policy analysts and

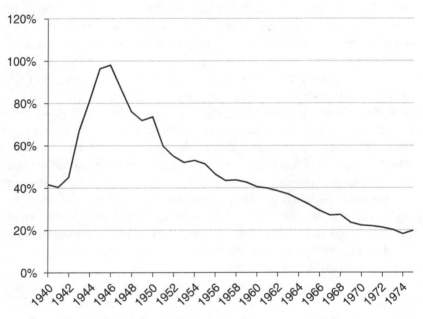

Figure 5.15.   U.S. federal debt held by the public as a percentage of gross domestic product, 1940–1975.

Source: Office of Management and Budget, 2013, Table 7.1.

officials as "proof" that failure to follow austerity policy would doom countries to economic decline.

The Reinhart and Rogoff paper had its critics from the beginning, who pointed out that their study had "direction of causation" limitations— that is, their statistical analysis did not determine whether countries with slow growth accumulated high debt as a result of the slow growth or rather that high debt caused slow growth as the austerity advocates claim. This technical debate did not reach beyond the specialists. How- ever, in April 2013 a graduate student in economics, Thomas Herndon, was able to obtain Reinhart and Rogoff's data analysis and produced a working paper showing that several errors lay behind their conclusions. Once the errors were corrected, the association between high public debt and slow growth in their data disappeared (Herndon et al., 2013).[64]

The spectacle of a lowly graduate student finding a fatal flaw in an influential study by two elite Harvard professors proved irresistible to the mass media.[65] The Herndon critique suddenly appeared in the *New York Times,* the *Wall St. Journal,* and the *Financial Times,* and the author appeared on National Public Radio and the popular Colbert Report tele- vision show.[66] As the Herndon critique went viral on the internet, many influential commentators suggested that the case for austerity policy had now collapsed.[67] It appears that the Herndon critique emerged at a moment when evidence of severely harmful outcomes for countries pursuing austerity was mounting, and many were looking for a way to break with it. Greece and Spain followed austerity and plunged into de- pression-level unemployment, while Iceland refused to adopt austerity following its financial collapse and emerged with relatively little pain, with its unemployment rate dropping to 5.8% by 2012. In Greece a new left-wing socialist party was rising rapidly in the polls, as was a neo- Nazi party. The mass media became more skeptical toward austerity in the late spring of 2013, although its advocates did not give up.

Some critics of austerity view it as an irrational, self-defeating re- sponse. However, it can be seen in another light. First of all, austerity shifted the target of public anger. As the crisis—and bank bailout—un- folded, millions of people became outraged at the banks. It appeared that banker speculation had first earned billions for the bankers, then destroyed the economy along with millions of jobs and trillions of dol- lars in homeowner equity. The bankers had been saved from the conse- quences of their folly by the taxpayers.

Bush's treasury secretary, Henry Paulson, who arranged the financial bailouts, had previously served as CEO of Goldman Sachs. Not only did he preside over saving his old firm, he also arranged the unorthodox bailout of insurance company AIG. Thanks to an $85 billion rescue package given to AIG by the government, AIG was able to make good on its credit default swap obligations to Goldman Sachs at 100% on the dollar. The bailout made good on $44 billion in credit default swap obligations of AIG to nineteen big banks, including $8.1 billion for Goldman Sachs.[68] Neither AIG nor the Treasury Department insisted on some discount from the amount owed to the banks, as would seem normal in a bankruptcy.

In 2008–09 the rich and powerful faced a rising tide of public anger, and where it might lead was unpredictable. Then the austerity view suddenly redirected the focus of public anger, by telling people, "It's not the banks that have done this to you, it's the government and greedy public sector workers and their powerful unions." In the United States, where "big government" is always an easy target, this transformation of the politics of the crisis was quite successful. Secondly, a dominant set of ideas is not dislodged easily, even when it appears to be discredited by events. Neoliberal ideas and policies have been a central part of the overall neoliberal form of capitalism, which worked very well for business and wealthy households over several decades. While a structural crisis of a social structure of accumulation presumably eventually leads to its replacement, that does not necessarily happen quickly. The groups that have benefited from the existing regime always mobilize to try to preserve it even when it has produced a crisis. The promotion of austerity can be seen as the second step in a two-step response by some actors: first support whatever is necessary to save the banks and stop the free-fall of the economy, then demand a shift to austerity to try to revive the neoliberal form of capitalism.

The decision to bail out the banks, along with their CEOs and shareholders, enabled them to emerge stronger than ever from the initial phase of the crisis. Not only were the largest banks bailed out, they were allowed, and even encouraged, to absorb other slightly smaller institutions. As a result, bank concentration rose substantially, further boosting the power of the big banks. In the Great Depression no such bank bailouts occurred, and the banks not only suffered financially but largely lost their political clout. This was followed by the imposition of a strict regime of state regulation over them. By contrast, the banks emerged from the financial crisis of 2008 with the power to lobby the Dodd-Frank reregulation bill in ways that weakened its impact, and many resurgent bankers who had supported the Obama presidential campaign in 2008 backed the Republicans in 2010 and 2012, helping invigorate the growing Republican pursuit of austerity policy.[69]

However, four years after the shift to austerity, it had produced nothing but economic decline. It does not appear to be a sustainable basis for promoting rising profits and economic expansion over the long run. It is possible that austerity may be nearing the end of its period of dominance.

Structural Crisis

The characterization of the crisis that began in 2008 as a structural crisis is not just a matter of semantics. If the crisis is fundamentally a financial crisis, resulting from ill-advised financial deregulation, then it could be fully resolved by imposing new financial regulations, leaving the other institutions that arose with neoliberal capitalism unchanged. If the crisis is fundamentally a severe recession, then a Keynesian stimulus should be able to fully resolve it. Both policies have been tried, at least to some extent, but the crisis has continued with a very sluggish recovery, continuing high unemployment, and millions of home mortgages still under water. In our view, although there are strong arguments for both reregulation of finance and Keynesian stimulus, neither one, nor the two together, would be sufficient to restore normal profitability and economic expansion.

The social structure of accumulation theory does not in itself provide a detailed explanation of why a particular form of capitalism eventually descends into a structural crisis. The analysis of the crisis offered here, stemming from growing inequality, asset bubbles, and speculative financial institutions—which in turn arose from the fundamental institutions of neoliberal capitalism—explains how the particular operation of this form of capitalism gave rise to a severe crisis in 2008. For neoliberal capitalism to resume functioning effectively as a social structure of accumulation, it would have to remain able to promote rising profitability by keeping wages down while solving the resulting demand problem through debt-fueled consumer spending arising from further speculative and risky activities by financial institutions and a new giant asset bubble. Such a prospect appears highly unlikely.

Neoliberal capitalism in the United States has so far retained the ability to keep wages down and raise profits. From the bottom of the recession in 2009 through 2012, the average hourly wage declined at the rate of -0.6% per year while output per hour rose at 1.7% per year (*Economic Report of the President*, 2013, Tables B-47 and B-49).[70] As Figure 5.16 shows, since 2009 the profit rate in the U.S. nonfinancial corporate business sector has recovered rapidly, almost reaching its 2006 pre-crisis high by 2011–12.[71]

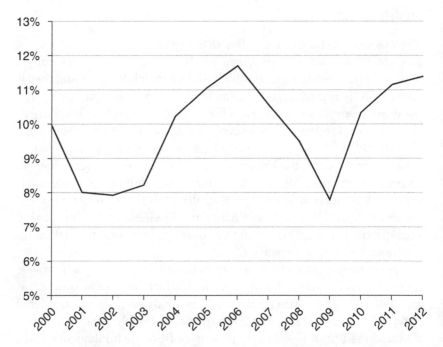

Figure 5.16. Rate of profit of the nonfinancial corporate business sector, 2000–2012.

Source: U.S. Bureau of Economic Analysis, 2013, NIPA Table 1.14, Fixed Assets Table 4.1.

Note: The rate of profit is pre-tax profit plus net interest and miscellaneous payments divided by fixed assets.

The major U.S. banks have continued to engage in speculative, risky activities. Several examples came to light in 2012–13. The so-called London Whale scandal in 2012 involved a London-based trading group of JPMorgan Chase, which accumulated a huge position in credit derivatives while overvaluing them on its books, then selling them, resulting in a distortion in the market price. The bank incurred a $6 billion loss. The bank had to admit wrongdoing and pay fines of over $1 billion to U.S. and British regulatory authorities.[72]

A second example involved Goldman Sachs, which took advantage of the repeal of the former Glass-Steagall Act barrier against financial institutions engaging in nonfinancial activities to invest in aluminum stockpiles. Goldman bought Metro International Trade Services, a warehousing firm that holds more than a quarter of U.S. aluminum supplies, which are used to manufacture a wide range of consumer products such as drink containers, cars, electronics, and house siding. After Goldman Sachs bought the firm in 2009, the length of time for manufacturers to get delivery of aluminum from the firm rose from six weeks to sixteen months. Under the obscure pricing rules for aluminum overseen by an overseas commodity exchange, this enabled Goldman Sachs to raise the price, increasing the cost of the final products to American consumers by an amount estimated at more than $5 billion over the following three years. To comply with the pricing regulations, the company ordered forklift drivers to constantly move pallets of aluminum from one warehouse to another.[73]

These examples suggest that the passage of the mild Dodd-Frank bill has not prevented the banks from continuing their speculative activities. However, nothing approaching the scale of the huge expansion in high-risk lending of the pre-crisis period has emerged, nor does a repeat of that experience seem likely in the near future. The high-risk activities of the financial sector contributed to growing consumer demand prior to 2008 by enabling households to engage in debt-financed consumption, but after 2007 household debt reversed its long rise, declining from 126.7% of after-tax household income in 2007 to 103.4% in 2012 as households were compelled to pay down, or default on, their outsize debt (see Figure 4.20 in Chapter 4).

Giant asset bubbles represent the third component of neoliberal capitalism's previous ability to promote rising profits and economic expansion over the long run. The aftermath of the collapse of the real estate bubble is still with us, in the form of millions of underwater mortgages, greatly diminished values of mortgage-related financial assets, and a less credulous attitude toward claims of eternally rising asset prices on the part of investors. It seems highly unlikely that a new large asset bubble will arise under these conditions. Thus, despite the recovery of the rate of profit and the continuation of some speculative activities by the big banks, it appears that the neoliberal form of capitalism has exhausted its ability to function as an effective social structure of accumulation. It is justified to regard the crisis that began in 2008 as the structural crisis of neoliberal capitalism.

Further reinforcing this view is the evidence that, while the rate of profit has fully recovered, capital accumulation, which is the rate of increase of the capital stock, has not. Figure 5.17 shows that the annual rate of capital accumulation fell to 0.4% in 2009, which is just above one-fourth of its previous post-World War II low in 2003. After 2009 it increased, but by 2012 it had reached only a rate of 1.3%, which is only 47% of its immediate pre-crisis high in 2007, despite the full recovery of the rate of profit.[74]

As a result of rising profits, along with low interest rates, nonfinancial corporations in the U.S. accumulated huge holdings of cash after 2009. In mid-2010 U.S. corporations' cash holdings were reported to be $943 billion, more than enough to cover a year's worth of investment as well as dividends.[75] In 2012 their cash holdings had reached a record $1.45 trillion, yet investment remained lackluster and job growth slow for a period following a sharp recession.[76] While neoliberal institutions continue to create conditions for a high share of profit in national income, they are no longer bringing normal capital accumulation or economic expansion. Without a normal rate of economic expansion, the rate of profit cannot remain high for very long.

Like the crisis that began in 2008, the Great Depression of the 1930s emerged from a liberal form of capitalism, as we will argue in Chapter 6. As has been noted above, capitalism in 2008 differed from that of 1929, in that there was a state and a central bank powerful enough to intervene effectively and prepared to do so quickly. That explains why the current crisis, despite an initial trajectory of output decline that paralleled that of

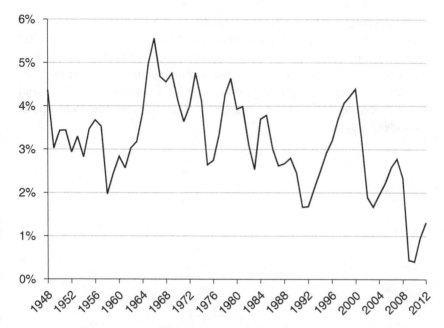

Figure 5.17. Annual rate of capital accumulation, 1948–2012.

Source: U.S. Bureau of Economic Analysis, 2013, NIPA Table 5.2.5, Fixed Assets Table 4.1.

Note: The rate of capital accumulation is net private nonresidential investment as a percentage of net private nonresidential fixed assets, both corrected for inflation.

1929–30, did not become as severe as the earlier one. In the Great Depression output in the U.S. declined by some 30% over three-and-a-half years of contraction while the unemployment rate reached 25%. However, a similarity is found in the depressed rate of business fixed investment in both crises. In 1939, ten years after the start of the Great Depression, while GNP had slightly surpassed its 1929 level, business fixed investment was only about 58% of its 1929 level. The depressed rate of capital accumulation may well have stemmed from the same cause in both cases: the large amount of excess capacity revealed by the collapse of a giant asset bubble that initiated the crisis. A large overhang of fixed capital can depress the incentive to invest for a long time.[77]

If the crisis that began in 2008 is indeed a structural crisis of the neo-liberal form of capitalism, then there is reason to expect that some kind of major economic change lies ahead. However, before proceeding to a consideration of possible new developments to come, we will undertake a brief review of some earlier periods in U.S. history that have potential lessons for the likely future course of change in economic institutions and ideas.

6

Lessons of History

The social structure of accumulation theory argues that every structural crisis is followed by major institutional restructuring. However, no social theory can tell us exactly how economic institutions and ideas will evolve in the future. The analysis presented so far has offered an explanation of the processes in neoliberal capitalism that gave rise to the crisis that began in 2008, as well as tracing the course of the crisis, and state responses to it, since its inception. This provides a basis for considering the possibility and likelihood of various future directions of change. However, earlier history can supply further clues about the likely direction of economic change in the future.

History is not simply a recurring cycle. Over time the economic, political, and cultural features of society change, which makes every new period different in various ways from any in the past. Nevertheless, if long-term changes are taken into account, useful lessons can be drawn from an examination of history. Past periods in which liberal institutions prevailed, the transitions to a different form of capitalism that followed, and past periods in which finance played a special role all have something to teach us about the possible directions of economic change in the near future, as well as adding some insights about the nature of the neoliberal era and the crisis that began in 2008.

The neoliberal era is not the first period in U.S. history in which liberal, or free-market, institutions predominated. A highly competitive form of capitalism characterized the post-Civil War decades through about 1900. That period is often called the Gilded Age, a term coined by Mark Twain and a co-author in a novel about the new wealthy class that arose in that period (Calhoun, 2007, 1). The period has also been referred to as the "Robber Baron" era because of the prominent role played by a new group of wealthy capitalists who used bare-knuckles tactics in pursuit of profit.[1]

The Gilded Age was followed by the first episode of regulated capitalism in U.S. history, known to historians as the Progressive Era, which lasted from about 1900 to 1916.[2] The state began to take a much more active role in the economy after 1900, and bankers assumed a new position in that period. The major financiers of the day, based mainly in New York City, became a powerful force in the economy, which justifies using the concept of "finance capital" to define the new relation that arose between financial and nonfinancial institutions. Finance capital refers to a close association between financial and nonfinancial institutions, with large financial institutions playing the dominant role.[3]

A few years after the end of World War I, U.S. capitalism changed again as another era of free-market institutions and ideas took hold at the start of the 1920s.[4] We will argue that, in addition, the role of financial institutions changed significantly in the 1920s, shifting from the financial dominance of the Progressive Era to a form of financialization bearing similarities to the contemporary period. The 1920s free-market period in the United States, sometimes called the "Roaring Twenties," gave rise to a number of phenomena that were similar to what we have observed in the neoliberal era.[5] Like the neoliberal era, the 1920s liberal period eventually gave rise to a financial crisis and a severe real sector recession, starting in 1929.

This chapter briefly considers in turn the late nineteenth free-market Gilded Age, the regulated capitalism of the Progressive Era/finance capital era after 1900, and the return of free-market institutions in the Roaring Twenties. The last section summarizes the lessons for an evaluation of the possible future directions of economic change today.

The Gilded Age

The U.S. economy was radically transformed in the period from the end of the Civil War through 1900. A capitalist economy had already arisen in the northeastern United States in the decades before the Civil War, but in 1865 the economy outside the southern United States was still predominantly made up of small farmers and local businesses. Even the new railroads were small local companies, as were manufacturing firms.[6] Only the railroads had adopted the corporate form of organization. Over the following decades new technologies drove a rapid increase in firm size. From 1870 to 1890 rail mileage nearly quadrupled, and by 1900 there were more than 1.3 million telephone units in operation. Steel production rose from 77,000 tons in 1870 to 11.2 million in 1900 (Calhoun, 2007, 2). By 1900 giant, nationwide companies in manufacturing, mining, rail transportation, and telephone communication, now organized as corporations, sat astride the U.S. economy, which had become a major manufacturing power in the world.

The federal and state governments did not entirely follow a laissez-faire policy in this period. The federal government subsidized railroad construction and imposed high protective tariffs against superior European manufactured goods, while encouraging an inflow of immigrant workers. State governments were even more active in promoting and subsidizing transportation improvements. All levels of government intervened on the side of management in the frequent confrontations with labor. The federal government continued to extinguish the land claims of native peoples, which posed an obstacle to economic expansion.

However, the new capitalists who arose in this period were unhindered by state intervention in their pursuit of profit. The economy was intensely competitive during the 1870s to 1890s, as the new, rapidly growing companies fought battles for survival and dominance. Banks were unregulated. An ideology of rugged individualism and "survival of the fittest" prevailed. This era can be considered one of free-market, or liberal, capitalism.[7]

This period of highly competitive, unregulated capitalism had several features that are relevant for the concerns of this book. While the long-term economic growth rate of the major European economies of the day slowed during the 1870–90s, the United States underwent several decades of relatively rapid economic expansion in this period of early U.S. industrialization.One study estimated that real output in the United States grew at 3.7% per year during 1878–1894, a high growth rate for that era (Gordon et al., 1982, 43).[8] Unlike the long-run inflation, gradual or rapid, that has characterized Western economies since World War II, the late nineteenth-century United States saw long-term deflation. The wholesale price index for the U.S. economy in 1890 was 39.2% *below* its level in 1870 (U.S. Bureau of the Census, 1961, 115). The intense competition of the period, with rival producers driving down prices over time, was probably a contributor to the long trend of declining prices.[9]

The macroeconomy was highly unstable. There were seven depressions, as they were then called, between 1870 and 1900, with 179 months of economic contraction over the period, almost matching the 181 months of expansion. A depression that started in 1873 lasted for five-and-a-half years, and another in the early 1880s lasted more than three years (National Bureau of Economic Research, 2013). The depression that began in 1893 led to a double-digit unemployment rate that lasted from 1894 to 1898, and real GDP per capita did not surpass its 1893 level until 1899 (Romer, 1986; Whitten, 2013). Bank failures were common. A major financial panic occurred in 1873, set off by speculation in railroad securities, which was followed by the longest contraction in U.S. history (National Bureau of Economic Research, 2013). Another major financial panic broke out in 1893, which was followed by the severe depression noted above.[10]

Most of the individuals who became known as robber barons got their start in business in the 1860s and 1870s. The famous names include John D. Rockefeller, Andrew Carnegie, Cornelius Vanderbilt, J. P. Morgan, and Jay Gould. There were three distinct types of new capitalists. One type, industrial entrepreneurs, built growing companies in railroads, manufacturing, and mining. Andrew Carnegie, the steel capitalist, is the prototype of the industrial entrepreneur. These actors were fiercely competitive and drove their managers and workers hard. While they used hard-nosed tactics to build their companies—breaking contracts, buying judges, maintaining private armies, sabotaging rival companies—they undeniably built up increasingly productive enterprises (Josephson, 1962; Morris, 2005, chaps. 3–5).[11]

The second type of capitalist was the speculator, of which the prototype was Jay Gould.[12] The most famous of these actors did not just buy and sell securities in hopes of profiting from price changes. They took advantage of the new corporate form of business organization to essentially steal from the company rather than build it up. In one famous example, Jay Gould prevailed on the Union Pacific Railroad's board, which he controlled, to buy a new rail company that appeared to be a potential competitor. However, Gould had secretly organized the rival company, which turned out to be a worthless shell. He made an estimated $10 million profit on the deal, and since he had already sold his

Union Pacific shares, he effectively robbed the other shareholders (Josephson, 1962, 196–201).[13]

The third type was the banker. A new institution of investment banking arose after the Civil War, from the humble origin of dry goods merchants. Initially the investment banks assisted governments in the sale of bonds. In the 1870s they began to handle railroad bonds, and in the 1890s they added the securities of manufacturing companies. Over the course of the period, the leading investment banks, which controlled access to the major sources of long-term capital in Britain and Germany, established control first over the major railroads and later the major manufacturing and mining companies. J. P. Morgan was the most famous and powerful of the investment bankers. Jacob Schiff of Kuhn, Loeb was also a major figure (Kotz, 1978, chap. 3).[14] New technologies gave rise to large, nationwide companies, but that process did not directly lead to monopoly. Instead, in railroads, and later in manufacturing, a loose oligopoly typically arose, with five to fifteen major companies competing in an industry. This kind of industrial structure was highly unstable. Price wars were common in both railroads and manufacturing, wreaking economic destruction on all parties.

As the major bankers gained control over nonfinancial companies, they sought to eliminate the intense competition that led to overbuilding, price wars, and bankruptcies, which harmed the bondholders represented by the investment bankers. J. P. Morgan and the other major bankers believed that the short-run profit-seeking of the industrial entrepreneurs gave rise to what they regarded as "ruinous" competition.[15] The bankers also despised the predatory behavior of the speculative capitalists such as Jay Gould and Daniel Drew. The three-way conflict among bankers, industrial entrepreneurs, and speculators, operating against the background of an increasingly unstable and highly competitive economy, played an important role in the emergence of the first regulated form of capitalism in the United States after 1900.

Finance Capital and the Progressive Era

The regulated capitalism that emerged after 1900 involved the restriction of market activity both by newly powerful bankers and by the state. We will consider first the expanded role of bankers and then the new state role in this period.

J. P. Morgan and the other major bankers represented the broadest capitalist interests of the three types of capitalists cited above. The industrial entrepreneurs sought to advance their own companies, fighting one another in the process. The speculators stole from other capitalists as well as from one another. Starting in the 1890s, the major bankers began to gain control over nonfinancial companies. In the depression following the Panic of 1893, the bankers took control of the major railroads, combining them to reduce their numbers and imposing a policy of "community of interest"—that is, avoidance of price competition and over-building. Next they moved into manufacturing, gaining control of the leading firms and promoting a wave of acquisitions that culminated in a huge merger wave in 1898–1903. In 1899 alone, 1,028 firms disappeared into consolidations, and the market value of newly merged manufacturing firms that year was $2.3 billion out of a total estimated value of $10 to $15 billion for the U.S. manufacturing capital stock as a whole (Edwards, 1979, 226–227). Unlike the typical two-firm merger of recent times, during 1895–1904 75% of firm disappearances were in mergers involving five or more firms (Scherer, 1980, 119). Out of that process emerged industrial giants that were to dominate the U.S. economy for decades to come, including General Electric, United States Steel Corporation, American Telephone and Telegraph, International Harvester, Aluminum Company of America, and Anaconda Copper Company.[16]

The conflict between banker and industrial entrepreneur was captured by the battle between J. P. Morgan and Andrew Carnegie in the steel industry starting in the late 1890s. Carnegie's company, based in Pittsburgh, was the most efficient in the industry. Carnegie was famous for undercutting rivals and double-crossing customers with last minute price increases. The leading steel firms would regularly agree to hold the line on prices, then Carnegie would break ranks. In 1898 Morgan organized Federal Steel, a big rival to Carnegie's steel company, then pressured Carnegie to sell out to him. In 1901 Carnegie settled, selling his company to Morgan for some $300 million. Morgan combined Carnegie's company with his own holdings to create the United States Steel Corporation (Josephson, 1962, 416–426).[17]

Upon its formation U.S. Steel produced about 65% of the industry's output, and it was able to impose cooperative pricing practices on its remaining smaller rivals. This was the beginning of the practice of co-respective competition. After 1900 the long-term price trend shifted from deflation to inflation, as the wholesale price index rose by 23.9% from 1900 to 1915, which was the last year before World War I began to affect U.S. prices (U.S. Bureau of the Census, 1961, 116–117).

By shortly after 1900, J. P. Morgan and the other major bankers had, in their view, established stability and order in American industry. They had expelled many of the intensely competitive industrial entrepreneurs, installing banker nominees as CEOs of the new giant companies. They had marginalized the speculative capitalists. The era of finance capital, referring to a close association of financial and industrial institutions with the banks at the center, had begun in the U.S.[18]

J. P. Morgan began to function as the de facto central banker for the U.S. economy. When financial panics struck, everyone turned to Morgan to bring matters under control. In a famous incident during the financial panic of 1907, Morgan locked the leading bankers of the day in his private library, keeping them there until they had all agreed to contribute funds aimed at stopping a major bank run.

The period 1900–16 gained the name "Progressive Era" from the changes in the role of the state in that period, changes that were driven by new social movements. While some historians treat the new social movements of that period as a single entity, it had two main strands, a reform movement and a socialist movement.[19] The Progressive movement, referring to the reform strand, arose after 1900 with a base among small farmers, small business, and middle class social reformers, demanding that the government take action to protect ordinary people against the depredations of the robber barons.

After 1900 a socialist movement also grew rapidly in the United States. The Socialist Party, formed in 1901, drew support from workers, small farmers, and intellectuals. The Socialist Party presidential candidate, the well-known labor leader Eugene V. Debs, drew a small but rising percentage of votes for president, reaching 6% of the vote in 1912. In that year Socialists held 1,200 municipal offices, and in the pre-World War I years Socialist candidates won the mayoralty in many cities including Milwaukee and Minneapolis (Weinstein, 1967, 93–103, 115–118). There were more than a hundred Socialist Party newspapers across the country, and the most influential of them, *Appeal to Reason*, had a circulation of 762,000 in 1913 (Weinstein, 1967, 95–102). The Socialists supported, not economic reform, but a radical reconstruction of the economy based on public ownership of large enterprises, with cooperation to replace competition.

A major part of the Progressive reform movement demanded that the government break up the new concentrations of economic power. The Socialist Party called instead for the nationalization of the new big corporations and banks. Both posed threats to the interests of the new large corporations and finance capitalists. The two movements had an impact both on mainstream political figures and on some of the leading capitalists.

Theodore Roosevelt, who served as president from 1901 to 1909, expressed fear of the growing socialist movement in a 1905 letter, writing that the "growth of the Socialist Party in this country" was "far more ominous than any populist movement in times past" (Weinstein, 1968, 17). Roosevelt began to identify with the less threatening Progressive reform movement, but he argued for a policy of government regulation of the large corporations rather than breaking them all up into smaller companies. While anti-trust suits were initiated during his presidency aimed at breaking up some of the monopolies that had arisen, such as the Standard Oil Trust and the American Tobacco Company, Roosevelt had a friendly relationship with such new big corporations as U.S. Steel, which did not seek to eliminate its rivals.[20] Like the finance capitalists, Roosevelt emphasized cooperation rather than competition:

> It is preposterous to abandon all that has been wrought in the application of the cooperative idea in business and return to the era of cutthroat competition. . . . The man who wrongly holds that every human right is secondary to his profit must now give way to the advocate of human welfare, who rightly maintains that every man holds his property subject to the general right of the community to regulate its use to whatever degree the public welfare may require it. (Schlesinger, 1963, 61)

During Roosevelt's presidency, the federal government established new laws to regulate the food and drug industries in 1906, as was noted in Chapter 2.

Some of the new finance capitalists also began to support an active role for the government in regulation of industry. George W. Perkins, a partner in J. P. Morgan and Company and a leading representative of the Morgan interests, came to favor government licensing of all interstate corporations, with federal standards for trade practices and prices

(Schlesinger, 1963, 60). In remarkable testimony before a House committee in 1911, the Morgan-appointed CEO of U.S. Steel, Elbert Gary, stated that he wanted a way to go

> to a governmental authority, and say to them, 'here are our facts and figures . . . now you tell us what we have the right to do and what prices we have the right to charge'. (Weinstein, 1968, 84)

In the same year Cyrus McCormick, head of International Harvester, also indicated approval of government fixing of the prices of his products (Weinstein, 1968, 85). It appears that at least some of the new finance capitalists sought to steer the emerging active state role, which they could not reverse given the strength of the reform movement, in a direction that would not harm their interests. A system of orderly price leadership is not easy to maintain, and it appears that U.S. Steel's CEO was suggesting the government could help to sustain it.

Roosevelt's successor as president in 2009, fellow Republican William Howard Taft, took up a vigorous trust-busting program, filing ninety-nine anti-trust suits in his four-year tenure as president, including one calling for the breakup of U.S. Steel (Miller Center, 2013). This led Roosevelt to break with him and run for president on the Progressive Party ticket in 1912. The Democratic candidate Woodrow Wilson won the election, and thereafter the state role moved away from trust-busting and toward regulation. In 1913–14 the Federal Trade Commission Act and the Clayton Anti-Trust Act embodied the movement in anti-trust policy away from breaking up big companies and toward regulation of their behavior to prevent destabilizing kinds of competition.[21] The Federal Reserve Act of 1913 established government oversight of the banking system.

The National Civic Federation, founded in 1900, played a role in shaping new dominant ideas in this period. It promoted the idea that every group in society had responsibilities to one another. Although it had labor and public members, it was dominated by big business. Several partners in J. P. Morgan and Company were active in the organization (Weinstein, 1967, 7–8). Although the National Civic Federation talked about cooperation between business and labor, little came of it, and the big business members of the organization, such as U.S. Steel, fought against unions in their companies. There was no capital-labor compromise in the regulated capitalism of this period.

Lessons from the Gilded Age and the Progressive Era/ Finance Capital

Three lessons emerge from the above developments for the concerns of this book. First, the liberal institutional structure, or social structure of accumulation, of the late nineteenth century gave rise, from its own internal dynamics, to important elements of a new regulated social structure of accumulation after 1900, as bankers acted to regulate economic relations, reducing the role of market forces. Free competition in the preceding period had led to growing economic concentration, and bankers completed the process. This led to a very high rate of economic concentration, banker control of industry, and co-respective competition, which formed part of the new regulated social structure of accumulation after 1900. This raises the question of whether an eventual resolution of the structural crisis of the contemporary neoliberal capitalism that began in 2008 might involve similar developments. The neoliberal era has seen increased concentration in a number of sectors, including banking, as was noted in previous chapters. We shall consider this possibility in Chapter 7.

Second, the introduction of state regulation of the economy after 1900 was driven by powerful social movements, based among ordinary people, demanding reform or radical reconstruction of society. Without those social movements, it is uncertain whether either big business leaders or mainstream political figures would have supported the shift to regulated capitalism. This has implications for the likely course of economic change today.

Third, the provocative claim by some analysts that contemporary financialization is in important ways analogous to the finance capital relation that emerged after 1900 is not supported by the historical evidence (Dumenil and Levy, 2004; Arrighi, 1994). The similarity between the two phenomena extends only to the important role played in the economy by financiers and their great enrichment. However, the particular role of the financiers is quite different in the two periods. The era of finance capital saw the bankers rise to a position of long-run domination over individual large nonfinancial enterprises. The bankers pursued long-term interests, seeking to stabilize competition to gain secure long-term profits. Finance capital was associated with an expanded role for the state.

By contrast, financialization in the neoliberal era, as we showed in earlier chapters, involved a separation of finance from the nonfinancial sector. The financiers found ways to make profits that were independent of long-term relations with large nonfinancial corporations, and they made no effort to gain long-term control over them. Contemporary financiers have engaged in increasingly speculative and even rapacious activities, as we saw in Chapter 5. Today's major bankers appear to be closer to contemporary incarnations of Jay Gould rather than J. P. Morgan. This suggests that these figures have been part of the problem that led to the current structural crisis rather than potentially part of the solution. If bankers are to play a role in constructing a new and viable social structure of accumulation today, they would have to adopt a long-term outlook quite different from the dominant financier behavior to date in the neoliberal era.

The Roaring Twenties

Shortly after the end of World War I, another major change took place in the institutional form of U.S. capitalism. Around 1920 a new period of free-market institutions and ideas emerged, lasting through the early 1930s. Rather than a structural crisis of the existing social structure of accumulation ushering in the new period of free-market capitalism, the effects of World War I in the United States played the key role in this transition.

As the United States entered World War I in April 1917, an atmosphere of super-patriotism and intolerance engulfed the nation. Germany, and people of German ancestry, were vilified and crudely stereotyped in the mass media. In this atmosphere, the Progressive movement quickly atrophied. The Socialist Party, which strongly opposed U.S. entry into the war, was severely repressed by a combination of government prosecutions and private vigilante violence. Its leaders were given long prison sentences for speaking out against the war and the draft under the newly passed Espionage Act of 1917. Its newspapers were confiscated, and its offices in some parts of the country were destroyed by mobs. While the Socialist Party survived the wartime repression, it was weakened further after the war ended as a more generalized anti-foreigner mood arose associating radicalism with immigrant status. In 1919–20 the FBI conducted raids leading to mass deportation of suspected foreign radicals.[22]

With the near-disappearance of both the reform and socialist movements, the brief period of regulated capitalism ended. Three successive conservative Republican presidents were elected. The activist state role was replaced by laissez-faire, and little effort was made to enforce the Progressive Era regulations of business or the anti-trust laws. The Federal Reserve System, created in 1913, was largely passive in the 1920s. An ideology of rugged individualism displaced the earlier call for cooperation and social responsibility.

The New York bankers saw their control over the economy recede somewhat in the 1920s. New centers of finance arose in Chicago and San Francisco, and new major industries arose outside the bankers' control, such as the automobile industry pioneered by the fiercely anti-Wall Street Henry Ford (Kotz, 1978, 41–47). A speculative mania of get-rich-quick schemes blossomed. The practice of co-respective competition, and the avoidance of price reductions that it entailed, came under pressure, particularly after 1929. Deflation returned, as the consumer price index declined by 14.4% in 1920–29 despite a growing economy over the period.

As had occurred at the start of the neoliberal era, the defeat of a strike played a key role in the emergence of the 1920s liberal institutional structure. In September 1919 steel workers went on strike across several states, but in the changed political atmosphere the strike was crushed, with intervention by state police and the National Guard in Pennsylvania, Delaware, and Indiana. From 1920 to 1925 union membership fell by more than 25%, from 4.7 to 3.5 million (Public Purpose, 2013).

Although much of the world economy became depressed after the mid-1920s, the U.S. economy grew rapidly for the entire decade. From 1920 to 1929 real gross national product (GNP), a measure of national output used in earlier times that is similar to GDP, rose at 4.1% per year. Consumer spending and business fixed investment both grew more rapidly, at 4.6% and 5.2% per year, respectively (calculated from Gordon, 1974, 24).

In Chapter 4 we identified three important developments in the neoliberal era: growing inequality, big asset bubbles, and speculative financial institutions. Each of the three also emerged from the liberal institutional structure in the 1920s.

With business resurgent and unions in decline in the 1920s, one would expect little real wage growth. However, immigration to the

United States, which had averaged one million per year during 1905–14, was sharply reduced after the passage of restrictive immigration legislation in 1924. From 1925 to 1929 only 296,000 immigrants arrived per year (U.S. Bureau of the Census, 1961, 56). Rapid economic growth along with limited immigration kept the unemployment rate relatively low, in the range of 1.75% to 5% during 1923–29 (Romer, 1986, 31). This tended to strengthen workers' bargaining power despite the absence of union representation. While the nominal wages of production workers in manufacturing barely changed during 1920–29, declining consumer prices caused their real hourly wage to rise at 2.0% per year. However, output per hour in manufacturing rose much faster, at the remarkably rapid rate of 5.5% per year (U.S. Bureau of the Census, 1961, 92, 126, 601). That was a decade when assembly line methods were widely introduced. This suggests that income was shifting from wages to profits over the decade. One study found that the ratio of total profits to total wages rose from 27.3% in 1923 to 32.8% in 1929 (Devine, 1983, 15). The share of income received by the richest 1% rose from 14.8% in 1920 to 22.4% in 1929 (Piketty and Saez, 2010). Thus, the 1920s was a decade of increasing inequality.

The 1920s also saw a series of large asset bubbles. In the early 1920s a large real estate bubble arose, most famously in residential properties in Florida, some of which reportedly changed hands as often as ten times in a day. The real estate bubble was nationwide, particularly affecting commercial properties in New York City and other major cities (Historical Collections, Harvard Business School Baker Library, 2013). The estimated value of nonfarm dwellings in the United States rose by more than 400% from 1918 to 1926. In Miami the value of a building permit rose from $89,000 in January 1919 to $8.0 million in September 1925 (Goetzmann and Newman, 2010, 2). The real estate bubble began to deflate in 1926.

As is well known, a very large bubble arose on the U.S. securities market starting in the mid-1920s. From the beginning of 1925 to its peak in September 1929, the Dow Jones Industrial stock price average rose more than three-fold, while the total profits of a sample of large manufacturing corporations over that period rose by only 42% (Federal Reserve Bank of St. Louis, 2013; U.S. Bureau of the Census, 1961, 591). In 1928 nearly a billion shares changed hands on the New York Stock Exchange (Gordon, 1974, 34). Many stock investors believed they were getting rich.

In the 1920s the financial sector became increasingly speculative. A series of "financial innovations" were introduced that appeared to be magical money-making machines. One was the public utility holding company, a highly pyramided institution that enabled a relatively small investment to control many large power utilities. By 1929 ten large public utility holding companies controlled about 75% of U.S. electric power and light (Bonbright and Means, 1932, 91). Investment bankers who organized these holding companies sold shares and bonds in the various levels of the holding company to the public and were able to monopolize the bond business of the power utilities. These institutions were highly complex, with interest on bonds from one unit in the holding company paid out of revenues from other units. Another "financial innovation" was the closed-end investment trust, a speculative investment vehicle pioneered by individual investment managers and promoters. Investment banks that sponsored investment trusts used them as a source of borrowed funds and a place to sell the securities they floated (Kotz, 1978, 48–49).

In the 1920s there was even a forerunner of the mortgage-backed securities of the neoliberal era, as financial institutions created bonds backed by commercial real estate. These bonds were issued by mortgage companies and sold by investment banks. The interest on the bonds was to be paid out of the rental income from new commercial developments.[23] From 1921 to 1925 bonds backed by real estate rose from 2.5% to 22.9% of all U.S. bond issues. These highly speculative bonds were closely tied to the commercial real estate bubble of the period (Goetzmann and Newman, 2010, 24).

At first the new speculative vehicles were created by individual financial operators, but as their profitability became apparent, the big bankers could not resist joining in. The Morgan financial group came to control the two largest public utility holding companies by 1929. Goldman Sachs and other large investment banks sponsored investment trusts, as did major commercial banks (Kotz, 1978, 47–48). The largest commercial banks established security affiliates, enabling them to join in the profit opportunities from speculative dealings in securities (Carosso, 1970, 272).

The 1920s saw a retreat of finance capital and the emergence of a process of financialization. The role of finance in the neoliberal era has not been identical to that of the 1920s, but it bears far more similarity to it than to the era of J. P. Morgan and finance capital at the start of the twentieth century.

Rising inequality, big asset bubbles, and increasingly speculative behavior by financial institutions all characterized the Roaring Twenties.[24] After the stock market bubble began to deflate in October 1929, the U.S. economy descended into the Great Depression.[25] As the depression wore on, the financial innovations of the 1920s collapsed. By March 1933 the Dow Jones average had fallen to 13.8% of its September 1929 high, and that month the American banking system shut down.

Despite the similarities between the Roaring Twenties and the neoliberal era, the U.S. economy in 1929 was not the same as in 2008. The federal government was very small in 1929, with its total spending only about 3% of GNP in that year (*Economic Report of the President*, 1967, 213, 284). The government had no experience in leaning against a recession, and in any event to do so effectively would have required a huge increase in spending from its small base in 1929, which finally did occur only after the country entered World War II. Also, the time sequence for financial collapse and real sector decline went in opposite directions in the two crises. While an asset bubble deflation set off both crises, in the 1930s the long real sector decline led to a financial collapse only several years later in 1932–33, whereas in 2008 an impending financial collapse emerged at the start of the crisis, although it was halted by state intervention.

The long crisis that emerged from the 1920s liberal form of capitalism was eventually resolved by the construction of regulated capitalism after World War II. That raises the question of whether a similar institutional transformation, to a new form of regulated capitalism, is likely in the years ahead.

Lessons of History

Our brief sketch of the Gilded Age, finance capital and the Progressive Era, and the Roaring Twenties—and the transitions between them—has suggested possible lessons for our consideration of the likely scenarios of economic change at this time. The current crisis is not the first but the third crisis of a liberal form of capitalism in the United States. Each of the previous two crises was followed by a regulated form of capitalism. Big business played an important role in the shift to regulated capitalism both in 1900 and in the late 1940s, with large social movements creating a context that led big business leaders to support or acquiesce in an expanded state role. Increased economic concentration also played a role in the transition to the first period of regulated capitalism after 1900, although not the second one after World War II. The major bankers played a special role in the first of the transitions to regulated capitalism around 1900, although bankers did not play a special role within big business as a whole in the rise of the post-World War II episode of regulated capitalism, as noted in Chapter 3. These historical experiences should be kept in mind as we turn to a consideration of likely future economic developments.

7

Possible Future Paths

Every past structural crisis of capitalism before the one that began in 2008 has eventually led to major institutional restructuring. This was true of the crisis of the late nineteenth century, the Great Depression of the 1930s, and the crisis of the 1970s. In each case, a new social structure of accumulation eventually emerged from the crisis of the preceding form of capitalism. The relevance of the concept "structural crisis"—a crisis that cannot be resolved without major institutional restructuring—draws support from this history.

In a period of crisis that affects the major world powers, such as that of today, a viable restructuring would have to take place not just within individual countries but in global economic institutions as well. This complicates any process of restructuring that might emerge today. Since political power has resided at the nation-state level in the capitalist era, past restructuring of the global economy has been led by one or a few powerful states, as occurred after World War II.

There are several requirements for any new social structure of accumulation that might arise in the current period. It would have to effectively promote profit-making and stable economic expansion. To do so, it must assure growing demand for the output of the economy over the long run, as well as promoting a profitable production process. It must bring about a stabilization of the main class relations of capitalism, particularly the capital-labor relation. It must include a coherent and compelling set of ideas to provide the glue that holds a social structure of accumulation together and gives it the stability required to promote profitability and stable expansion for a long period of time.

Chapter 6 drew several lessons from U.S. history about past institutional transitions following a liberal social structure of accumulation. In both previous cases—the transitions after the Gilded Age and after the Roaring Twenties—the following transition was to a regulated form of capitalism, with big business playing a leading role. In both cases, reformist and radical social movements spurred the shift to regulated capitalism. In the transition following the Gilded Age, increased economic concentration played an important role, as did the assertion of power by bankers, although neither of those developments was a factor in the second transition following the Roaring Twenties.

We will consider four possible future directions of change—or absence of change—in the institutional form of the economy. The first is a continuation of the neoliberal form of capitalism, perhaps with some adjustments to it. The second is the rise of a form of regulated capitalism in which business alone regulates the economy, through some combination of state and non-state institutions. The third is a form of regulated capitalism based on capital-labor compromise. The fourth is the replacement of capitalism by an alternative socialist system. Of the four alternatives, the first two would maintain a capital-labor relation of thorough capitalist domination of labor, the third is defined by a relation of compromise between capital and labor, and the fourth would pass beyond an economy centered around the capital-labor relation as it exists in a capitalist system.

A Neoliberal Future

At the time of this writing, neoliberalism has survived the crisis in the United States, despite a brief period of highly interventionist policies at the height of the financial and real sector crisis that seemed contrary to neoliberal theories and policy prescriptions and modest new government regulations over the financial sector. As was shown in Chapter 5, inequality has continued to increase in the United States, and the banks have continued to find ways to make profits from speculative activities. The rate of profit largely recovered as of 2011, as Figure 5.16 showed. However, no new big asset bubble has arisen, nor is one likely to emerge. Household debt has been falling instead of rising. Lacking a big asset bubble and the associated debt-fueled consumer spending, neoliberal capitalism cannot promote stable economic expansion.

Capital accumulation remained depressed through 2012, as Figure 5.17 showed. If the neoliberal social structure of accumulation remains in place, it promises a future of stagnation and instability.

Nevertheless, one cannot exclude the possibility that no major institutional restructuring will take place any time soon. The social structure of accumulation theory holds that in a structural crisis there is a powerful tendency for a new social structure of accumulation to eventually emerge, but it is only a tendency. The possibility of the crisis going on for a very long time, or even indefinitely, cannot be excluded. Such a result would spell long-run economic decline, but that has occurred in history from time to time. Japan, which had seemed to be conquering the world economy in the 1970s and 1980s, sank into a severe economic crisis in 1989 but, despite much talk about the need for major changes, little has actually changed after some twenty-five years of stagnation.

A continuation of neoliberal capitalism, lacking its former ability to bring stable economic expansion, would continue to degrade the living and working conditions of the majority. The claim that "there is no alternative" would wear thin, and various forms of radicalization and political instability would be likely to follow. While corporations might enjoy high profits and and their CEOs continue to gain great wealth, one would expect that a turn toward support for economic change would eventually emerge even from within big business.

Viewing the economic and political landscape in the United States today, one does not detect the beginnings of any impending major change. However, it is normally difficult to foresee, or even to imagine, a radical break from past institutions in advance. After all, institutions are effective partly by virtue of their ability to create the belief that they are permanent. Yet radical breaks do occur. In the 1890s, as the robber barons gobbled up smaller businesses and operated outside of any government regulation, one could not have foreseen the great changes about to unfold in the United States after 1900. In 1932 one could not have predicted the remarkable transformations in the state and the capital-labor relation that would begin to develop a few years hence.

If a new institutional structure arises in capitalism in the coming years, we can expect it to take the form of some type of regulated capitalism. History shows a pattern of a regulated form of capitalism arising from the crisis of a liberal one. Given the small number of cases, this could be a coincidence. However, there are reasons why such a pattern is observed. The last two liberal forms of capitalism, in the 1920s and after 1980, eventually gave rise to a big-bang type of structural crisis, including a financial crisis, while the first liberal form of capitalism in the Gilded Age saw recurring severe depressions and financial crises. The high level of inequality and the speculative financial sector during a liberal period are implicated in its structural crisis, which eventually lead the search for a solution toward institutions that would address those developments. An active state role is a way to reduce inequality and it also can solve the demand problem other than through problematic asset bubbles. State intervention, or monopolistic control by a small group of powerful private economic actors (as in the case of finance capital), appear to be the only ways to reign in speculative behavior by the financial sector. The high costs to society of unrestrained profit seeking become apparent after a long period of liberal institutions, which builds support for institutions that can restrain market behavior.[1]

Hence, both historical evidence and theoretical considerations suggest a strong likelihood that economic restructuring will emerge that restricts the market as regulator of economic activity. However, there are several different forms that such economic change might take. Two of them would bring a new period of regulated capitalism, while the third would move beyond capitalism.

Business-Regulated Capitalism

Labor and citizen movements are weak in the United States at the present time. Big business and its allies have a great deal of influence in politics and in the formation of public opinion. If a new form of regulated capitalism develops under these conditions, it would be most likely one that perpetuates the domination of business over labor but with institutional changes designed to reign in the market in various ways. We refer to this as business-regulated capitalism.

A major institutional change is normally preceded by the rise of newly influential ideas that support the change. In recent times neoliberal ideas have maintained their hegemony. In the austerity period since 2009, more extreme neoliberal policy positions have appeared. A significant number of the Republican representatives in the U.S. Congress have adopted a bold anti-government position, regarding the maximum possible reduction of taxes and public spending as the highest aim of politics and threatening to force the federal government into bankrupt-cy by refusing to increase the debt ceiling.[2] Some candidates for federal office have even demanded abolition of the Internal Revenue Service.[3]

However, a rethinking of neoliberal ideas has appeared recently in the writings of some well-known conservative analysts. In the depth of the financial crisis in December 2008, William Kristol, an icon of con-servative thought in the United States, wrote a remarkable op-ed col-umn in the *New York Times* titled "Small Isn't Beautiful" (Kristol, 2008). He argued that "conservatives should think twice before charging into battle . . . under the banner of 'small-government conservatism,'" add-ing an inevitability argument by saying that "the public knows that gov-ernment's not going to shrink much no matter who's in power." After an approving reference to the Medicare drug benefit introduced by Presi-dent George W. Bush, he came out in favor of increased public spending but on military infrastructure rather than civilian. He concluded by likening small-government conservatism to the famous charge of the Light Brigade, a symbol of unthinking disastrous action based on tradi-tion rather than reason.

In 2012 another conservative icon, Francis Fukuyama, offered a model of conservatism based on "a renewal of the tradition of Alex-ander Hamilton and Theodore Roosevelt that sees the necessity of a strong if limited state and that uses state power for the purposes of national revival" (Fukuyama, 2012). He attributed distrust of the state both to the political left and the right, denouncing the contemporary right for taking it "to an absurd extreme, seeking to turn the clock back . . . before the progressive era at the turn of the twentieth century." He recommended that contemporary conservatives should "get over their ideological aversion to the state" and support state investments in military power and "rebuilding of the economy as a precondition for a reassertion of military power over the long run." It is notable that Alexander Hamilton is known for his support of a strong central gov-ernment against Jeffersonian opposition after the American Revolution, while Theodore Roosevelt was an architect of the first wave of regulated capitalism after 1900, as we saw in Chapter 6.

In April 2013 it was reported that a major conservative advocacy organization, the American Conservative Union, had formed a part-nership with business lobbyists to oppose cuts in military and infra-structure spending. That organization had a previous record of fighting for reduced government spending and arguing for limiting the size of government.[4]

Positive references made to Theodore Roosevelt by Kristol and Fukuyama make sense for pro-business intellectuals, since business played an active role in the transformation of government policy in that era and Roosevelt ended up endorsing "responsible" big corporations, opposing their dissolution through anti-trust action. The Progressive Era reforms involved little in the way of labor rights or welfare programs. In light of the major role played by finance capitalists in that era, along with the absence of any significant change in labor relations or any major social welfare programs, one could consider the Progressive Era social structure of accumulation to be a precedent for a business-regulated form of capitalism.[5]

There have been other examples of regulated capitalism that involved little power for labor, in the case of developmental state models. Japan starting in the 1870s and South Korea from the 1950s introduced a developmental state model to rapidly build capitalism, which entailed state guidance of the economy. In Japan that model was initially built by a section of the old feudal ruling class, and later a group of state bureaucrats was in charge. In South Korea the military organized a similar developmental state. Both were economically very effective, bringing rapid economic advance. Labor remained repressed, although it cannot be said that business dominated the state, but rather was subordinate to the state. However, in a developmental state the business class is not well developed at the start, a condition quite different from that of a developed capitalist country.

Table 7.1 lists the dominant ideas and institutions of a hypothetical contemporary business-regulated form of capitalism in the United States. The labor market would continue in its current form, and the capital-labor power relation would still be characterized by thorough capitalist domination of labor. The interface with the global economy would not undergo major change. However, the role of government would change, as would the main institutions in the corporate sector and the dominant ideas. The main divergences from neoliberal capitalism in the role of government would be regulation of the financial sector to overcome financial instability and to direct credit to productive uses; expanded public investment in military and civilian infrastructure; promotion of innovation; and an expansion of private-public

Table 7.1. The Ideas and Institutions of Business-Regulated Capitalism

1. Dominance of ideas of nationalism and responsibility of individuals and organizations toward society and the state

2. The Global Economy
   a) Pursuit of free trade agreements
   b) Pursuit of control over natural resources around the world
   c) Maintenance of military superiority

3. The Role of Government in the Economy
   a) Expansion of public-private partnerships
   b) Government regulation of the financial sector
   c) Government investment in military and civilian infrastructure
   d) Promotion of innovation to achieve national superiority
   e) Low taxes on business
   f) Limited social programs
   g) Limited social regulation based on cost-benefit analysis
   h) Limited enforcement of anti-trust laws

4. The Capital-Labor Relation
   a) Further marginalization of collective bargaining, perhaps with employer-dominated employee associations
   b) Further casualization of jobs

5. The Corporate Sector
   a) Return of co-respective competition
   b) Shift of corporate aims toward long-run performance
   c) Return to bureaucratic principles within corporations
   d) Financial institutions return to focus on providing financing for nonfinancial business

partnerships. The corporate sector would assume a shape similar to that of post-World War II regulated capitalism.

The dominant ideas that could hold together such a social structure of accumulation are those of nationalism and individual responsibility. Such ideas justify a stronger role for the state. They also offer ordinary people a sense of being part of a powerful entity, which would facilitate acceptance by the majority in the face of limited material benefits for them.

Such a set of institutions is not only coherent but could also potentially promote profitability and stable economic expansion over a long period of time. While employer domination of labor would bring rising profits, growing state spending would solve the demand problem that would otherwise arise due to growing inequality. Regulation of finance would promote national success in the global competitive struggle as well as financial stability.

One possible objection to the feasibility of such a social structure of accumulation is the high level of public debt in the United States. An austerity advocate might argue that such a model would bankrupt the nation. However, the example given in Chapter 5 of the U.S. post-World War II debt experience, when debt relative to GDP shrank steadily due to economic growth, shows the weakness of that objection (see Figure 5.15). If such a regime succeeded in bringing relatively rapid economic growth, then a rising level of state spending, moderated by limited social welfare spending, would be consistent with a stable or even falling public debt ratio.

A business-regulated form of capitalism could come in either of two variants. The right-wing version would emphasize building up the military, an aggressive foreign policy, and a repressive policy toward dissenters. The centrist version would focus on building up civilian infrastructure, a foreign policy that worked through international coalitions, and greater respect for civil liberties.[6]

Neither variant of this form of capitalism would be favorable for working people, most of whom would experience stagnating or falling living standards. The right-wing version might bring significant repression. There would be a serious threat of regional or even global war emerging from the nationalist ideology and the pursuit of economic dominance in the world.

It is not clear how such a form of capitalism could emerge from current conditions. An active state role in the economy is always potentially dangerous to business, since state power might end up being used to pursue goals not favored by business. Hence, constructing such a model is a complex and difficult undertaking.

U.S. big business has always found it difficult to organize to carry out a common program. In every capitalist society the basic institutions of capitalism tend to pit capitalists against one another, and the conflicting interests of different segments of business present an obstacle to the emergence of a business-regulated form of capitalism. The rapid increase in concentration in some industries in the recent period might facilitate the development of such a social structure of accumulation. As was noted above, banking has become highly concentrated. Perhaps this will lead to the emergence of financial leaders more like J. P. Morgan than the inheritors of the tradition of Jay Gould who have dominated the financial sector in recent times.

Perhaps the biggest obstacle to the emergence of this or any form of regulated capitalism is the weakness of social movements at this time. Paradoxically, there may not be a path to even a business-dominated variant of regulated capitalism in the United States unless the business class perceives a threat to its long-run interests coming from a popular movement, either reformist or radical. Put baldly, capitalists are not very good at actively running capitalism over the long run, unless they are pushed into doing so by a perceived threat to their core interests.

Social Democratic Capitalism

Labor leaders and left-of-center political figures have been advocating a return to something like the regulated capitalism that prevailed in the United States in the post-World War II decades. Some Keynesian economists have endorsed such a transformation (Palley, 2012). If the labor movement revives and expands in the coming years, this could be a possible direction of economic change. We use the term "social democracy" here to refer to a regulated form of capitalism in which a compromise between capital and labor plays a central role.[7]

As we saw in Chapter 3, the post-World War II regime of regulated capitalism based on capital-labor compromise arose in the context of a strong and militant labor movement, as well as a threat from significant socialist movements around the world. Those developments, along with fear of another big depression, led big business leaders to compromise with labor and support regulated capitalism in the late 1940s. The labor upsurge of the 1930s did not begin until around 1934–35, which was five or six years after the start of the Great Depression. The immediate response of working people to a big economic crash is to try to survive as individuals and families. Only after some period of crisis does the response turn to collective action. It is possible that a rebirth of labor activism will occur in this crisis, a response that has already emerged in Greece, Spain, and some other countries. In the United States there have been outbreaks of labor militancy, including the 2012 labor occupation of the state capitol building in Wisconsin in a confrontation between unions and an anti-union governor, and the unprecedented brief nationwide strikes at the major fast food chains in 2013.

Table 7.2 presents the dominant ideas and institutions of a hypothetical new social democratic form of capitalism. It has only modest differences from Table 3.1 showing the ideas and institutions of the previous regulated capitalism. The main differences are revisions in intellectual property law (3d), public investment in green technologies (3f), and strengthened rights of workers to organize (4a). We know from history that such a set of ideas and institutions was able to promote a long period of high profit and rapid economic expansion after World War II. The higher minimum wage and strengthened protections of the right of workers to organize and join unions indicated in Table 7.2, along with other provisions on the list, could result in wages and profits rising at similar rates. This would help solve the demand problem of long-run economic expansion while allowing profits to rise. If this regime gave rise to a high rate of capacity utilization, that would also contribute to producing a high rate of profit. Capital-labor compromise, along with counter-cyclical fiscal and monetary policy, can create stability and predictability that is favorable for making long-run productive investments. Public expenditure on infrastructure and new technologies also promotes economic growth.

A social democratic form of capitalism would be much more favorable for the majority than either the neoliberal or business-regulated form of capitalism. It holds the promise of decreasing inequality, rising living standards, and greater economic security for the majority. Some analysts argue that, while such a form of regulated capitalism was workable decades ago, it is no longer viable today due to irreversible changes in the global economy. However, the form that globalization has taken in the neoliberal era is not immutable. As was noted in Chapter 2, history shows that a strong trend toward global economic integration before World War I was reversed in the period from World War I to World War II, after which a more controlled globalization process emerged under the Bretton Woods system. If unregulated globalization was reversed once before, it could be again. It is hypothetically possible to institute a new global system in which trade is somewhat regulated, with strong

Table 7.2. The Ideas and Institutions of Social Democratic Capitalism

1. Return of dominance of Keynesian ideas and theories

2. The Global Economy

    a) Shift to regulated trade agreements

    b) Barriers to free movement of financial capital

    c) Multinational approach to access to global resources

3. The Role of Government in the Economy

    a) Return of Keynesian fiscal and monetary policies aimed at a low
        unemployment rate and an acceptable inflation rate

    b) Reregulation of the financial sector

    c) Strengthened social regulation: environmental, occupational safety
        and health, and consumer product safety

    d) Return to strong anti-trust enforcement along with revised
        intellectual property laws, to reduce monopoly power in
        intellectual products as well as in other products.

    e) Expansion of provision of public goods and services including
        infrastructure and education

    f) Public investment in new technologies including green technologies

    g) Expanded welfare state including a higher minimum wage

    h) Return to a progressive income tax system

4. The Capital-Labor Relation

    a) Return to collective bargaining between companies and unions
        sanctioned by strengthened rights of workers to organize

    b) An increased proportion of stable, long-term jobs

5. The Corporate Sector

    a) Return of co-respective competition

    b) Shift of corporate aims toward long-run performance

    c) Return to bureaucratic principles within corporations

    d) Financial institutions return to focus on providing financing for
        nonfinancial business and households

controls over potentially destabilizing financial capital movements. If capital is entirely free to move around the globe, the result is to play off workers in every country against one another in a race to the bottom. A new social democratic form of capitalism such as suggested in Table 7.2 could not work without agreement by the major world powers on a new global architecture appropriate to such a system. Achieving such agreement would not be easy, which represents a significant obstacle, although not an insurmountable one, to the emergence of such a regime.

Another potential objection is the claim that the technological developments of recent decades make a new social democratic regime unworkable. Chapter 3 offered a critique of the claim that new technologies in information processing and communication require neoliberal institutions for their effective utilization. There is no persuasive argument that these new technologies could not continue to develop under a social democratic form of capitalism. Those technologies would make the more planned system of regulated capitalism potentially more effective.

Another objection to this future for capitalism is that it was tried before, and it eventually led to an economic crisis that destabilized that form of capitalism. While this form of capitalism would be much better for the majority than either neoliberal capitalism or business-regulated capitalism, the social structure of accumulation theory argues that no form of capitalism can last more than a few decades before giving rise to a structural crisis and another round of restructuring. However, most advocates of a new social democratic regime do not agree with that assessment, believing that the undoing of the previous round resulted from accidental economic and political developments that could be avoided this time.[8]

A social democratic form of capitalism would include an effort to restore some job stability in place of the neoliberal trajectory toward casualization of jobs. This would be a difficult objective to achieve, given that corporations have found the substitution of casual jobs for stable jobs to be very profitable. However, it might be possible to make some progress toward this goal through a combination of labor union demands and state regulation of the labor market.

If the labor movement revives and grows strong, there is no insurmountable economic or political obstacle to the emergence of another round of social democratic capitalism. However, there is a serious problem that would arise from the long-run consequences of such a development. The problem stems from the likely success of that form of capitalism in again promoting a long period of rapid economic growth. As we observed above, society changes over time, and one difference between today and the late 1940s is that environmental constraints are operative today that were not yet binding in the earlier period.

It has been well documented that human economic activity is the cause of global climate change that, based on the current trajectory, will lead to global economic disaster for humanity within the next fifty to one hundred years. The earth's supply of natural resources used in economic activity is also coming under strain. Another period of twenty-five years or more of rapid economic growth in the United States, accompanied by accelerated growth in the other developed economies, would threaten the future of human civilization.

Some supporters of social democratic capitalism hope that a shift to green technologies can render rapid economic growth compatible with environmental constraints. However, it does not appear that the introduction of green technologies, desirable though they may be, can outweigh the carbon emission effects of rapid economic growth. A full treatment of this problem would require taking account of various proposed methods for preventing large-scale global climate change, such as efforts to remove carbon from the atmosphere. We cannot look into this complex debate here, but it can be said that decades of rapid economic growth would pose a serious challenge to the effort to avert major global climate change.[9]

A social democratic form of capitalism requires that wages and profits both rise at a robust rate. This is possible only if output also rises rapidly. The danger of environmental catastrophe is linked to another period of social democratic capitalism by the latter's basic mode of operation.

Moving beyond Capitalism

There are grounds for considering one more possible future direction of economic change, namely moving beyond capitalism to an alternative socialist system, despite the seemingly very low likelihood of such a development at this time. Before capitalism arose several centuries ago, no previous socioeconomic system lasted forever. In the nineteenth century Marxist theory predicted that capitalism, like the systems that preceded it, would one day be superseded by a new socioeconomic system, variously referred to in that era as socialism or communism.[10] After the Russian Revolution of 1917, a socialist system came to be widely viewed as a possible alternative to capitalism, both by advocates and opponents of socialism. Its supporters viewed socialism as a higher form of society, while its opponents feared that socialism would bring a new Dark Age of political repression and economic decline.[11] For much of the twentieth century, a contest between the two systems unfolded, with the outcome appearing to be uncertain for many decades. Even some critics of socialism feared that it might eventually supplant capitalism, for such reasons as the possibility that socialism would bring rapid economic growth, full employment, and a high degree of economic security for workers.[12]

The rapid demise of almost all of the Soviet-type socialist systems during 1989–91, followed by transitions to capitalism, radically changed the dominant views about socialism. The more gradual evolution since 1978 of China, the most populous Communist Party-ruled state, from its traditional socialist model toward one based on markets and private enterprise has had a similar effect. The dominant conclusion from these developments was that the socialist challenge to capitalism had ended, with a complete victory for capitalism. Even in the heyday of the socialist movement, from 1900 through the 1970s, it did not achieve a large following in the United States compared to its popularity in Europe and other parts of the world. As we saw in Chapter 6, during the Progressive Era the Socialist Party did grow rapidly, but it never won more than a small share of the vote nationally. In the next wave of radical upsurge in the U.S. in the 1930s and 1940s, the Communist Party was the largest socialist organization. While the Communist Party played a major role in the building of new industrial unions in that period, and for a time gained a significant following among intellectuals and in the African-American community, it was able to win only a small percentage of the population to its banner. This contrasts with the rise of mass-based Socialist and Communist parties in Europe in the twentieth century.[13]

Today socialist movements are weak in almost all parts of the world and particularly in the United States. However, despite the history of the rise and fall of Soviet-type socialism and the weakness of socialist movements in the world and in the United States today, the possibility that socialism will again come to represent a viable alternative future, even in the United States, should not be discounted. There are several reasons for this conclusion. First, after decades of improving material conditions for the majority in the era of postwar regulated capitalism, the process went into reverse in the neoliberal era. As we have seen, the average worker's material conditions have stagnated or declined in the United States during the neoliberal era. Since the crisis began in 2008, the worst sides of capitalism have been on vivid display, as millions lost their jobs and millions faced the loss of their homes. While median income has not recovered to its pre-crisis level, corporate profits and the income of the richest 1% have soared. This provides fertile ground for a revival of interest in an egalitarian alternative to capitalism.

Second, as was noted in Chapter 4, in some Latin American countries where the economic conditions of the majority plummeted well before the global crisis struck, new attempts to build a "Twenty-First Century Socialism" have emerged, in Venezuela and Bolivia. Despite the widespread discrediting of socialism, the idea has lived on as the egalitarian alternative when capitalism inflicts unbearable hardships on people.

Third, even in the United States there is evidence that a larger-than-expected percentage of the population has a favorable view of socialism. In the spring of 2009 during the depth of the economic crisis, the mainstream public opinion survey company Rasmussen conducted a survey of the American people's views of capitalism and socialism. They undoubtedly expected to find little in the way of positive views of socialism. The results, released on April 9 of that year, were so surprising that they were widely reported in the major media, stirring vigorous commentary. The survey found that only a slim majority of 53% preferred capitalism while 20% favored an undefined "socialism" and 27% were undecided. Among respondents under age thirty, the results were 37% for capitalism, 33% for socialism, and 30% undecided (Rasmussen Reports, 2009). An analysis of the Rasmussen data by survey expert Nate Silver found that support for socialism was almost as great as for capitalism in the lowest income group, with support for capitalism rising steeply with income (although dipping slightly above an income of $100,000 a year) (Silver, 2013).

Similar surveys were conducted over the following years by the other leading American survey companies, with various wordings of the questions, and they all reported roughly similar results. A Pew Center survey released on May 10, 2010, found that 52% reacted positively to the word "capitalism" while 29% did so to the word "socialism." The percentage of positive reactions to socialism was 33% for women, 43% for those aged eighteen to twenty-nine (the same percentage as those viewing "capitalism" positively in that age group), and 44% for those with family incomes less than $30,000 (Pew Center, 2010). A later Pew Center survey with the same questions in December 2011 found little change, although the percentage of those aged eighteen to twenty-nine with a positive view of socialism rose from 43 to 46% (Pew Center, 2011).

Numerous commentators argued that the larger-than-expected percentage expressing a favorable view of socialism probably resulted from interpreting the term to refer to European social democracy, with its generous social programs and low levels of inequality, along with a market economy. Some pointed out that the (misleading) application of the label "socialist" to President Obama by right-wing commentators might have increased the positive identification with the term among his supporters. Also, it was noted that people under thirty would not remember the repressive socialism of the Soviet variety. Nevertheless, the survey results do suggest that a substantial percentage of the U.S. population, especially among young people and low income families, has serious doubts about what they understand "capitalism" to be, while having a positive view of something called "socialism" presented as an alternative to capitalism.

Fourth, the sudden outbreak of the Occupy Wall Street movement in September 2011 was the first significant avowedly anti-capitalist protest movement in the United States within memory. Its demonstrations took place in at least 150 U.S. cities and towns (as well as abroad), claiming to represent "the 99%" against the power of "the 1%" (Silver, 2011). While this movement did not explicitly call for socialism, most of its (unofficial) leaders held some variety of anarchist or socialist views.[14] The Occupy movement, which did not create any stable organization or formulate clear demands, largely dissipated in 2012, but it did demonstrate the existence of a potential mass base for a radical movement against capitalism in the United States.

It is possible that no significant radical movement will arise in the United States in the near future. However, that would not bode well for any of the possible alternatives to neoliberal capitalism. History suggests that a radical movement provides an important part of the political pressure that can lead to some type of regulated economy, even one within the capitalist system. If a significant radical movement does emerge, then it would open the possibility not just of prodding big business to accept some form of regulated capitalism but of passing beyond capitalism.

What might a contemporary socialist alternative to capitalism look like, as distinguished from a social democratic form of capitalism? Table 7.3 outlines the ideas and principles of a hypothetical "twenty-first

Table 7.3. The Ideas and Principles of Democratic Participatory Planned Socialism

1. Dominance of ideas of cooperation, equality, popular sovereignty, and the right to economic security

2. Social ownership of productive enterprises

    a) Ownership by national, regional, and local governments

    b) Worker ownership

    c) Cooperative ownership

3. Economic activity determined not by profitability but the aim of satisfying individual and collective wants and needs

4. Participatory economic planning guides the allocation of resources and the distribution of income

5. Income distribution assures that everyone can live at a socially acceptable living standard

6. Every working-age person who is able to work is guaranteed a job

7. A high level of provision of free or low-cost public goods including education, health care, and public transportation

8. Democratic political institutions

9. Guarantees of free speech and free association

century socialism." The version of socialism in Table 7.3 is sometimes called democratic participatory planned socialism, since it would involve a democratic state and a participatory form of economic planning.[15] Since this is not a form of capitalism but an entirely different socioeconomic system, Table 7.3 provides the general principles of such a system rather than the more concrete institutions given for the various forms of capitalism, which assume that in the background the fundamental relations of capitalism are in place. While most of the features listed in Figure 7.3 are relatively self-explanatory, the fourth one on the list—participatory economic planning—requires some clarification, which is provided below. Advocates of a contemporary socialism, whose structure would be influenced by an effort to avoid the negative features of twentieth-century socialism while learning from its successes, cite several advantages of a socialist alternative.

First, since socialism is based on production to meet individual and collective wants and needs rather than to make profit for owners, there would not be a problem of how to assure adequate aggregate demand, nor would there be a conflict between employers and workers that can be resolved in capitalism only by employer domination or a tenuous compromise between opposing classes. In twentieth-century socialism there was no demand problem. However, there were serious problems of adequate supply both regarding quantity and quality. Advocates of a new socialism argue that the supply problem in twentieth-century socialism resulted from the highly centralized, hierarchical form of economic planning that concentrated decision-making power at the top, leaving ordinary consumers with no way to make the system respond to their needs. Supporters of a new socialism argue that such problems would be solved by a participatory form of planning in which workers, consumers, and community members would be represented in the economic decision-making process.[16] Supporters add that the recent advances in information-processing and communication technologies would make a form of economic planning involving wide participation by millions of workers, consumers, and community members, which might have been unworkable in the past, now a potentially feasible way to make resource allocation decisions.[17]

Second, advocates of socialism argue that a new socialist system should be able avoid the kinds of damage inflicted on various groups by the profit-seeking economic activity of capitalism. The "negative externalities" of economic activity under capitalism—environmental destruction, unsafe jobs, harmful consumer products—should in principle be internalized and avoided, or minimized, in a participatory planned economy. An enterprise manager whose firm created such effects would presumably be demoted, not rewarded for the extra profit that can be gained by imposing costs of production on others, since those others would be represented on the enterprise board of directors. Advocates argue that the insertion of socially responsible aims into the evaluation criteria for economic decision-makers is far more effective than efforts to regulate or tax anti-social behavior by private profit-seeking enterprises.[18]

Third, advocates of socialism argue that it would guarantee a job for everyone who wants to work, eliminating unemployment and the large costs it imposes on the unemployed as well as the waste it represents for society. This was a positive lesson of twentieth-century socialism— the Soviet economy achieved continuous full employment for several decades after World War II. Since a socialist system assumes responsibility for the support of all of its citizens, it is economically rational to provide productive work for everyone rather than putting people on the dole. By contrast, a purely capitalist system only creates jobs when the labor can generate an expected profit for a capitalist, although social democratic capitalism has been able to bring full employment for extended periods of time as well in some European countries.

Fourth, advocates argue that the organization of production in a socialist system can take account of the impact of the production process on the lives of people at work, as well as on the products that are produced. People spend a large part of their lives at work, and human welfare is greatly affected by the experience at work as well as by leisure and consumption. With input from representatives of workers in decisions about technological development, such development can take account of the impact on work as well as cost savings and the effectiveness of products. In a participatory planning system, all three would be taken into account in the design and development of the labor process and could be balanced against one another.

Fifth, advocates argue that a socialist system can generate a distribution of income that provides a comfortable and secure living standard for everyone while allowing income differentials based on criteria considered fair by society. For example, the least desirable kinds of labor, which typically also are the lowest paying, would not be imposed on particular individuals who have no alternative, as occurs under capitalism. Through participatory economic planning a humane means of getting the undesirable kinds of work done could be found, such as through higher, rather than lower, pay for such work, or through rotation of such work over time among the population.

Sixth, while capitalism generates a robust process of technological innovation, advocates of socialism argue that technological innovation aimed at social benefit would produce a superior process of technological innovation compared to one aimed at profit for investors. Profit-driven technological innovation has many problems, which are perhaps most acute in the allocation of innovative resources in medical research. For example, the pharmaceutical companies have recently been financing little research aimed at developing new antibiotics, despite the rapid spread of deadly drug-resistant bacteria, because the financial payoff from antibiotics, which can fully cure a person in a matter of days, is much smaller than that for drugs that must be taken for the lifetime of the patient. As a result, several governments have been granting large subsidies to pharmaceutical companies to develop medications against antibiotic-resistant bacteria.[19] In a socialist system more scarce research and development efforts would go into finding cures for life-threatening diseases that afflict people in low income countries rather than new treatments for facial acne. Technological innovation in a socialist system could be directed more evenly across the production of public and private goods, rather than just toward privately consumed goods. Because of the severe defects of the profit motive in directing and financing innovation, states and other non-profit institutions play a major role in the innovation process even under capitalism.

Advocates of a new socialism argue that it could bring forth a greater outpouring of new technologies and products than capitalism can produce (Kotz, 2002). A socialist system could guarantee to any individual or group that has an idea for a new product, process, or service access to resources to develop it and try it out by setting up a new (socially owned) enterprise. Even Soviet socialism had institutions that were intended to encourage individual inventors and innovators, but they did not work effectively in the highly centralized and authoritarian form of economic planning in the USSR. Advocates of participatory planning claim that such efforts would be successful under the alternative form of planning envisioned here.

Seventh, a socialist world system should in principle be organized based on cooperation among nations. A rising China, once among the poorest nations in the world, should not pose a threat to the living standard of residents of richer nations in a socialist world system. The elimination of the pursuit of profit should also remove a powerful factor leading to wars in the capitalist era, resulting from the efforts by governments to assure that their capitalists gain control of markets and raw materials sources.[20]

Eighth, and not least in importance, advocates of socialism argue that, while a socialist system can bring rapid economic growth, as the Soviet case demonstrated, economic growth is not built into the basic institutions of a socialist system. A democratic socialist system could aim for rapid growth, slow growth, a constant level of output, or a declining level of output, depending on the priorities that emerge from the political process. That means a socialist economy could operate in an environmentally sustainable manner. Given the threat of global climate change, the citizens of a socialist economy in a developed country could opt for gradual decrease in the production of goods, along with declining work hours.

A case can be made that a continuing increase in the production of goods is not necessary for improving economic welfare in the economically developed countries today. In the early period of capitalist development, economic growth undeniably led to substantial welfare gains, which eventually were shared by the majority. However, in recent decades the link between economic growth and human welfare is not so clear. If goods and services were distributed relatively equally, and public goods expanded relative to individually consumed goods, increasing human welfare might well be compatible with gradually declining output of goods along with decreasing work hours. This may be the only sustainable future in light of the earth's limited natural resources and its finite ability to absorb the waste products of production.

The critics of socialism offer an opposite assessment. First, they argue that socialism, whatever the intentions of its founders, inevitably leads to concentration of political and economic power in a few hands, with the citizens coming under the domination of a small elite and the abolition of all individual rights and liberties. That was clearly the outcome in twentieth-century socialism. Second, they claim that private ownership of productive wealth is the only guarantee of individual freedom and autonomy. Third, they claim that the profit motive of owners producing for sale in competitive markets represents the only rational and efficient means of organizing a modern economy. They argue that traditional central planning proved to be cumbersome and inefficient, stifled innovation, and was unable to respond to consumer wishes. They argue that a participatory form of economic planning would be too complex and slow to function effectively, leaving a market system as the only effective means for allocating resources. Fourth, critics argue that an egalitarian system that guarantees everyone a job and a comfortable living standard would lack the incentives necessary to drive either efficiency or economic progress.

Fifth, critics of socialism argue that industrial managers would come to constitute a powerful lobby against socially responsible production decisions, leading to an even more serious problem of negative external effects such as environmental destruction. They cite the dismal environmental record of the USSR as evidence. Sixth, critics point to the armed conflicts that arose among Communist Party-ruled states, such as the border clashes between the USSR and China in the 1960s and the brief war between China and Vietnam in 1979, as examples that run counter to the claim that socialism would eliminate international conflict and war. Seventh, they note that the domination of the Soviet Union over its Communist Party-ruled East European allies belies the socialist claim that cooperative relations would be the norm in a global socialist system. Eighth, they point out that any transition to socialism would be bound to entail high costs of economic disruption and possibly violent conflict—a conclusion shared by many socialists as well.

Unlike the other possible futures considered here, a democratic participatory planned socialism would be a new type of socioeconomic system. Such a system has not existed previously on a large scale, although one can identify small-scale examples of some of the principles of this type of socialism. Examples are the internal organization of cooperatives and in some public bodies such as elected local school boards that allocate resources based on the aim of providing a needed service. Advocates of this proposed new system argue that it is a viable socioeconomic system, while critics contest that claim based on the arguments cited above.

This author finds the claims of the critics of socialism to be unconvincing. Some of the criticisms are directed at the authoritarian and highly centralized form of socialism of the twentieth century, not at the alternative form proposed here, while others reflect assumptions about human nature and society that are based more on ideology than evidence. While the criticisms should be taken seriously when considering how a future socialism might work, so as to avoid past problems of actually existing socialism, they do not constitute a compelling case against the socialist alternative to capitalism. Among the alternative futures we have considered, only a new socialism has the potential to bring about a society with economic justice, universal economic security, and a genuine, welfare-improving economic progress that is environmentally sustainable.

Concluding Comments

The analysis offered in this book suggests that capitalism is not only in a period of structural crisis at this time but in a structural crisis that has no easy path to a desirable resolution. This historical moment may indeed be a turning point for humanity. Consider the future courses we have examined:

- Continuation of neoliberal capitalism: This promises continuing stagnation, further increase in inequality and declining living standards for many, and the likelihood of growing political instability. This path appears unlikely to continue for long.
- Transition to a business-regulated form of capitalism: This promises a return of economic growth but with few if any material benefits for the majority, while it would carry the threat of restriction of civil liberties at home and war abroad.
- Transition to social democratic capitalism: This promises a period of balanced growth and rising material living standards for the majority, but at the possible cost of long-run disaster from global climate change. The latter cost is also attached to the neoliberal and business-regulated forms of capitalism.
- Transition to democratic participatory planned socialism: Its advocates promise a new period of advances in human welfare based on a superior socioeconomic system, with the potential to avert the threat of global climate change and create a humane, environmentally sustainable economy. However, even its advocates admit there would be a cost, possibly high, of the transition, while its critics predict wholly negative consequences from the adoption of socialism with no benefit to offset the high cost of transition.

The path that will be followed in the years ahead cannot be predicted based on social theory or historical evidence. The economic changes—or absence of changes—that lie ahead will be the outcome of struggles among various groups and classes in the coming years, which will occur in the realm of ideas, economics, politics, and culture. However, those struggles will not take place in a vacuum. They will be influenced by the effects of decades of neoliberal capitalism and by the character of the crisis it has produced. They will also be informed by the participants' understanding and interpretation of the current crisis, its causes, and its possible resolutions.

Appendix: Data and Data Sources

The data used in this book to construct figures and tables were obtained from the major U.S. government and international institutional sources. The data sources are cited below each figure or table. The acronym NIPA is used in figure and table sources throughout this book for the National Income and Product tables provided by the U.S. Bureau of Economic Analysis. Most references to economic data in the text include a source citation, but for well-known economic data series (such as GDP or the unemployment rate) in some cases the source is not cited in the text to avoid an excessive number of such text citations.

The U.S. Commerce Department's Bureau of Economic Analysis (BEA) did a major revision of a key data series just after the data analysis for this book had been largely completed. Many of the figures and tables in this book use data from the BEA, which produces the series on GDP and other commonly used macroeconomic variables. The BEA periodically revises its methodology for constructing its various data series, and occasionally it undertakes a major redefinition of widely used variables. On July 30, 2013, the BEA introduced a major revision in its definition of business investment, adding a new broader category of investment in intellectual property. Previously the BEA had counted as investment only one form of intellectual property, computer software.

Since the data analysis for this book was largely completed prior to July 30, 2013, the figures and tables in this book that cite the BEA are based on the pre-revision data series. The sole exception is Figure 5.17 on the rate of capital accumulation, for which one of the pre-revision data series needed to construct that figure only went through 2011. In order to carry that series through 2012, we had to do an estimation procedure that made use of the revised series for investment in intellectual property to get a consistent series based on the pre-revision definition of investment. An explanation of the estimation procedure is available from the author upon request.

Notes

1. Introduction

1. This quote from Lucas has been reproduced with slightly different wording in various places. The wording here is from Krugman (2009a).
2. *New York Times*, January 13, 2012, A3. When Yellen was nominated for the Federal Reserve chairmanship, there were claims in the mass media that she had warned long in advance that developments in the housing market might cause a serious recession. Yellen herself did not claim such prescience, and it does not appear to be supported by the record (*New York Times*, October 10, 2013, A19). In a speech on October 21, 2005, Yellen, then president of the San Francisco Federal Reserve Bank, raised the question "if the [housing] bubble were to deflate on its own, would the effect on the economy be exceedingly large?" Her answer was a clear "no," arguing that "it could be large enough to feel like a good-sized bump in the road, but the economy would be able to absorb the shock" (Yellen, 2005).
3. The term "neoliberalism" has become widely used in the academic literature about contemporary capitalism, and outside the United States in the mass media as well. However, it is less commonly used—and can be confusing—in the United States. This matter is discussed at the beginning of Chapter 2.
4. As noted in Chapter 2, the state always plays an important role in a capitalist economy, since the market relations of capitalism depend on the definition and protection of property rights, which are functions of the state. However, the state economic role can remain limited or it can expand well beyond protecting property rights.
5. Gordon et al. (1982) argued that a social structure of accumulation must stabilize each of the key steps in the capitalist profit-making process: the purchase of workers' labor time and non-living inputs, the subsequent production process, and the last step of selling the final products.
6. It happens that in 1966 the U.S. economy had a low unemployment rate of 3.8% and other features associated with a business cycle peak.
7. While officially another business cycle peak was reached in July 1981, that peak year is anomalous for the post-World War II period in various ways, including the brevity of the preceding contraction and expansion. The contraction following the 1979 peak (whose monthly date is January 1980) lasted only six months until July 1980, and the following expansion

lasted only twelve months, until July 1981, after which the economy headed down again for sixteen months through November 1982. The monthly unemployment rate rose from 5.6% in May 1979 to 10.8% in December 1982, and at the official peak of July 1981 the unemployment rate was 7.2%. There are good grounds for regarding the period 1980–82 as one long recessionary period.

2. What Is Neoliberalism?

1. The term "neoliberal" has a long history, dating back at least to the 1920s and 1930s when small groups of European and American intellectuals met to discuss ways to revive liberal thought against the growing influence of socialist ideas and the advance of state economic planning. More recently the term "neoliberal" was used by critics of the economic policies of the Pinochet government in Chile in the mid-1970s, which were designed by economic advisors from the University of Chicago. The term appeared in books and journal articles with increasing frequency in Latin America in the 1980s and 1990s, and in the 2000s neoliberal came into common use throughout the world. See Mirowski and Plehwe (2009).
2. The early years of post-Soviet Russia provided a vivid demonstration of the chaos and violence that result if the state largely withdraws from its essential functions. While various factors explain that disastrous development, one was a belief on the part of some influential actors that the state should play virtually no role in society (Kotz and Weir, 1997, chaps. 9–10).
3. This does not mean that no difference exists in the United States between Democratic and Republican administrations (or between social democratic and liberal or conservative parties in Europe). Left-right differences remain, but in each period these differences, once a party is in office, are constrained by the form of capitalism. The Clinton administration was able to do some things that were beneficial for its constituencies of working people, women, and minorities, but it did not reverse the main direction of economic policy, as will be shown in Chapter 4.
4. There is some dispute about the extent to which what became known as "Keynesian economics" through the presentations in post-World War II economics textbooks accurately reflected Keynes' writings. Some argue that Keynes's critique of capitalism was more thoroughgoing and radical than "textbook Keynesianism." See Crotty (1999). In this book we use the expression "Keynesian economics" to refer to the textbook version that became the dominant theory of the economy after World War II.
5. The term "fiscal policy" refers to government spending and tax policies. This is distinguished from monetary policy, conducted by the Federal

Reserve System, which regulates the supply of money and credit and the level of interest rates.

6. Keynes focused on the economy as a whole—the "macroeconomy"—but the new economic orthodoxy after World War II also included a version of the older "neoclassical" microeconomics. The latter viewed a market system as the most effective means of allocating resources but also viewed "market failures" as a significant problem requiring state intervention. The awkward term "neoclassical-Keynesian synthesis" has been used for the economic theory that became dominant after World War II.

7. *New York Times,* January 4, 1971. The statement "We are all Keynesians now" is often mistakenly attributed to Nixon, but that statement actually surfaced in *Time Magazine* on December 31, 1965, attributed to Professor Milton Friedman of the University of Chicago, who responded by complaining the quote had been taken out of context. Friedman was undoubtedly correct, given his unremitting battle against Keynesian ideas during the 1950s and 1960s.

8. A quotation widely attributed to British prime minister Margaret Thatcher has her stating, "There is no society, there are only individuals and their families." This appears to be derived from a lengthy statement in which she said ". . . who is society? There is no such thing! There are individual men and women and their families . . ." The full quote, with no date, is from *The Spectator,* April 8, 2013, available at http://blogs.spectator.co.uk/coffeehouse/2013/04/margaret-thatcher-in-quotes/.

9. Other organizations that can obstruct competitive market relations are also opposed, such as trade unions and standard-setting professional associations.

10. While neoliberal theorists did not deny that some market failures could occur, they argued that attempts by the state to correct them only make matters worse and that market solutions rather than state intervention are the only effective way to deal with market failures.

11. For several decades after World War II, neoclassical economists sought to provide a rigorous proof of the optimal efficiency of a competitive market system. This effort never succeeded without making assumptions that even the economists admitted were highly unrealistic, such as infinite knowledge on the part of market participants (Ackerman, 2002). The claim of optimal income distribution derives from the idea that every market participant receives an income that reflects the marginal product of whatever factor of production is supplied (labor, capital), as well as compensating for the marginal disutility to the owner of that factor of production from supplying it to production—a claim that suggests that the most unpleasant types of labor should have the highest rates of pay if all else is equal.

Neoclassical theory, which focuses on economic equilibrium, has had difficulty deriving any definite propositions about the advantages of competitive markets for economic growth or innovation.

12. This system is sometimes called a "dirty float," based on the neoliberal view that the only "clean" force that operates in the economy is that of the market while the hand of government is necessarily "dirty."

13. Free movement of labor—that is, free migration—has not been a goal of the new system.

14. After the economic crisis that began in 2008, the behavior of the Fed changed again, as did government fiscal policy. In 2008 the Fed shifted its focus first to preventing the collapse of major financial institutions and the financial system, and later to encouraging economic expansion as the economy experienced very sluggish recovery with little inflation. Since 2008 fiscal policy has gyrated between Keynesian fiscal stimulus and neoliberal austerity policy (see Chapter 5).

15. The Reagan administration also sharply increased military spending. While the rationale was to increase U.S. military strength, Keynesians could argue that the effect, if not the intent, was to stimulate the economy through increasing total demand. As a combination of tax cuts and military spending increases took hold in the early 1980s, the economy did expand at a relatively rapid pace, growing at 4.0% per year from the recession year of 1982 through the next cyclical peak in 1990.

16. One segment of neoliberal economists—the supply side economists such as Arthur Laffer—argued that it was not necessary to cut spending when cutting tax rates, since a reduction in income tax *rates* would produce such a large increase in private sector economic activity that tax *revenues,* even at the new lower rates, would increase rather than decrease. Few other economists accepted this claim, which was scoffed at even by most academic neoliberal economists. Yet this was part of the public justification cited for the big tax rate cuts pushed through Congress by the Reagan administration in 1981. What followed was large and growing budget deficits, as the promised increase in tax revenues failed to materialize.

17. Another key regulated sector was crude petroleum, although the elaborate system created to stabilize its price prior to the early 1970s, operated by a combination of state and federal governments in cooperation with the major oil companies, was a more informal institution than that for the other regulated sectors.

18. In Europe such industries were often state owned rather than privately owned but state regulated. Even in the United States there has been some state ownership in the electric power sector.

19. See Benston (1983) for a thorough presentation of the economic case for financial deregulation.

20. In 1984 this author testified before the House Banking Committee about the dangers of financial deregulation, arguing that it would lead to the return of bank failures and financial panics (Kotz, 1984). To anyone familiar with banking history, this was an obvious conclusion, but the neoliberal economists paid little attention to history.

21. These two laws, the 1980 Depository Institutions Deregulation and Monetary Control Act and the 1982 Garn-St. Germain Depository Institutions Act, started the reversal of state control over interest rates and restrictions on the services that financial institutions could offer.

22. In 1998 Brooksley Born, then head of the Commodities Futures Trading Commission, called for discussion of regulation of financial derivatives, warning that they were potentially dangerous. However, her call was stymied by Treasury Secretary Robert Rubin and his successor Lawrence Summers. Secretary Summers then supported a ban on any regulation of derivatives that was inserted into the final financial deregulation bill of the era, the Commodity Futures Modernization Act of 2000, sponsored by a Republican, Senator Phil Gramm of Texas. The result was rapid growth of unregulated financial derivatives in the 2000s, which is discussed in Chapter 5.

23. The act created the new Occupational Safety and Health Administration, whose mission is to "assure safe and healthful working conditions for working men and women" (http://www.dol.gov/compliance/laws/comp-osha.htm).

24. In economic theory, such market failures result from "negative externalities," that is, costs imposed on third parties such as air and water pollution due to production processes or products, and from asymmetric information, whereby one party to a transaction knows the consequences of the transaction while the other does not, as in the case of dangerous products or jobs. Conventional economic theory teaches that unregulated market decisions do not result in an efficient allocation of resources if there are externalities or asymmetric information.

25. In the 1970s Watt founded the anti-environmentalist Western States Legal Foundation. Ann Gorsuch, a former attorney for Mountain Bell and then a conservative member of Congress from Wyoming, saw her role as EPA head to be easing environmental regulation and downsizing the agency.

26. The personnel declines cited are based on estimated positions in fiscal year 1984.

27. This decision was leaked to Congress, which held a hearing on the matter, producing headlines about widows' and orphans' lawsuits as the proposed

means of deterring production of unsafe products. The resulting wave of criticism forced the Federal Trade Commission to allow the regulatory action to go through in this case (Kotz, 1987, 166).

28. Senate Bill 1167 was introduced in 1967 (Martin, 2005, 11).

29. In the mid-1990s between 70% and 80% of mergers reported to the Federal Trade Commission were intra-industry mergers, the type of merger that increases monopoly power in markets. By contrast, about 40% of mergers in the 1980s were intra-industry (Federal Trade Commission, 2013). A merger wave in the 1960s was largely a conglomerate one, with little impact on monopoly power.

30. There have been some important state-owned enterprises in U.S. history, mainly in power generation, transportation, and arms manufacturing.

31. *New York Times,* February 4, 2007, 1, 24.

32. Actual tax rates paid by high-income taxpayers often were below the listed rates, due to various loopholes, so that the effective tax rates in the regulated capitalist era in the United States were not as progressive as Figure 2.5 suggests.

33. In Chapter 3, which concerns the rise of neoliberal capitalism, it will be argued that on the whole big business was never enthusiastic about the significant role of labor unions and the collective bargaining process. Historical conditions in the late 1940s caused big business to accept the new relation with labor as the best available option at the time.

34. Dwight D. Eisenhower Presidential Library, 2013. The quote is from a speech to the American Federation of Labor in New York City on September 17, 1952.

35. The decline in the private sector unionization rate from 1953 to 1973 reflected primarily changes in the sectoral composition of employment, as employment in traditionally non-union sectors expanded relative to total employment, and a shift in the geographical location of some industries toward parts of the United States that had proved inhospitable to unions— the Southeast and Southwest.

36. Caterpillar had a record $4.9 billion profit in 2011 but in the following year the company provoked a strike at its factory in Joliet, Illinois, by demanding a six-year wage freeze. The company, which gave big raises to its executives, complained that the unionized workers were paid above market rates. In the previous year Caterpillar closed a factory in London, Ontario, after workers refused a 55% wage cut (*New York Times,* July 23, 2012, A1).

37. See Uchitelle (2013), in which the noted *New York Times* economics writer recounts the spread of low-wage two-tier union contracts.

38. Not all of the OECD countries were found to have a significant percentage of temporary employees. Such workers were 5% or less of the total in Ireland, Austria, and the U.K. in 2006.

39. Baran and Sweezy (1966, chap. 2) is one of many books that describe the co-respective competition of the regulated capitalist era.
40. *New York Times,* July 18, 1999, D4.
41. Intensifying international competition in the late 1960 and 1970s played an important role in the demise of co-respective competition and its replacement by an unrestrained form of competition. This is discussed in Chapter 3.
42. One study found that the percentage of new CEO hires from outside the company in S&P 500 firms rose from an average of 15.5% in the 1970s to 32.7% in 2000–05 (Murphy and Zabojnik, 2007, 34).
43. Market principles also eventually intruded into non-capitalist sectors of the economy, including institutions of higher education. Faculty pay, previously largely independent of discipline, diverged based on earning potential outside the university. It became popular for university heads to seek to measure the "performance" of departments and programs, promising to reward those that scored high while withdrawing funds from those judged to be underperforming.
44. This description of financial institution activities in the regulated capitalist era is somewhat oversimplified. For example, commercial banks, particularly the largest ones, engaged in other activities besides making loans to business. However, the account in the text captures the main role in the domestic economy of each type of financial institution in that period.
45. In Chapter 7 we use the term "social democracy" more broadly to refer to a form of capitalism with features that were common to the regulated capitalism of the United States and Western Europe in the post-World War II decades.
46. For an overview of financialization, see Orhangazi (2008) and Epstein (2005).
47. A related analysis explains the rise of neoliberalism as the result of the ascendance of finance, or financial capitalists. This view is considered in Chapter 3.
48. The total volume of foreign exchange transactions in the world rose from about $15 billion per day in 1973 to about $80 billion per day in 1980 (Bhaduri, 1998, 152).
49. The process of financialization also involved an expansion of financial services provision by nonfinancial corporations and an increase in their holdings of financial assets.
50. While financial profit as a share of total profit fell steeply from 2003 through 2006, financial profit still continued to rise but nonfinancial profit rose faster. In 2007 both financial and nonfinancial profit declined, followed by a collapse of financial profit in 2008 as the financial crisis struck. However, financial profit rapidly rebounded after 2009 thanks to the government's bailout of the large financial institutions.

51. If contemporary capitalism could be understood as essentially financial-ized capitalism, it would imply that the problems it has produced could be resolved by reregulation of the financial sector. However, if financialization is an outgrowth of neoliberalism, that suggests that broader changes would be required to address the problems of the current form of capitalism.

52. Some analysts who emphasize globalization regard it as an inexorable pro-cess that cannot be regulated. Critics argue that globalization, which has been reversed before in history, could be slowed or even reversed again.

53. The narrower measures are government value added, which includes com-pensation of government employees and depreciation on government-owned capital goods; and government consumption and investment, which adds the value of government purchases from the private sector to government value added.

54. The broad measure government expenditure is not actually a part of GDP, since one major component, transfer payments, represents a redistribution of buying power rather than part of the goods and services that make up the GDP. Nevertheless, common practice compares government expendi-ture to GDP to estimate the size of government relative to the economy.

55. As noted in Chapter 1, we do not regard 1981 as a business cycle peak year, despite its identification as a peak year by the National Bureau of Economic Research.

56. As the economy expands, private sector output grows rapidly while some types of government spending contract, such as unemployment compen-sation. In recessions, the reverse happens. This effect can be seen in the cyclical movement of the measures of government spending in Figure 2.10.

57. The term "capital-labor relation" in Table 2.1 refers to institutions (prac-tices) that characterize the relation between capital and labor, such as mar-ginalization of collective bargaining, which is not the same as the capital-labor class relation, which we interpret as a power relation.

58. See Wolfson and Kotz (2010) for a related discussion of this point.

3. The Rise of Neoliberal Capitalism

1. The University of Chicago economics department, dominated by free-mar-ket economist Milton Friedman and a few others of like mind, did not join in the Keynesian revolution but stuck with the earlier dominant economic ideas. The term "Chicago School" economics came to mean free-market economic ideas and theories.

2. In graduate courses in macroeconomic theory, one or more journal articles by Milton Friedman might be included on the syllabus, to demonstrate

some diversity, but few if any outside of the University of Chicago considered Friedman's theories to be valid at that time.

3. Rogers (2011, chap. 2) offers a detailed account of the rise of free-market economic ideas and theories in that period.

4. Two days after the strike began, President Reagan ordered the firing of over 11,000 striking air traffic controllers, leading to the decertification of the union on October 22.

5. While the shift of big business to support for neoliberal restructuring in the 1970s is viewed here as the cause of that transformation, the economic and political context in that period provides the reasons why big business made such a shift. Thus, the context and its effects are essential parts of the explanation.

6. The word "coalition" has various meanings including a relatively unified association, but that meaning is not intended here. In this context, the meaning of coalition is a coming together for common action of different groups or factions, as in the case of a coalition government that includes several parties that may have quite different constituencies and/or political outlooks. A coalition of big business and organized labor in support of the key institutions of regulated capitalism does not imply that the two groups had the same interests or that they no longer fought one another over those issues on which their interests diverged.

7. Opponents of regulated capitalism also included some medium-sized business interests, whose operations were domestic rather than international, as well as a few big businesses. The assertion that big business supported regulated capitalism means that most of the major large corporations—a decisive part of the group—supported it. Such groups are never entirely unanimous on any issue.

8. Maddison (1995) provides data for the period 1950–73, rather than the 1948–73 period used in this book to represent regulated capitalism.

9. For example, see *The Golden Age of Capitalism* (Marglin and Schor, 1990).

10. Foster (2007) offers a related explanation of neoliberalism, arguing that a stagnation tendency inherent in monopoly capitalism prompted a shift of capital into financial activities, leading to the financialization of monopoly capitalism. Neoliberalism is then seen as the ideology of financialized monopoly capitalism. This view interprets neoliberalism more narrowly that we do, seeing it as an ideology rather than encompassing a whole set of institutions.

11. The Marxist theory of social change, known as historical materialism, is a subject of much controversy in the Marxist literature, where one finds debates over several different interpretations of the theory.

12. Another example of a historical step backward occurred when capitalism was bringing rapid economic progress in the sixteenth to nineteenth centuries, yet an archaic slave-based economic system arose and expanded in close association with it in the Americas.

13. Actual history is messier than a theory of how it develops might suggest. While the social structure of accumulation theory can be taken to assert that an entire coherent set of accumulation and profit-promoting institutions arise in a relatively compressed time period, history shows that each past social structure of accumulation has developed over a somewhat extended period of time out of a complex series of events (Kotz, 1994).

14. Table 3.1 shows the main institutions of regulated capitalism but not all of them. For an expanded list, see Kotz (1994).

15. The practice of co-respective competition among large corporations had its origin in the early 1900s when J. P. Morgan and other major bankers introduced it in industries over which they had gained control (see Chapter 6). The practice weakened in the 1920s and 1930s, but then became a standard practice after World War II.

16. Some of the key parts of the Bretton Woods system did not begin to fully function until the late 1950s (Kotz, 1994).

17. Associated with the Bretton Woods system were several other important new institutions that emerged in the second half of the 1940s, including the newly powerful military role of the United States in the world and the active provision of foreign economic aid.

18. Among the leading founders were Paul G. Hoffman, president of the automaker Studebaker Corporation; William Benton, co-founder of the advertising firm Benton & Bowles; and Marion B. Folsom, the treasurer of Eastman Kodak Company (McQuaid, 1982, 109–121).

19. As is the case for corporate boards of directors, the CED trustees also included some members from outside the business world, such as college presidents.

20. The report received widespread attention and was published in its entirely in the October 1944 issue of *Fortune* (McQuaid, 1982, 119).

21. Ferguson and Rogers (1986) argue that big financial institutions and capital-intensive corporations were the major big businesses that made peace with the New Deal, partly because their labor costs were a small part of total costs. They also argue that the more internationally oriented big banks and corporations also tended to take this position, since support for free trade became associated politically with acceptance of the New Deal reforms. However, by the 1960s big corporations in autos and textiles, which were relatively labor intensive, were associated with the CED, and Henry Ford endorsed its policies early on.

22. Although the document states that it does not necessarily represent the views of trustees of the CED, it is an official statement of the CED's Research and Policy Committee, which at that time included among its members the CEOs of Libbey-Owens-Ford Glass, Eastman Kodak, New York Life Insurance, Studebaker, Geo A. Hormel and Co, Federated Department Stores, Scott Paper, General Electric, R. H. Macy, and Northwest Bancorporation (CED, 1947).

23. At the time the 1964 statement was issued, the CED's Research and Policy Committee was composed of fifty out of the two hundred trustees of the CED (CED, 1964).

24. The Landrum-Griffin Act of 1959 imposed new rules on the internal organization of unions.

25. This CED report advocated tax reductions rather than government spending increases when it became necessary to counteract the effect of declining business investment, a form of Keynesian policy often called "conservative Keynesianism." In the 1960s, considered the high point of open use of Keynesian policy by the federal government in the United States, it was this version of Keynesian stimulus, in the form of a broad-based tax cut, that was proposed by the Kennedy administration and then passed by Congress during the Johnson administration.

26. While similar conditions in the other developed capitalist countries led to big business support for such measures, the exact course of the process of establishment of regulated capitalism differed across countries, as did the exact form of regulated capitalism. In some European countries labor-based political parties played the leading role in establishing a form of regulated capitalism with more generous social programs than was the case in the U.S.

27. By the late 1930s a few big companies, when faced with determined union drives by their workers, quickly gave in and recognized the union, as in the case of United States Steel Corporation in 1937. However, most big companies resisted in that period. The United Auto Workers won union recognition from General Motors only after a lengthy and dramatic sit-down strike in 1936–37, while several of the major steel companies other than U.S. Steel fought violent battles against the Steel Workers Union in 1937.

28. By contrast, the U.S. Chamber of Commerce, the majority of whose members were small businesses, opposed Keynesian stimulation of the economy after World War II, even when a recession struck in 1949 (Collins, 1981, 127–128).

29. The many negative features of the system in the Communist-ruled states ended up seriously limiting its appeal to workers in the West.

30. Joseph Kennedy, the father of President John F. Kennedy and Senators Robert and Edward Kennedy, reportedly explained why a wealthy capitalist such

as himself was supporting Roosevelt's New Deal by saying he would "give up half his wealth in order to be assured his family could enjoy the other half in peace and safety" (Whalen, 1963). He was speaking metaphorically—as far as is known, he did not give up half of his fortune, but he did support the New Deal's redistributive policies. This widely cited quote from Kennedy is reported in the Whalen article but without identifying the date or context.

31. In an unusual anti-trust suit in the 1930s, the U.S. government forced Du-Pont Chemical to sell its controlling interest in General Motors. The ostensible reason was a claim that DuPont Chemical was using its control of GM to monopolize its purchases of paint. Many observers believed that the real reason for that anti-trust action was the openly pro-Nazi sympathies of the DuPonts. With World War II approaching, and with it the prospect that GM would soon become a major weapons manufacturer, leaving GM in the hands of the Du Ponts might have seemed unwise to the Roosevelt administration. The forced sale of its GM holdings did nothing to soften the DuPonts' hostility to regulated capitalism.

32. Some analysts have argued that big business inevitably favors some form of actively state-regulated capitalism. While this argument had significant historical support prior to the 1970s, the later history makes such a view difficult to sustain.

33. The real wage here refers to the hourly earnings of production or non-supervisory workers in the private sector, corrected for inflation.

34. The inflation-corrected value of pre-tax corporate profits actually fell from 1966 to 1973, by 9.3%.

35. While the du Pont family had been diehard opponents of regulated capitalism in the 1940s, in the 1970s the chemical company's CEO, Irving Shapiro, steered the company into the political mainstream of U.S. big business.

36. The Business Roundtable was not the only instrument of big business lobbying in the 1970s. Individual corporations set up, or upgraded, governmental relations departments, naming high officials to run them and giving them larger budgets. Individual CEOs also became more active in lobbying in that decade (Vogel, 1989, 195–199).

37. The shift to a focus on stopping inflation in 1980 was undoubtedly influenced by the accelerating rate of inflation over the preceding years. As we noted earlier, the inability of Keynesian techniques to resolve the economic problems of the 1970s tended to weaken the hold of the dominant Keynesian ideas.

38. The failure of Keynesian policy interventions to solve the escalating economic problems of the 1970s also undermined support for Keynesian economics and gave an opening to advocates of free-market economic theory in academia.

39. Goldwater also demanded a more aggressive foreign policy.

40. In those years, Republican presidential nominees did not challenge the institutions of regulated capitalism.

41. Mizruchi (2013) presents an analysis of the relation between big business and institutional change since World War II that has some similarities to our account. However, he views the rise of neoliberal capitalism as indicating an abdication of leadership by the business class, which gave up its former ability to shape events in favor of the pursuit of short-run profit. In our view, the neoliberal form of capitalism has served the interests of big business effectively, but the nature of a free-market form of capitalism makes it unnecessary for business to continue to actively shape events.

42. There were some conflicts between public interest groups and the labor movement over environmental protection, but on the whole the two groups were allied on these issues.

43. The wording cited was directed at solving the problem of rising wages, falling profits, and inflation, but it might have been intended to suggest a more general position.

44. While Figure 3.4 gives a rough indication of rising import competition, the ratio of goods imports to goods-only GDP is not a perfect measure of the intensity of import competition faced by U.S. companies. Part of goods imports are inputs used by U.S. producers that are not available from U.S. companies.

45. The success of the Bretton Woods system also undermined that system itself in 1967–73. The recovery of Western Europe and Japan was a major factor that eventually caused the U.S. trade surplus to turn into a trade deficit in 1971. This made the fixed value of the U.S. dollar relative to gold and other major currencies unsustainable.

4. How Has Neoliberal Capitalism Worked?

1. Our dating of regulated capitalism and neoliberal capitalism was explained at the end of chapter 1.

2. As was noted in Chapter 2, in neoclassical economic theory under perfect competition every agent who supplies labor or capital to production will receive a payment that reflects the marginal product of the resource supplied by that agent.

3. In the United States and United Kingdom this experiment was overseen by an elected political leadership. However, in some parts of the world—in Africa, Asia, and Latin America—this experiment was forced on many countries by the IMF, backed up by the U.S. government. In the formerly Communist Party-ruled states of Central and Eastern Europe, neoliberal

restructuring was effectively urged on the new governments that emerged by the IMF, the World Bank, and Western economic advisors.

4. The three Western European countries are Germany, France, and the United Kingdom (Dumenil and Levy, 2004, 24).

5. While the profit rate data presented in the figures in this book are for the pre-tax rate of profit, as is common in the literature, here we provide data on after-tax profit in order to take account of the effect on profit of one plank in the neoliberal program, reductions in taxes on business.

6. As the appendix to this chapter explains, the rate of profit can be expressed as the product of the share of profit in income (or output) and the ratio of output to capital. Hence, an increase in the rate of profit over a period can be accounted for by a rise in the profit share, a rise in the output-capital ratio, or a combination of the two.

7. The measure of output per labor hour (labor productivity) reported here differs from the labor productivity measure in Figure 4.5, in two ways. The former is for the nonfinancial corporate business sector, while the measure in Figure 4.5 is for the entire nonfarm business sector. Second, the measure reported in the text here is derived from data from the U.S. Bureau of Economic Analysis, which can be used to analyze the factors that underlie the profit rate increase in the neoliberal era. The data for Figure 4.5 are for the standard labor productivity growth series from the U.S. Bureau of Labor Statistics.

8. A serious conceptual problem arises for defining a profit rate for the entire corporate sector, including the financial sector, from the difficulty in finding an appropriate measure of the capital stock for the whole corporate sector. That problem does not arise for the annual volume of profit for the corporate sector. Hence, we present the profit rate for the nonfinancial corporate business sector (Figure 4.1) but supplement it with data on the rate of growth of the volume of profit for the entire corporate sector. See Figure 4.12 for the source for the growth rate of the volume of profit.

9. In Figure 4.2 the bars reach to slightly below 4% and 3% because of rounding. The average annual growth rate rounds off to 4.0% in the first period and 3.0% in the latter two periods. Percentage growth rates in GDP are not accurate to beyond one decimal place.

10. Maddison passed away in 2010, but his group has continued to update estimates of world economic growth using the methodology he developed. Constructing GDP growth rates for the entire world economy requires making simplifying assumptions necessary to combine the GDP growth of many countries that have many economic differences.

11. Net private investment is derived by subtracting the depreciation of the capital stock from gross (total) private investment, where gross private

investment is the production of structures and equipment and software, plus the increase in business inventories. Net domestic product, obtained by subtracting depreciation from gross domestic product, is the appropriate measure of output for comparing net private investment to output.

12. The rate of capital accumulation is the better measure of the two. The share of private investment in output is affected not only by how vigorous private investment is but also by the behavior of the other components of output, which are consumer spending, government consumption and investment, and net exports.

13. A boom in residential investment contributed to the first half of the expansion of 2001–07.

14. Figure 4.11 showing the income shares of the richest 1% and richest 0.1% includes income from realized capital gains, which make up a significant part of the income of the very rich. Realized capital gains are not included in the income shares from the U.S. Census Bureau shown in Figure 4.10.

15. CEO pay is the average for the 350 largest firms ranked by sales, including realized stock options. Worker pay is the average compensation of production and nonsupervisory workers in the industries of the firms in the sample.

16. While we normally use the period 1948–73 to represent the regulated capitalist era, the shorter period through 1966 is appropriate for analyzing growth in profits, since, unlike such series as GDP, profit growth and the rate of profit turned down decisively after 1966 rather than 1973. As was noted earlier, judged by the series for profits or the rate of profit, postwar regulated capitalism was no longer working effectively during 1966 to 1979 rather than just 1973 to 1979.

17. The Bureau of Labor Statistics revised the methodology for the series for average hourly earnings in 2004, and as a result there is no consistent series available from 1948 to 2007. Figure 4.13 presents the old and new series for the subperiods over which they are available. While the two series move similarly for the years of overlap, it is possible that a consistent series for the whole period would show either a somewhat smaller or somewhat greater difference between the growth rates in average earnings in the two subperiods.

18. To compare average values of the unemployment rate for the three contiguous periods, one cannot include the turning-point years in two periods, which would double-count such years. Thus, the neoliberal era must start in 1980, not 1979, when the data are averages of values such as for the average unemployment rate. For growth rates of variables, this problem does not arise, since a growth rate over the period 1979–2007 actually starts with the growth from 1979 to 1980.

19. Full-time equivalent jobs include part-time jobs weighted by the hours worked as a percentage of full-time hours.

20. In recent decades changes in family structure have also played a role in rising household inequality, particularly the increase in both single-parent families and families with two wage earners.

21. In the days when the CEO was promoted from within, CEOs often received only a moderate boost in pay when they ascended to the top step on the corporate ladder. However, recruiting CEOs from the outside enabled potential candidates to bargain for a small share of the company's profit, claiming they could boost profit if hired. For large corporations with huge annual profits, this led to a rapid escalation of CEO pay, although other factors also played a role.

22. Some analysts point to low interest rates to explain the emergence of asset bubbles. A critique of this view is offered in Chapter 5.

23. See Chapter 6 for a discussion of earlier historical periods in the United States when financial institutions behaved in ways similar to their recent behavior.

24. Speculative activity, which refers to buying an asset in the expectation of later reselling it at a higher price, is viewed as performing useful functions by neoclassical economic theory. Advocates of that theory claim that speculation moves an asset price toward its equilibrium value while also spreading the risk of holding assets. Hence, the profit from speculation is seen as a return for a positive economic contribution by the speculator. Non-mainstream economists, including those following a Keynesian, institutionalist, or Marxist approach, generally regard speculation as serving no useful economic purpose while having a number of negative effects. The latter schools view profit from speculative activity as deriving from luck, trading on insider information (illegal under the securities laws), or fraud (when the seller does not disclose negative information about the asset being sold). Consistently high profits from speculation suggest to the latter group of analysts the likelihood of insider trading or fraud. This book follows the latter non-neoclassical interpretation of speculative activity.

25. Chapter 5 gives examples of high-risk activities by the largest U.S. banks, which landed them in serious legal difficulty after the crash.

26. Keynes presented a persuasive case that Say's Law is simply false, but some versions of textbook Keynesian economics view Say's Law as invalid "only in the short run" whereas in the long run Say's Law is presumed to be valid. The belief that in the long run only supply matters, and not demand, brought back an element of the pre-Keynesian "Classical" theory of the economy that Keynes had sought to overthrow.

27. Beginning in 2006 the Federal Reserve included student loans in its break-down of additions to consumer debt. In 2010 student loans surpassed auto and credit card loans to become the largest category of additions to consumer credit. In 2012 student loans outstanding increased by $1.1 trillion, which was 38.7% of total additions to consumer debt that year (Board of Governors of the Federal Reserve System, 2013).

28. In the later part of the 2001–07 expansion, business fixed investment also grew rapidly, spurred by the rising rate of profit as well as the euphoria induced by the real estate bubble.

29. The mean house price index for the United States also rose at its fastest rate from 2002 to 2005 (see Figure 5.5 in Chapter 5)

30. By contrast, Kotz (2009, 184, Table 13.4) found that in the late stage of business cycle expansions during 1948–73, real wages grew substantially faster than labor productivity growth in the nonfinancial corporate business sector. The growth rates of compensation and labor productivity cited in the text are for the nonfinancial corporate business sector.

31. The paradox mentioned earlier—that consumer spending relative to income rose over time, despite increasing inequality, which should have reduced that ratio—involves forces that work in opposite directions. Rising inequality in itself does tend to reduce the consumer spending ratio, but that ratio tends to rise due to the other forces analyzed above—the stimulative effect of asset bubbles on consumer spending, the hard-pressed middle and low income families who found borrowing the only way to maintain their living standard, and the active promotion of household borrowing by financial institutions. The data, which show a sharp upward trend in consumer spending relative to income over the neoliberal era, confirm the view that the latter forces overwhelmed the effect of rising inequality on the consumer spending ratio.

32. Greenspan gave this warning in a speech on December 5, 1996, at the American Enterprise Institute(http://www.federalreserve.gov/boarddocs/speeches/1996/19961205.htm).

33. Jeff Faux, personal communication, July 18, 2013. Faux, an economic policy analyst, attended the 1993 summit meeting and met with AFL-CIO representatives during the meeting.

34. Between 1993, when Clinton took office and the deficit began to decline, and the year 2000, the interest rate on AAA corporate bonds varied little, remaining about 7.5%, while the prime rate on bank loans rose from 6.0% to 9.2% (*Economic Report of the President,* 2002, 406, Table B-73).

35. *New York Times,* July 3, 1997.

36. *The Times* [London], February 20, 2002, 23.

37. The United States never had an aristocracy, but in the United Kingdom part of the Thatcher government's appeal was the image that it was fighting for middle class rights against old class privileges. Some aristocratic elements of the British upper class had qualms about Thatcherism for this reason (Harvey, 2005, 31).

38. This interpretation of the demise of state socialism is not supported by the historical evidence. See Kotz and Weir (1997). Nevertheless, it became the dominant mainstream interpretation.

39. The difference between wage growth and labor productivity growth is not exactly equal to the growth of the wage share because we measure the growth rates as compounded average annual growth rates, and as a result an interaction term between wage growth and productivity growth can account for a small percentage of the growth rate in the wage share.

5. Crisis

1. The measure of household debt used in this book (Figure 4.20)—outstanding debt relative to disposable income—is one of several possible measures of the extent of household debt. A second, the ratio of principal and interest payments to household income, measures the current burden of the debt, but that measure is lowered when interest rates on the debt are low, and it can suddenly jump up when rates rise as they normally do after a period of economic expansion. A third measure, the ratio of outstanding debt to the market value of household assets, shows the extent to which households are leveraging their home value to build up debt. That measure is depressed during a real estate bubble, when the market value of homes is elevated, and it will rise suddenly when the bubble bursts. The first measure, the ratio of household debt to household income, is the best one for indicating the long-run degree of household indebtedness independent of the current interest rate and current value of real estate.

2. *New York Times,* October 3, 2008, A1, A23. Of the five, after 2007 one went bankrupt (Lehman Brothers), two had to be acquired by larger institutions to avoid failure (Merrill Lynch and Bear Stearns), and two required bailouts by the Federal Reserve (Goldman Sachs and Morgan Stanley).

3. We use the general term "financial instruments" rather than "securities," since some of the new financial products that arose in this period, such as credit default swaps, were not securities.

4. Fannie Mae is the informal name for the Federal National Mortgage Association, created by the federal government in 1938 to encourage home buying. In 1968 Fannie Mae was privatized, although it retained some

connections to the government, so that it is sometimes called a "government sponsored enterprise."

5. An antecedent of mortgage-backed securities arose in the 1920s, in the form of real estate-backed securities, which played a role in the real estate bubble of the mid-1920s; see Chapter 6.

6. According to a legal expert who testified before Congress in 2003, "By shifting the credit risk of the securitized assets (for a price) to . . . mortgage backed securities investors, financial institutions can reduce their own risk. As the risk level of an individual institution declines, so does systemic risk, or the risk faced by the financial system overall" (Cowan, 2003, 7).

7. The origination of a mortgage refers to the creation of the initial mortgage loan to the homeowner. The company that makes the original mortgage loan is called the originator.

8. Immergluck and Wiles (1999) is the study cited by Chomsisengphet and Pennington-Cross (2006).

9. *New York Times,* June 7, 2009, 15. In that same article Wells Fargo denied the charges, stating, "We have worked extremely hard to make homeownership possible for more African-American borrowers."

10. Mortgage-backed securities are usually also issued in tranches.

11. *New York Times,* February 17, 2008, 1, 17. Since credit default swaps are not traded on exchanges but are created by a two-party contract, the value of outstanding credit default swaps can only be estimated. Bosworth and Flaaen (2009) estimated that credit default swaps rose from about $1 trillion in 2000 to over $50 trillion in mid-2008.

12. In addition to the difficulties of accurately evaluating the risk and return of the complex new securities created in the neoliberal era, it is inherently impossible to "accurately" determine risk and return on any security since it depends on future events that cannot be known in advance but only guessed at. The best that can be attained in evaluating securities is an impartial and informed guess.

13. *New York Times,* November 12, 2013, B1, B6.

14. *New York Times,* December 24, 2009; April 17, 2010; March 19, 2012.

15. *New York Times,* January 29, 2009.

16. *New York Times,* December 26, 2008.

17. Freddie Mac is the informal name of another government-sponsored home mortgage market enterprise, whose formal name is the Federal Home Loan Mortgage Corporation. It was created in 1970.

18. *New York Times,* June 7, 2010; October 24, 2013, B1; October 26, 2013, B1.

19. *New York Times,* October 20, 2013, 1, 18. Some of the mortgage securities in question were inherited by JPMorgan when it took over failing Bear Stearns

and Washington Mutual in 2008, but others had been sold by JPMorgan prior to those takeovers.

20. *Financial Times,* July 9, 2007. This famous quote was actually about participation in leveraged buyouts in light of developing problems in the U.S. subprime mortgage market, but it captures the logic that kept sophisticated players involved in investments of all types that were bound to fail at some point.

21. The broader industrial capacity utilization index, available only from 1967, shows the same pattern.

22. For the entire nonfinancial corporate business sector, the ratio of output to the capital stock declined by 8.1% during 1979–2007, although that ratio reflects technological changes as well as changes in capacity utilization.

23. One might expect that another cause of excess capacity would come from the rising inequality of neoliberal capitalism, on the grounds that rising inequality should lead to slow growth of consumer spending relative to output. However, as we saw in Chapter 4 (Figure 4.8), neoliberal capitalism in the United States produced a rise rather than a fall in consumer spending relative to GDP, as households borrowed heavily to support their spending.

24. The rate of profit on capital is the product of the ratio of profit to output and the ratio of output to capital. Decreasing capacity utilization implies a falling ratio of output to capital which, for a given ratio of profit to output, reduces the profit rate.

25. The process described here, in which creation of excess productive capacity, or fixed capital, eventually leads to a big drop in investment and hence a recession, is called "over-investment" (Kotz, 2013).

26. While a need to increase productive capacity to be able to increase production is a major reason for firms to invest, firms also invest to take advantage of new technologies.

27. The sources for the sequence of events in the financial crisis are, unless otherwise noted, timelines from Federal Reserve Bank of St. Louis (2013) and BBC News (2009).

28. *New York Times,* September 24, 1998, A1, C11; September 25, 1998, A1, C4; October 2, 1998, A1, C3.

29. Later the Federal Reserve did decline to bail out one failing major financial institution, Lehman Brothers, in September 2008.

30. *New York Times,* June 6, 2008, C1, C4.

31. *New York Times,* February 22, 2008, A1, A16.

32. *New York Times,* March 15, 2008, A1, A12; March 16, 2008, Business Section 1, 9.

33. The U.S. economy reached a business cycle peak in the fourth quarter of 2007, and the recession is considered to have begun in the following calendar quarter, that is, the first quarter of 2008.

34. The other large contributor to the GDP decline in the first quarter of 2008 was residential construction, which had been falling since the fourth quarter of 2005 following a slowdown in the rate of home price inflation.

35. Banks are required to hold reserves that are a certain percentage of their loans and investments. If they are holding excess reserves, it means they are not fully using their reserves to make loans and investments but instead are keeping them in non-earning liquid forms.

36. The government component of GDP, which had been 72% of GDP during the last wartime year of 1945, fell precipitously by 65% in 1946, to 28% of GDP in that year. The impact of the sudden contraction of government in 1946 caused an 11.6% drop in GDP in that year, giving one more (negative) lesson in support of the Keynesian claim that increased government spending increases GDP.

37. *New York Times,* October 15, 2008, A1, A25.

38. *New York Times,* October 15, 2008, A1, A25. It was not clear why Paulson went through this ritual, other than to claim the historical mantle of the famous J. P. Morgan and to show that he was in charge. As we shall see in Chapter 6, in 1907 J. P. Morgan locked up the leading bankers to pressure them to contribute substantial sums to stem a tidal wave of bank runs, whereas Paulson came bearing $250 billion to contribute *to* the banks, although some of them were reluctant to accept even a non-voting government share in their ownership.

39. *New York Times,* November 26, 2008, A1, A24.

40. *New York Times,* December 20, 2008, A1; November 3, 2010, B1.

41. This author attended Feldstein's presentation, delivered on January 4, 2009.

42. The remark about the fundamentals of the economy remaining strong was in the form of expressing agreement with a quote from Republican presidential candidate John McCain.

43. *New York Times,* October 24, 2008, B1, B6.

44. The exception was Turkey, whose economy was not significantly affected by the crisis.

45. The Obama administration's economic policy-makers and advisors had disagreed among themselves about the size of the stimulus bill that should be introduced. Some argued that a larger bill was needed to reverse the recession, while others warned that a larger bill would not get through Congress. Lawrence Summers, the former advocate of deregulation in the Clinton administration who was serving as director of Obama's National Economic Council in 2009, argued forcefully for the lower amount that was sent to Congress.

46. Calculated from U.S. Bureau of Economic Analysis, 2013, NIPA Table 1.1.6.

47. *New York Times,* November 10, 2008, A1.
48. The Chinese authorities were able to initiate a big stimulus program without having to obtain approval by a recalcitrant legislature or defend it against domestic critics.
49. *New York Times,* February 9, 2009.
50. Sluggish GDP growth has continued past the first quarter of 2013. The GDP growth rate was 2.2% per year through the latest quarter for which data are now available, the first quarter of 2014 (U.S. Bureau of Economic Analysis, 2014, NIPA Table 1.1.6). However, in the summer of 2013 the U.S. Bureau of Economic Analysis completed a major revision of the national income and product accounts, and as a result the growth rates of GDP and its components that can be calculated extending beyond the first quarter of 2013 are not strictly comparable to the growth rates reported in the figures and tables in this book, which use the pre-revision series.
51. The 2012 income data from Saez (2013) are preliminary. The income gains cited are for pre-tax family market income including realized capital gains. The recovery of the stock market during 2009–2012 made large capital gains possible for the richest families.
52. *New York Times,* November 24, 2008, A14.
53. *New York Times,* September 5, 2013, A1, A3.
54. *New York Times,* August 27, 2013, B1, B2.
55. After 2009 Germany's unemployment rate fell continuously to 5.5% in 2012, for reasons that involve Germany's relation to the rest of the European Union economies.
56. *New York Times,* July 6, 2009, B1. However, the Center for Automotive Research claimed that government aid to GM and also Chrysler saved a total of more than 1.1 million jobs in 2009, including jobs in supplier industries and dealerships (*New York Times,* November 18, 2010, A1).
57. Martin Feldstein, presentation, annual Allied Social Science Associations convention, Atlanta, January 2, 2010.
58. *New York Times,* November 23, 2009, A1, A4; May 23, 2010, 1, 4; July 10, 2013, 18.
59. The big economic contractions in Greece, Ireland, and Spain have been directly caused by severe austerity programs, but the context involves particular problems that arise from the eurozone common currency arrangements, which are beyond the scope of this text.
60. *New York Times,* October 5, 2008, 1, 30.
61. The austerity advocates' arguments focus on the danger of large public deficits and public debt, arguing that public spending must be sharply reduced to lower the deficit. In practice many austerity advocates seem more interested in cutting public spending than in reducing deficits, since most of them

oppose tax increases that are an alternative way to reduce a public deficit. Some Scandinavian governments have followed a policy of high levels of public spending combined with low deficits, achieved by high tax rates.

62. The full debate among economists about crowding out is more complex than the account given here.

63. For "advanced economies" the median long-term growth rate for those with public debt ratios over 90% was about one percentage point lower than lower-debt economies, while the average long-term growth rate of the high-debt economies was negative (Reinhart and Rogoff, 2010, 574).

64. Herndon found an Excel coding error and the unexplained omission of some data points (country-year information) that were contrary to their claim.

65. A typical media report, by the BBC World News, was headlined "Reinhart, Rogoff . . . and Herndon: The Student Who Caught Out the Profs" (http://www.bbc.com/news/magazine-22223190).

66. The paper had two faculty co-authors, but graduate student Herndon was the principal author.

67. A follow-up study to the Herndon critique found that the Reinhart and Rogoff data contained evidence that there was a link running from slow growth to later high debt, but not vice versa (Dube, 2013).

68. *New York Times,* March 16, 2009, A14.

69. In the 2012 election cycle the American Banking Association reportedly sent 80% of its political action committee donations to Republicans, compared to 58% in the 2008 election cycle (*New York Times,* October 10, 2013, A15).

70. Hourly earnings are for production or nonsupervisory workers in the non-agricultural private sector, and output per hour is for all persons employed in the nonfarm business sector. Data for 2012 are preliminary.

71. Figure 5.16 is for the pre-tax profit rate. The after-tax profit rate rose above its 2006 level by 2011.

72. *The Guardian,* September 19, 2013; *New York Times,* October 16, 2013.

73. *New York Times,* July 21, 2013, 1, 14, 15. A third example involved alleged bank manipulation of the market for ethanol credits, which are part of the government effort to reduce dependence on imported oil and help U.S. agriculture. JPMorgan Chase and other big financial institutions were reported to have accumulated vast holdings of ethanol credits, driving their price up twenty-fold at the moment when refiners had to buy them under expanded federal ethanol requirements. JPMorgan denied the charge (*New York Times,* September 15, 2013, 1, 16).

74. The rate of capital accumulation in 2012 is estimated, using the Bureau of Economic Analysis definition of investment prior to the revision of July 30, 2013, and the new series value of investment in 2012.

75. *New York Times,* October 27, 2010.
76. *Forbes,* March 19, 2013.
77. There is no agreement among economists about the cause of depressed investment either in the 1930s or today. However, the explanation offered here appears to fit the historical evidence.

6. Lessons of History

1. The term "robber barons" apparently first arose in the 1870s. It was later popularized by a book with that title by Josephson (1962 [1934]).
2. Recently some historians have challenged the breakdown of the years 1870–1916 into these two periods, arguing that significant reform occurred prior to 1900, such as the initiation of the federal civil service and railroad regulation in the 1880s (Edwards, 2006). See Johnston (2011, 97–101) for a discussion of this debate. In our view the reforms in the 1880s were too limited to sustain the view of Edwards that the entire period starting in 1870 was one long Progressive Era. The dominant business practices and government economic policies before 1900 fit our conception of free-market or liberal capitalism.
3. The term "finance capital" was introduced by Hilferding (1981) in a book originally published in German in 1910, drawing mainly on developments in Germany in that period. The concept of finance capital used in this book, applied to the U.S. experience, has slight differences from Hilferding's original formulation.
4. Most works of the social structure of accumulation school regard the period from about 1900 through the early 1930s as based on a single social structure of accumulation (Gordon et al., 1982, chap. 4). In our view, there is strong evidence that a new social structure of accumulation emerged after World War I in the U.S.
5. The term "Roaring Twenties" traditionally refers to the economic prosperity and cultural change of that decade in the United States.
6. The only exception was the predominance of large cotton textile companies in New England. In 1865 Pittsburgh had twenty-one rolling mills and seventy-six glass factories while Cleveland had thirty oil refining companies.
7. While capitalists were free to pursue profits in any way they saw fit in this period, the U.S. government had created conditions in which the individual profit motive of the industrial entrepreneurs led them to make productive investments in new technologies, bringing rapid economic development. The state-financed investments in new transportation systems created a large internal market, the high protective tariffs made investment in the development of U.S. industry profitable by enabling U.S. industry to

compete against more advanced European rivals, and the state encouragement of immigration provided a labor force. Thus, although the capitalism of this period can be considered a liberal type of capitalism, state actions were sufficient to promote rapid economic development. History shows that rapid industrialization has always required a state that supports it. In the twentieth century the state role required to promote the development of an underdeveloped economy expanded compared to the nineteenth century, since later developers faced much stronger competition from already developed economies. See Chang (2002).

8. By contrast, the annual growth rates of real output during 1878–94 in the U.K., France, and Germany were 1.7%, 0.9%, and 2.3%, respectively, all slower than in the preceding decades in those countries (Gordon et al., 1982, 43).

9. Economists do not agree about the cause of the late nineteenth-century deflation. Some attribute it to monetary factors related to the nature of the banking and broader financial system of the period.

10. Despite the rapid output growth in the U.S. economy in the late nineteenth century, social structure of accumulation advocates have made a case that there was a structural crisis in the United States in that period, based on the large proportion of years of recession and the probable decline in the rate of profit over the period. See Gordon et al. (1982, 41–47). Many scholars view the period from the 1870s to the 1890s in Europe, where growth did slow down in that period, as the first Great Depression.

11. An independent oil refining company that refused to sell out to Rockefeller was blown up, and in the 1887 trial the act was blamed on a subordinate official who had exceeded his instructions (Josephson, 1962, 269–270).

12. See Morris (2005) and Josephson (1962) for accounts of the business practices of Jay Gould. Daniel Drew was another example of the speculative capitalist in that era.

13. Jay Gould's famous exploits were rather extreme examples of fraud and insider information as the basis of gaining large speculative profits at the expense of others. However, in Chapter 4 it was noted that we regard speculative activity in general as serving no useful economic purpose but rather as a harmful activity, one that can gain sizeable profit over time only through trading on insider information or misleading the buyer about the item being sold.

14. J. P. Morgan had ties to British capitalists, who invested in American securities through Morgan's investment bank. German-Jewish capitalists invested in America through Kuhn, Loeb and other investment banks run by German-Jewish immigrants. Goldman Sachs and Lehman Brothers, both small New York investment banks in the 1890s, began to handle the

securities of light manufacturing and retail companies after 1906. Those sectors had been ignored by the major investment banks (Kotz, 1978, 34–35). See also Roy (1997, chap. 5) and Chernow (1990, pt. I).

15. Economists developed the concept of "destructive competition," believed to particularly afflict industries with high fixed costs and low costs of additional output from existing capacity, such as railroads and steel. This concept disappeared from economics textbooks in the neoliberal era.

16. Roy (1997, chaps. 5, 8) discusses the rise of investment banks and giant corporations in this period.

17. Carnegie, the son of a radical Scottish weaver, had long been plagued by doubts about his single-minded pursuit of wealth. In 1885 he shocked established opinion by voicing support for socialism as the future of the new industrial society (Nasaw, 2006, 1, 256). After selling out to J. P. Morgan, he retired from industry to become a leading philanthropist.

18. John D. Rockefeller followed a unique trajectory. Starting as an industrial entrepreneur, he achieved a monopoly of the oil refining industry for his Standard Oil Trust. In the 1890s the Rockefeller fortune formed the basis for a new financial group centered around Citibank of New York. In the 1920s a second financial group emerged from the Rockefeller fortune, based on Chase Manhattan Bank (Kotz, 1978, 37, 50–51).

19. Dawley (1991, 128) refers to a single progressivism encompassing all factions, but it is useful to distinguish the different aims and constituencies of the reform movement and the socialist movement (Weinstein, 1968).

20. The suits against the very unpopular Standard Oil Trust and American Tobacco Company were successful, and both were broken up.

21. The shift in anti-trust policy away from breaking up large corporations to regulating their behavior so as to stabilize the new big business capitalism was consolidated by the 1920 U.S. Supreme Court decision dismissing the government suit calling for the breakup of U.S. Steel (Justia U.S. Supreme Court Center, 2013). The court ruled that U.S. Steel should not be broken up since it had not sought a monopoly by driving its competitors out of business or acquiring all of them. This was interpreted as legal acceptance of large and even dominant corporations as long as they behaved in a cooperative way toward competitors rather than trying to drive them out of business.

22. After World War I the Socialist Party was also weakened by other factors, including a split in the organization over whether to endorse the new Bolshevik regime in Russia. Many members who supported the Russian revolutionary government left the Socialist Party to form what became the Communist Party.

23. The real estate-backed securities of the 1920s differed from the mortgage-backed securities of the neoliberal era, in that the former were backed by

the income generated by the real property itself rather than interest on the mortgages on real property.

24. Those three development in the 1920s might account for the relatively rapid and stable economic growth of that decade, in a similar manner to the neoliberal era. However, this author had not done the research necessary to determine whether that is supported by the evidence.

25. The economy began to contract in August 1929, but the decline accelerated after the stock market deflation (Gordon, 1974, 41).

7. Possible Future Paths

1. This argument was made long ago in a famous work by Polanyi (1944). Similarly, there is an argument that the crisis of a regulated form of capitalism tends to lead to a liberal social structure of accumulation.

2. Big business groups have not supported this extreme anti-state position, instead exerting pressure against it in congressional lobbying in some cases.

3. Equally extreme anti-state positions were voiced in the first Reagan administration, before a shift to more moderate neoliberalism. Perhaps neoliberal ideas are at their most provocative when they are first achieving hegemony and again when their protagonists sense that their hegemony may be slipping away.

4. *New York Times,* April 6, 2013, A12.

5. As we saw in Chapter 6, the Progressive Era opened with big business on the defensive. Big business only gradually gained the power to direct the state role in the economy in ways favorable to its interests.

6. In some European countries the recent rise of neo-fascist movements and political parties suggests that a highly repressive and ultra-nationalistic form of business-regulated capitalism might emerge.

7. A narrower meaning of social democracy refers to the very generous welfare states established in Europe after World War II under the leadership of labor-based social democratic political parties. That form of regulated capitalism is sometimes contrasted to the regulated capitalism of the United States after World War II in which no labor-based social democratic party was present and the welfare state was more limited, although a capital-labor compromise was also worked out.

8. Examples of such "accidental developments" include the 1973 Arab oil embargo that contributed to rapid inflation and the effects of white racism in undermining the political coalition that had supported regulated capitalism.

9. Li (2013) makes a case that even optimistic estimates of the future rate of reduction in carbon emissions per unit of GDP would still require that the world economy *contract* at 1% per year to avert climate catastrophe.

10. After the nineteenth century the term "socialism" became the usual one to refer to a new socioeconomic system to displace capitalism, while the political parties advocating socialism were named either Socialist or Communist parties (or other names in some cases). Followers of the Marxist version of socialist thought have reserved the term "communism" for the ultimate stage of socialism, achievable only after a long period of post-capitalist evolution. Both Socialist and Communist parties at first advocated not just the reform of capitalism but its replacement by the an alternative socialist system. Over time many Socialist parties gave up that aim and became reformist, but here we use the term "socialism" to refer to an alternative socioeconomic system to capitalism.

11. Hayek's *The Road to Serfdom* (1944) presents the view that socialism leads inevitably to the denial of human freedom and creativity.

12. The famous economist Joseph Schumpeter of Harvard in the 1940s disliked socialism but feared it represented the future.

13. In the Progressive Era and during the Great Depression in the United States, many trade union leaders became Socialists or Communists, but relatively few of the rank and file did so. In Western Europe during that period, a large percentage of ordinary workers were won over to socialist views. There is a large literature that seeks to explain this historical difference between the United States and Europe.

14. Most self-described anarchists envision a future without private ownership of productive enterprises, and some regard anarchism as a part of the broader socialist movement. However, a critique of the state is the centerpiece of anarchist theory, which leads to opposition to state ownership of enterprises.

15. The literature on democratic participatory planned socialism includes Devine (1988), Albert and Hahnel (1991), and Lebowitz (2010). Some advocates of socialism support a version that would rely on market forces rather than economic planning (Roemer, 1994; Schweickart, 2011). In our view, both theoretical considerations and historical experience with market socialism suggest that a marketized version of socialism tends eventually to revert to capitalism. In China the leadership explained the shift to market socialism after 1978 as necessary in light of China's low level of economic development, but that consideration is not relevant for the form of socialism appropriate to a developed economy such as that of the United States.

16. In the Soviet system those consumers who wielded significant decision-making power in the system, such as the defense ministry and some industrial ministries, were able to effectively demand high-quality products, which explains why Soviet weapons and some industrial machinery were at the world technological frontier. Since ordinary households had no

power in the system, consumer goods were often in short supply and of poor quality.

17. It is not assumed that democratic participatory planned socialism would eliminate conflicts of interest in society. There would undoubtedly be conflicts of interest among workers, consumers, and community members— roles occupied by each member of society at different times. However, advocates argue that a process of negotiation and compromise among representatives of those three interests is the best way to resolve such conflicts. See Devine (1988). What would be eliminated is the fundamental conflict of interest between labor and capital that characterizes a capitalist system.

18. Unforeseen effects of actions and decisions could still result in negative externalities in a socialist system, but advocates argue that such a system would not create incentives to push social costs onto others such as results from the profit motive in a capitalist system.

19. *New York Times,* June 2, 2013.

20. The hope of some analysts that capitalist globalization would eliminate state economic rivalries over access to markets and control over raw materials has not been realized.

References

Ackerman, Frank. 2002. Still Dead after All These Years: Interpreting the Failure of General Equilibrium Theory. *Journal of Economic Methodology* 9(2) (July): 119–139.

Aglietta, Michel. 1979. *A Theory of Capitalist Regulation: The U.S. Experience.* London: Verso.

Albert, Michael, and Robin Hahnel. 1991. *The Political Economy of Participatory Economics.* Princeton, NJ: Princeton University Press.

Arrighi, Giovanni. 1994. *The Long Twentieth Century.* London: Verso.

Arthur Andersen & Co. 1979. *Cost of Government Regulation Study for the Business Roundtable*, Vol. I. Chicago: Author.

Baker, Dean. 2007. *Midsummer Meltdown: Prospects for the Stock and Housing Markets.* Center for Economic and Policy Research. http://www.cepr.net

Baran, Paul, and Paul M. Sweezy. 1966. *Monopoly Capital.* New York: Monthly Review Press.

Barr, Michael S., and Gene Sperling. 2008. Poor Homeowners, Good Loans. *New York Times,* Op-Ed, October 18.

Barth, James R., Tong Li, Triphon Phumiwasana, and Glenn Yago. 2008, January. *A Short History of the Subprime Mortgage Market Meltdown.* Santa Monica, CA: Milken Institute. http://www.milkeninstitute.org/publications/publications.taf?function=detail&ID=38801037&cat=ResRep

BBC News. 2003. Buffet Warns on Investment "Time Bomb." http://news.bbc.co.uk/2/hi/2817995.stm

———. 2009, August 7. Timeline: Credit Crunch to Downturn. http://news.bbc.co.uk/2/hi/business/7521250.stm

Benston, George J. 1983. Federal Regulation of Banking: Analysis and Policy Recommendation. *Journal of Bank Research* (Winter): 211–244.

Benton, William. 1944. *The Economics of a Free Society: A Declaration of American Business Policy.* Supplementary Paper No. 1. New York: Committee for Economic Development.

Bhaduri, A. 1998. Implications of Globalization for Macroeconomic Theory and Policy in Developing Countries. In Dean Baker, Gerald Epstein, and Robert Pollin, eds., *Globalization and Progressive Economic Policy.* Cambridge: Cambridge University Press.

Block, Fred. 1977. *The Origins of International Economic Disorder.* Berkeley: University of California Press.

Board of Governors of the Federal Reserve System. Various Years. http://www.federalreserve.gov/

Bonbright, James C., and Gardiner C. Means. 1932. *The Holding Company: Its Public Significance and Its Regulation.* New York: McGraw-Hill.

Bosworth, Barry, and Aaron Flaaen. 2009, April 14, *America's Financial Crisis: The End of an Era.* Washington, DC: The Brookings Institution. http://www.brookings.edu/research/papers/2009/04/14-financial-crisis-bosworth

Bowles, Samuel, Richard Edwards, and Frank Roosevelt. 2005. *Understanding Capitalism: Competition, Command, and Change,* 3rd ed. New York: Oxford University Press.

Bowles, Samuel, David M. Gordon, and Thomas E. Weisskopf. 1990. *After the Wasteland: A Democratic Economics for the Year 2000.* Armonk, NY: M.E. Sharpe.

Business Roundtable. 1972. Membership List. Charles B. McCoy Papers, Hagley Museum and Library, Wilmington, DE.

———. 1973. The Business Roundtable: Its Program and Purpose (founding document of the Business Roundtable, including text and slides). Charles B. McCoy Papers, Hagley Museum and Library, Wilmington, DE.

———. 1977, July 7. *Business Roundtable Task Force on Taxation Proposals, "Capital Formation: A National Requirement."* Wilmington, DE: Author.

———. 1979, July. *Social Security Position Statement.* Wilmington, DE: Author.

———. 1981, July. *Policies to Promote Productivity Growth.* Wilmington, DE: Author.

Calhoun, Charles W. 2007. *The Gilded Age: Perspectives on the Origins of Modern America.* Wilmington, DE: Scholarly Resources.

Carosso, Vincent P. 1970. *Investment Banking in America: A History.* Cambridge, MA: Harvard University Press.

CED (Committee for Economic Development). 1944. *A Postwar Federal Tax Plan for High Employment.* New York: Author. http://hdl.handle.net/2027/mdp.39015020813484

———. 1947. *Collective Bargaining: How To Make It More Effective.* A Statement on National Policy of the Research and Policy Committee. New York: Author.

———. 1948. *Monetary and Fiscal Policy for Greater Economic Stability.* Statement on National Policy of the Research and Policy Committee. New York: Author.

———. 1964. *Union Powers and Union Functions: Toward a Better Balance.* Statement on National Policy of the Research and Policy Committee. New York: Author.

———. 1972, July. *High Unemployment without Inflation: A Positive Program for Economic Stabilization.* Statement by the Research and Policy Committee. New York: Author.

———. 1976. *The Economy in 1977–78: Strategy for and Enduring Expansion.* Statement by the Research and Policy Committee. New York: Author.

———. 1979. *Redefining Government's Role in the Market System.* Statement by the Research and Policy Committee. New York: Author.

———. 1980, September. *Fighting Inflation and Rebuilding a Sound Economy.* Statement by the Research and Policy Committee. New York: Author.

Chang, Ha-Joon. 2002. *Kicking Away the Ladder: Development Strategy in Historical Perspective.* London: Anthem.

Chernow, Ron. 1990. *The House of Morgan: An American Banking Dynasty and the Rise of Modern Finance.* New York: Atlantic Monthly Press.

Chomsisengphet, Souphala, and Anthony Pennington-Cross. 2006. The Evolution of the Subprime Mortgage Market. *Federal Reserve Bank of St. Louis Review* 88(1) (January/February): 31–56.

Clawson, Dan, and Mary Ann Clawson. 1987. Reagan or Business? Foundations of the New Conservatism. In Michael Schwartz, ed., *The Structure of Power in America,* 201–217. New York: Holmes and Meyer.

Collins, Robert M. 1981. *The Business Response to Keynes, 1929–1964.* New York: Columbia University Press.

Council of Economic Advisors. 2013, February 1. *The Economic Impact of the American Recovery and Reinvestment Act of 2009.* Ninth Quarterly Report. http://www.whitehouse.gov/sites/default/files/docs/cea_9th_arra_report_final_pdf.pdf

Cowan, Cameron L. 2003, November 5. Statement on Behalf of the American Securitization Forum before the Subcommittee on Housing and Community Opportunity, United States House of Representatives, Hearing on Protecting Homeowners: Preventing Abusive Lending While Preserving Access to Credit.

Crotty, James. 1999. Was Keynes a Corporatist?: Keynes's Radical Views on Industrial Policy and Macro Policy in the 1920s. *Journal of Economic Issues* 33(3) (September): 555–578.

———. 2008, September. *Structural Causes of the Global Financial Crisis: A Critical Assessment of the "New Financial Architecture."* Political Economy Research Institute Working Paper 180. http://www.peri.umass.edu/fileadmin/pdf/working_papers/working_papers_151–200/WP180.pdf

———. 2009. Structural Causes of the Global Financial Crisis: A Critical Assessment of the "New Financial Architecture." *Cambridge Journal of Economics* 33: 563–580.

Curry, Timothy, and Lynn Shibut. 2000. The Cost of the Savings and Loan Crisis. *FDIC Banking Review* 13(2): 26–35.

Dawley, Alan. 1991. *Struggles for Justice: Social Responsibility and the Liberal State.* Cambridge, MA: Belknap Press of Harvard University Press.

Devine, James N. 1983. Underconsumption, Over-Investment and the Origins of the Great Depression. *Review of Radical Political Economics* 15(2): 1–28.

Devine, Pat. 1988. *Democracy and Economic Planning: The Political Economy of a Self-Governing Society.* Boulder, CO: Westview Press.

Dube, Arin. 2013, April 17. Reinhart/Rogoff and Growth in a Time before Debt. *Next New Deal: The Blog of the Roosevelt Institute.* Guest post. http://www.next-newdeal.net/rortybomb/guest-post-reinhartrogoff-and-growth-time-debt

Dumenil, Gerard, and Dominique Levy. 2004. *Capital Resurgent: Roots of the Neoliberal Revolution.* Cambridge, MA: Harvard University Press.

———. 2011. *The Crisis of Neoliberalism.* Cambridge, MA: Harvard University Press.

Dwight D. Eisenhower Presidential Library. 2013. http://www.eisenhower.archives.gov/all_about_ike/quotes.html#labor

Economic Report of the President. Various years. Washington, DC: U.S. Government Printing Office. http://www.gpo.gov/fdsys/browse/collection.action?collectionCode=ERP

Edwards, Lee. 1997. *The Power of Ideas: The Heritage Foundation at 25 Years.* Ottawa, IL: Jameson Books.

Edwards, Rebecca. 2006. *New Spirits: America in the Gilded Age, 1865–1905.* New York: Oxford University Press.

Edwards, Richard. 1979. *Contested Terrain: The Transformation of the Workplace in the Twentieth Century.* New York: Basic Books.

Eichengreen, Barry, and Kevin H. O'Rourke. 2009. A Tale of Two Depressions. *Vox: Research-Based Policy Analysis and Commentary from Leading Economists.* http://www.voxeu.org/index.php?q=node/3421

Epstein, Gerald. 2005. Introduction: Financialization and the World Economy. In Gerald Epstein, ed., *Financialization and the World Economy,* 3–16. Cheltenham, U.K.: Edward Elgar.

Federal Housing Finance Agency. 2013. *House Price Indexes.* http://www.fhfa.gov/Default.aspx?Page=87

Federal Reserve Bank of St. Louis. 2013. *The Financial Crisis: A Timeline of Events and Policy Actions.* http://www.stlouisfed.org/timeline/timeline.cfm

Federal Reserve Bank of St. Louis Economic Research. 2013. *Economic Data.* http://research.stlouisfed.org/fred2/

Federal Trade Commission. Various years. *Annual Report to Congress Pursuant to the Hart-Scott-Rodino Antitrust Improvements Act of 1976.* http://www.ftc.gov/bc/anncompreports.shtm

Ferguson, Thomas, and Joel Rogers. 1986. *Right Turn: The Decline of the Democrats and the Future of American Politics.* New York: Hill and Wang.

Ferris, Benjamin G. Jr., and Frank E. Speizer. 1980, July. *Business Roundtable Air Quality Project,* Vol. I, *National Ambient Air Quality Standards: Criteria for Establishing Standards for Air Pollutants.* Washington, DC: Business Roundtable.

Financial Times Lexicon. 2013. "asset-bubble" entry. http://lexicon.ft.com/ Term?term=asset-bubble

Foster, John Bellamy. 2007. The Financialization of Capitalism. *Monthly Review* 58(11) (April): 1–12.

Foster, John Bellamy, and Fred Magdoff. 2009. *The Great Financial Crisis: Causes and Consequences.* New York: Monthly Review Press.

Freeman, Richard B., and Brian Hall. 1998, March. *Permanent Homelessness in America?* National Bureau of Economic Research Working Paper No. 2013. http://www.nber.org/papers/w2013

Friedman, Milton, and Anna Schwartz. 1963. *A Monetary History of the United States, 1867–1960.* Princeton, NJ: Princeton University Press.

Fukuyama, Francis. 2012. Conservatives Must Fall Back in Love with the State. *Financial Times,* July 22, 7.

Geltner, David. 2012. Commercial Real Estate and the 1990–91 U.S. Recession. Powerpoint presentation of conference paper at Korea Development Institute Seminar on Real Estate Driven Systemic Risk, Seoul, December 13–14. http://mitcre.mit.edu/

Goetzmann, William N., and Frank Newman. 2010, January. *Securitization in the 1920s.* National Bureau of Economic Research Working Paper 15650. http://www.nber.org/papers/w15650

Gordon, David M., Richard Edwards, and Michael Reich. 1982. *Segmented Work, Divided Workers: The Historical Transformation of Labor in the United States.* Cambridge: Cambridge University Press.

Gordon, Robert Aaron. 1974. *Economic Instability and Growth: The American Record.* New York: Harper and Row.

Green, Mark, and Andrew Buchsbaum. 1980. *The Corporate Lobbies: Political Profiles of the Business Roundtable and the Chamber of Commerce.* Washington, DC: Public Citizen.

Greenspan, Alan, and James Kennedy. 2007. *Sources and Uses of Equity Extracted from Homes.* Federal Reserve Board Finance and Economics Discussion Series No. 2007–20. http://www.federalreserve.gov/pubs/ feds/2007/200720/200720pap.pdf. Updated data from Federal Reserve provided by Steven Fazzari.

Harvey, David. 2005. *A Brief History of Neoliberalism.* Oxford: Oxford University Press.

———. 2010. *The Enigma of Capital and the Crises of Capitalism.* Oxford: Oxford University Press.

Hayek, Friedrich A. von. 1944. *The Road to Serfdom.* Chicago: University of Chicago Press.

Herndon, Thomas, Michael Ash, and Robert Pollin. 2013, April. *Does High Debt Consistently Stifle Economic Growth? A Critique of Reinhart and Rogoff.* Political Economy Research Institute Working Paper 322, http://www.peri.umass.edu/236/hash/90f39d0f04acc9078afd636c6f2f0aa6/publication/596/

Hilferding, Rudolf. 1981. *Finance Capital: A Study of the Latest Phase of Capitalist Development.* London: Routledge & Kegan Paul.

Hirsch, Barry. 2007. Sluggish Institutions in a Dynamic World: Can Unions and Industrial Competition Coexist? *Journal of Economic Perspectives* 22(1): 153–176.

Hirsch, Barry, and David A. Macpherson. 2013. U.S. Historical Tables: Union Membership, Coverage, Density and Employment. 1973–2012. *Union Membership and Coverage Database from the CPS.* http://www.unionstats.com

Historical Collections, Harvard Business School Baker Library. 2013. The Forgotten Real Estate Boom of the 1920s. *Bubbles, Panics and Crashes.* http://www.library.hbs.edu/hc/crises/forgotten.html

Hoge, W. 1998. First Test for Britain's Camelot: Welfare Reform. *New York Times,* January 4.

Howard, M. C., and J. E. King. 2008. *The Rise of Neoliberalism in Advanced Capitalist Economies: A Materialist Analysis.* Basingstoke, U.K.: Palgrave Macmillan.

Immergluck, Daniel, and Marti Wiles. 1999. *Two Steps Back: The Dual Mortgage Market, Predatory Lending, and the Undoing of Community Development.* Chicago: The Woodstock Institute.

International Monetary Fund. 2013a. *World Economic Outlook Database.* http://www.imf.org/external/pubs/ft/weo/2013/01/weodata/index.aspx

————. 2013b. *International Financial Statistics Database.* http://www.imf.org/external/data.htm

Johnston, Robert D. 2011. The Possibilities of Politics: Democracy in America, 1877 to 1917. In Eric Foner and Lis McGirr, eds., *American History Now,* 96–124. Philadelphia: Temple University Press.

Josephson, Matthew. 1962 [1934]. *The Robber Barons: The Great American Capitalists 1861–1901.* New York: Harcourt Brace Jovanovich.

Justia U.S. Supreme Court Center. 2013. United States v. United States Steel Corp.—251 U.S. 417 (1920). http://supreme.justia.com/cases/federal/us/251/417/

Kallberg, Arne L. 2003. Flexible Firms and Labor Market Segmentation: Effects of Workplace Restructuring on Jobs and Workers. *Work and Occupations* 30(2): 154–175.

Keynes, John Maynard. 1936. *The General Theory of Employment, Interest, and Money.* New York: Harcourt, Brace.

Kotz, David M. 1978. *Bank Control of Large Corporations in the United States.* Berkeley: University of California Press.

——. 1984. The False Promise of Financial Deregulation. In U.S. Congress, House Committee on Banking, *How the Financial System Can Best Be Shaped to Meet the Needs of the American People: Hearings on H.R. 5734,* 98th Congress, 2nd Session, 195–209. Washington, DC: U.S. Government Printing Office.

——. 1987. Market Failure. In Center for Popular Economics, ed., *Economic Report of the People,* 159–184. Boston: South End Press.

——. 1994. Interpreting the Social Structure of Accumulation Theory. In David M. Kotz, Terrence McDonough, and Michael Reich, eds., *Social Structures of Accumulation: The Political Economy of Growth and Crisis,* 50–71. Cambridge: Cambridge University Press.

——. 2002. Socialism and Innovation. *Science and Society* 66(1) (Spring): 94–108.

——. 2003. Neoliberalism and the U.S. Economic Expansion of the 1990s. *Monthly Review* 54(11) (April): 15–33.

——. 2008. Contradictions of Economic Growth in the Neoliberal Era: Accumulation and Crisis in the Contemporary U.S. Economy. *Review of Radical Political Economics* 40(2) (Spring): 174–188.

——. 2009. Economic Crises and Institutional Structures: A Comparison of Regulated and Neoliberal Capitalism in the U.S.A. In Jonathan P. Goldstein and Michael G. Hillard, eds., *Heterdox Macroeconomics: Keynes, Marx and Globalization,* 176–188. London: Routledge.

——. 2013. The Current Economic Crisis in the United States: A Crisis of Over-Investment. *Review of Radical Political Economics* 45(3) (Summer): 284–294.

Kotz, David M., and Terrence McDonough. 2010. Global Neoliberalism and the Contemporary Social Structure of Accumulation. In Terrence McDonough, Michael Reich, and David M. Kotz, eds., *Contemporary Capitalism and Its Crises: Social Structure of Accumulation Theory for the Twenty First Century,* 93–120. Cambridge: Cambridge University Press.

Kotz, David M., Terrence McDonough, and Michael Reich, eds. 1994. *Social Structures of Accumulation: The Political Economy of Growth and Crisis.* Cambridge: Cambridge University Press.

Kotz, David M., and Fred Weir. 1997. *Revolution from Above: The Demise of the Soviet System.* London: Routledge.

Kristol, William. 2008. Small Isn't Beautiful. *New York Times,* Op-Ed, December 8, A29.

Krugman, Paul. 2009a. Fighting Off Depression. *The New York Times,* Op-Ed, January 5. http://www.nytimes.com/2009/01/05/opinion/05krugman.html

————. 2009b, February 19. Nobel Laureate Paul Krugman: Too Little Stimulus in Stimulus Plan. Interview, *Knowledge@Wharton*. http://knowledge.wharton.upenn.edu/article.cfm?articleid=2167

Lebowitz, Michael A. 2010. *The Socialist Alternative*. New York: Monthly Review Press.

Li, Minqi. 2013. The 21st Century: Is There An Alternative (to Socialism)? *Science & Society* 77(1) (January): 10–43.

Luhbi, Tami. 2009. Obama: Aid 9 Million Homeowners. *CNNMoney*. http://money.cnn.com/2009/02/18/news/economy/obama_foreclosure

Maddison, Angus. 1995. *Monitoring the World Economy, 1820–1992*. Paris and Washington, DC: Organization for Economic Cooperation and Development.

————. 2010. *Historical Statistics of the World Economy, 1–2008 AD*. http://www.ggdc.net/maddison/oriindex.htm

Marglin, Stephen A., and Juliet B. Schor, eds. 1990. *The Golden Age of Capitalism: Reinterpreting the Postwar Experience*. New York: Oxford University Press.

Martin, Stephen. 2005. *Remembrance of Things Past: Antitrust, Ideology, and the Development of Industrial Economics*. http://www.krannert.purdue.edu/faculty/smartin/vita/remembrance1205a.pdf

McQuaid, Kim. 1982. *Big Business and Presidential Power from FDR to Reagan*. New York: William Morrow and Company.

Miller Center. 2013. *American President: A Reference Resource, William Howard Taft Front Page*. University of Virginia. http://millercenter.org/president/taft/essays/biography/4

Mirowski, Philip, and Dieter Plehwe, eds. 2009. *The Road from Mont Pelerin: The Making of the Neoliberal Thought Collective*. Cambridge, MA: Harvard University Press.

Mishel, Lawrence, Josh Bivens, Elise Gould, and Heidi Shierholz. 2012. *The State of Working America*, 12th ed. Washington, DC: Economic Policy Institute.

Mitchell, Alison. 1995. Two Clinton Aides Resign to Protest New Welfare Law. *New York Times*, September 12.

Mizruchi, Mark S. 2013. *The Fracturing of the American Corporate Elite*. Cambridge, MA: Harvard University Press.

Morgenson, Gretchen. 2008. Debt Watchdogs: Tamed or Caught Napping? *New York Times*, December 7, 1, 32.

Morris, Charles R. 2005. *The Tycoons: How Andrew Carnegie, John D. Rockefeller, Jay Gould, and J.P. Morgan Invented the American Supereconomy*. New York: Henry Holt.

Mulligan, Casey B. 2008. An Economy You Can Bank On. *The New York Times,* Op-Ed, October 10, A29.

Murphy, Kevin J., and Jan Zabojnik. 2007, April. Managerial Capital and the Market for CEOs. *Social Science Research Network.* http://papers.ssrn.com/sol3/papers.cfm?abstract_id=984376

Nasaw, David. 2006. *Andrew Carnegie.* New York: Penguin Press.

National Bureau of Economic Research. 2013. *U.S. Business Cycle Expansions and Contractions.* http://www.nber.org/cycles/cyclesmain.html

Office of Management and Budget. 2013. http://www.whitehouse.gov/omb/budget/Historicals

Orhangazi, O. 2008. *Financialization and the U.S. Economy.* Cheltenham, U.K.: Edward Elgar.

Palley, Thomas I. 2012. *From Financial Crisis to Stagnation: The Destruction of Shared Prosperity and the Role of Economics.* Cambridge: Cambridge University Press.

Peschek, Joseph G. 1987. *Policy Planning Organizations: Elite Agendas and America's Rightward Turn.* Philadelphia: Temple University Press.

Peters, Gerhard, and John T. Wooley. 2013. Message to the Congress Transmitting the Annual Economic Report of the President, February 10, 1982. *The American Presidency Project.* http://www.presidency.ucsb.edu/ws/?pid=42121

Pew Center. 2010, May 4. *"Socialism" Not So Negative, "Capitalism" Not So Positive. Pew Center for the People and Press.* http://www.people-press.org/2010/05/04/socialism-not-so-negative-capitalism-not-so-positive/

————. 2011, December 28. *Little Change in Public's Response to "Capitalism," "Socialism." Pew Center for the People and Press.* http://www.people-press.org/2011/12/28/little-change-in-publics-response-to-capitalism-socialism/?src=prc-number

Philippon, Thomas, and Ariell Reshef. 2009. *Wages and Human Capital in the U.S. Financial Industry: 1909–2006.* National Bureau of Economic Research Working Paper 14644. http://www.nber.org/papers/w14644

Phillips-Fein, Kim. 2009. *Invisible Hands: The Making of the Conservative Movement from the New Deal to Reagan.* New York: W.W. Norton.

Piketty, Thomas, and Emmanuel Saez. 2010. Income Inequality in the United States, 1913–1998. *Quarterly Journal of Economics* 118(1) (2003): 1–39. Updated data revised July 17, 2010, http://www.econ.berkeley.edu/~saez/

Polanyi, Karl. 1944. *The Great Transformation.* New York: Rinehart.

Public Citizen. 2013. *NAFTA's Broken Promises 1994–2013: Outcomes of the North American Free Trade Agreement.* http://www.citizen.org/documents/NAFTAs-Broken-Promises.pdf

Public Purpose. 2013. *U.S. Private Sector Trade Union Membership.* http://www.publicpurpose.com/lm-unn2003.htm

Rasmussen Reports. 2009. *Just 53% Say Capitalism Better Than Socialism.* http://www.rasmussenreports.com/public_content/politics/general_politics/april_2009/just_53_say_capitalism_better_than_socialism

Reinhart, Carmen M., and Kenneth S. Rogoff. 2010. Growth in a Time of Debt. *American Economic Review: Papers and Proceedings* (May): 573–578.

Reuss, Alejandro. 2013. *Capitalist Crisis and Capitalist Reaction: The Profit Squeeze, the Business Roundtable, and the Capitalist Class Mobilization of the 1970s.* Ph.D. diss., University of Massachusetts, Amherst.

Roemer, John E. 1994. *A Future for Socialism.* Cambridge, MA: Harvard University Press.

Romer, Christina. 1986. Spurious Volatility in Historical Unemployment Data. *Journal of Political Economy* 94(1) (February): 1–37.

Rogers, Daniel T. 2011. *Age of Fracture.* Cambridge, MA: Belknap Press of Harvard University Press.

Roy, William G. 1997. *Socializing Capital: The Rise of the Large Industrial Corporation in America.* Princeton, NJ: Princeton University Press.

Saez, Emmanuel. 2013. *Striking It Richer: The Evolution of the Top Incomes in the United States.* http://elsa.berkeley.edu/~saez/saez-UStopincomes-2012.pdf

Saez, Emmanuel, Joel B. Slemrod, and Seth H. Giertz. 2012. The Elasticity of Taxable Income with Respect to Marginal Tax Rates: A Critical Review. *Journal of Economic Literature* 50(1): 3–5.

Samuelson, Paul M. 1948. *Economics: An Introductory Analysis,* 1st ed. New York: McGraw-Hill.

Scherer, F. M. 1980. *Industrial Market Structure and Economic Performance,* 2nd ed. Boston: Houghton Mifflin.

Schlesinger, Arthur M. Jr. 1963. The New Freedom Fulfills the New Nationalism. In Arthur Mann, ed., *The Progressive Era: Liberal Renaissance or Liberal Failure.* New York: Holt, Rinehart and Winston.

Schweickart, David. 2011. *After Capitalism,* 2nd ed. Lanham, MD: Rowman & Littlefield.

SIFMA (Securities Industry and Financial Markets Association). 2013. http://www.sifma.org/research/statistics.aspx

Silver, Nate. 2011. The Geography of Occupying Wall Street (and Everywhere Else). *New York Times,* October 17, http://fivethirtyeight.blogs.nytimes.com/2011/10/17/the-geography-of-occupying-wall-street-and-everywhere-else/

———. 2013, April 9. The Have-Nots Aren't Having It. *FiveThirtyEight,* http://www.fivethirtyeight.com/2009/04/have-nots-arent-having-it.html

Smith, Greg. 2012. Why I Am Leaving Goldman Sachs. *The New York Times,* Op-Ed, March 14, A25.

Stiglitz, Joseph E. 2010. *Free Fall: America, Free Markets, and the Sinking of the World Economy.* New York: W.W. Norton.

Stuckler, David, and Sanjay Basu. 2013. How Austerity Kills. *The New York Times,* Op-Ed, May 13, A21.

Sweezy, Paul M. 1994. The Triumph of Financial Capital. *Monthly Review* 46(2) (June): 1–11.

Uchitelle, Louis. 2013. Diminishing Expectations: 'Two-Tier' Union Contracts Have Opened a Gulf between Generations. *The Nation* 296(8) (February 25): 18–20.

U.S. Bureau of Economic Analysis. Various years. http://www.bea.gov/

U.S. Bureau of Labor Statistics. Various years. http://www.bls.gov/.

U.S. Bureau of the Census. 1961. *Historical Statistics of the United States: Colonial Times to 1957.* Washington, DC: U.S. Government Printing Office.

———. 2013. http://www.census.gov/

U.S. Chamber of Commerce. 2010, November 7. *Statement by Thomas Donohue.* http://www.uschamber.com/press/releases/2010/november/americans-voted-jobs-and-economic-growth-says-donohue

U.S. Department of Health and Human Services. 2013. *Indicators of Welfare Dependence,* Appendix A, Table TANF 6. http://aspe.hhs.gov/hsp/indicators 08/apa.shtml

U.S. Department of Labor, Wage and Hour Division. 2009. *History of Federal Minimum Wage Rates under the Fair Labor Standards Act, 1938–2009.* http://www.dol.gov/whd/minwage/chart.htm

Vogel, David. 1989. *Fluctuating Fortunes: The Political Power of Business in America.* New York: Basic Books.

Vosko, Leah F. 2010. *Managing the Margins: Gender, Citizenship, and the International Regulation of Precarious Employment.* Oxford: Oxford University Press.

Webster, Ben. 2005. Tube Costs 20 Times More . . . but It Is Still No Better. *The Times* [London], March 18, 35.

Webster, P. 1999. Blair and Schroder Unite on Hardline Spending Cuts. *The Times* [London], June 8, 1.

Weinstein, James. 1967. *The Decline of Socialism in America 1912–1925.* New York: Monthly Review Press

———. 1968. *The Corporate Ideal in the Liberal State: 1900–1918.* Boston: Beacon Press.

Whalen, Richard J. 1963. Joseph P. Kennedy: A Portrait of the Founder. *Fortune,* January. http://features.blogs.fortune.cnn.com/2011/04/10/joseph-p-kennedy-a-portrait-of-the-founder/

Whitten, David O. 2013. The Depression of 1893. *EH.net Encyclopedia.* http:// eh.net/?s=whitten

Wolf, Martin. 2009. Seeds of Its Own Destruction. *Financial Times,* March 9, 7.

Wolfson, Martin H., and David M. Kotz. 2010. A Re-Conceptualization of Social Structure of Accumulation Theory. In Terrence McDonough, Michael Reich, and David M. Kotz, eds., *Contemporary Capitalism and Its Crises: Social Structure of Accumulation Theory for the Twenty First Century,* 72–90. Cambridge: Cambridge University Press.

Woodward, Bob. 1994. *The Agenda: Inside the Clinton White House.* New York: Simon & Schuster.

Yellen, Janet. 2005. Housing Bubbles and Monetary Policy. Presentation to the Fourth Annual Haas Gala, October 21, San Francisco. http://www.frbsf .org/our-district/press/presidents-speeches/yellen-speeches/2005/october/ housing-bubbles-and-monetary-policy/

Zhu, Andong, and David M. Kotz. 2011. The Dependence of China's Economic Growth on Exports and Investment. *Review of Radical Political Economics* 43(1) (Winter): 9–32.

Index

adjustable rate mortgages, 131, 132, 146
AFDC (Aid to Families with Dependent
   Children), 23, 117; benefit, 46
AIG (American International Group), 141,
   147, 174
American Conservative Union, 201
American Economic Association, 1
American Enterprise Institute, 74, 239n32
American Recovery and Reinvestment Act
   of 2009, 158
anti-trust: enforcement, 20, 21, 41, 42, 51,
   207; law, 14, 20, 29, 192, 203; legislation,
   51; policy, 189, 248n21; suits, 188, 289,
   234n31
asset bubbles, 104, 105, 112, 142, 200; of
   1920s, 193; and business fixed investment, 113; and crisis of 2008, 103,
   198; definition of, 105; deflation, 195;
   development of, 169; effects on consumer
   spending, 239n31; and growing inequality and speculative financial institutions,
   107, 111, 114, 175, 192, 195 identification,
   106; of large sized, 128, 177–179; and
   neoliberal capitalism, 37, 106, 176
AT&T: Business Roundtable member, 68,
   69; CED affiliate, 54. See also Business
   Roundtable; CED

bank concentration, 174
Bank of America, 54, 68, 69, 138, 147
Bank of Japan, 147
Benton, William, 54, 55, 60, 232n18
Bernanke, Ben, 1, 89, 159, 160
Blair, Tony, 119, 120; government, 115, 119
Brookings Institution, 74
bubble-driven expansion, 114
budget crisis, 167
Buffet, Warren, 140
Bureau of Consumer Protection, 19

bureaucratic principles, 50, 51, 203, 207
Bush, George H. W., 9, 115, 118
Bush, George W., 154, 155, 174, 201
Business Council, 53, 75
business cycle, 54, 96; and capacity utilization, 141; expansions, 239n30; and
   government expenditure, 38; peak, 6, 7,
   223nn6–7, 230n55, 242n33
Business Roundtable, 68–72, 77–81,
   234n36

CACI International, 22
capital accumulation, 178, 199; neoliberal
   era,142; rate of, 93, 178, 179, 237n12,
   245n74; stable, 3, 103, 121, 123
capital-labor relation, 26, 197, 198, 202,
   230n57; institutional change, 28, 35;
   neoliberal era, 42; and neoliberal institutions, 43; and regulated capitalism, 51,
   202, 203, 205,207
Carnegie, Andrew, 184, 186, 248n17
Carter, Jimmy, 9, 15, 16, 18, 71, 72, 76, 115;
   administration, 17
CDS (credit default swap), 134, 138, 141,
   147, 240n3; AIG, 147, 174; definition of,
   133; and financial crisis, 131; value of,
   134, 241n11
CED (Committee for Economic Development), 53–56, 233n23
central planning, 32, 217
Chamber of Commerce (U.S.), 61, 167,
   233n28
Chicago school, 1, 230n1
Chinese Communist Party, 60, 61
Citibank, 54, 68, 147, 248n18
Citigroup, 139
class coalition, 80
Clayton Anti-Trust Act, 20, 189
Clean Air Acts, 18